Motorcycling

Across Ohio

Motorcycling Across Ohio

by William M. Murphy

Arbutus Press, Traverse City, MI

ISBN 1-933926-14-7
Manufactured in the United States of America
First Edition/First Printing

Photos are by the author unless otherwise noted.
Maps designed by Land Access Information Association, Traverse City, MI
Interior design and layout by Julie Phinney, Bozeman, Montana
  (406-586-1297 – mjphinney@msn.com)

Dedicated to my family

for accepting my time on the road and the long months

chained to my computer writing this book. It is also dedicated

to veterans of yesteryear and today for making and keeping

this country a place where we can explore its beautiful places

and meet its wonderful people in peace and safety.

Contents

Preface

OHIO: TO THE HEART OF IT ALL, the tourism folks proclaim. The Seneca tribe of the Iroquois Nation declared it "Ohiiyo: Good River" long before the first European laid eyes on this delightful land. There's no doubt about the Buckeye State being in the heart of our nation, strategically located on the crossroads of major highways and railroads. It is also the birthplace of many presidents (seven!); the home of major industrial giants that contribute immensely to our economy; contains plentiful farmlands and forests, universities and cities, and so many contributions to our nation and culture that they're too lengthy to list. There is also no doubt that the state's namesake, Good River, was rightfully ascribed centuries ago by folks who appreciated the river for its life-giving sustenance and water highway that allowed travel and trade among distant tribes.

The state is also at the heart of the history of our country, especially the Old Northwest Territory. Critical events and battles that took place in Ohio had an enormous impact on the expansion of the country. Perhaps more than any other Midwestern state, Ohio is filled with the drama of nation-building. During the period between 1770 to 1820, Ohio was the scene of dreams and of dreams cut tragically short. It is where the fate of two civilizations collided and one inevitably lost while the other prevailed. It is where men and women of incredible courage either struck out for a new beginning or fought to the death protecting what they had known for millennia and were about to lose.

The sweat and blood of thousands of brave men and women stained the soil of Ohio during this tumultuous period. Mostly it was the anonymous settler or Indian family, but it also included names of people who made it into the history books—people like Colonel Crawford and General William Henry Harrison, Simon Kenton and Simon Girty, Generals "Mad Anthony" Wayne and St. Clair, Tecumseh and Chief Blue Jacket. Not dismissing or minimizing the very real trauma of that period, I can easily imagine these brave and adventurous people riding their two-wheeler into the sunset were they alive today. They obviously had the courage and character to take the road less traveled.

But for the purpose of this book: What can Ohio contribute today for the discriminating motorcyclist? The answer is loud and clear: A lot! Don't let this state's location in the American Midwest fool you. Everything a motorcyclist dreams of is here—twisting roads, wonderful scenery, loads of natural and manmade attractions, fascinating history that includes old forts and battlefield sites, charming covered bridges, ghost towns, roads as old as the nation itself, canals used by the earliest settlers, and much more. So Ohio Motorcyclists, stand tall, stick your chest out and shout it loud and clear: *Ohio is a Great Motorcycling State!*

Take your pick—the attractions and history of Lake Erie; the forests, parks, caverns and waterfalls of the Appalachian country; the mighty Ohio River whose meandering currents define the entire southern state boundary; or the bucolic country roads and farmland of the northwest. Ohio really does offer everything a motorcyclist wants. This fact isn't as well known as it ought to be, however, which is precisely why I'm writing this book.

For thirty-five years I've been lucky enough to ride on some of the most exciting and beautiful roads North America has to offer. My motorcycling experiences have brought me delight and vastly broadened my knowledge and appreciation of this land, its history, and its people. I've been blessed with stunning scenic beauty, experienced the exhilaration only available to those who choose this mode of travel, and met the most wonderful and friendly people that you're likely to find anywhere. In short, motorcycles and motorcycle riding have enriched my life immeasurably.

My journey isn't complete, however. There are thousands of miles of made-in-motorcycle-heaven roads that I've yet to experience; there are hundreds of wonderful places yet to visit; and untold numbers of fellow bikers that I have yet to meet on the road and share stories with.

One of my only regrets about this wonderful activity is that it is misunderstood by too many people. Some folks are of the opinion that bikers must be antisocial; After all, they reason, why would we voluntarily participate in this dangerous and rebellious activity if we weren't? We may never be able to convince everyone that motorcycling is neither excessively dangerous nor a sign of rebellion, but slowly the message is getting out. It's hard to maintain a negative view of an activity that has become so commonplace that your dentist, lawyer, or pastor may well be an enthusiast. In fact, I fully expect one day to discover that motorcycles are the official vehicles of heaven.

Maybe motorcycling's vestigial "outlaw" image is part of the charm. After all, I think it's fundamental to the American spirit to want to be at least a bit of a nonconformist or iconoclast—to have some part of our life that separates us from the crowd and that makes a statement about who we are. For the majority of us, being a motorcyclist is much more than just owning and riding a motorcycle. It's a lifestyle. It's a manifestation of our desire to find freedom and adventure in an eight-to-five world of traffic jams and deadlines. Being a part of this lifestyle means associating with out-of-the-ordinary people who share the love of riding these wonderful machines, and gaining entry to the incredible wide world that opens up for us when we are on our bikes. Motorcyclists share many traits and reasons for riding, but in fact, they represent a cross-section of society and are a very diverse group.

I do believe that this cross-section has certain traits and qualities that make us different. We motorcyclists are willing to accept an increase in potential danger and discomfort for the incredible adventure and freedom that are its rewards. Blue-collar, white-collar or pink-collar, cowboy boots, wing tips, or high-heel shoes—it doesn't matter what we wear when we aren't riding. It's our love of the sport and the adventure and joy it brings us that count and that make us one community—and a community we are. Though there are many types and brands of machines available to meet the differing desires of enthusiasts, when you get right down to the basics, there are common threads that all bikers will mention when asked. These qualities include the incredible sense of freedom—the physical and emotional exhilaration that is very hard to describe or quantify—as well as a very real sense of adventure, and of course, the gut-level enjoyment that comes from being one with a most remarkable machine capable of providing the same thrills that many seek at amusement park rides, only the ride never ends. Joy with the twist of the wrist—if only all of life were so simple!

To the nonenthusiast all motorcycles may seem alike. Two wheels, handlebars, and a seat may be all that some folks notice when they see a motorcycle. Of course, bikers know that the variety of motorcycles that are on the road is nothing short of amazing. Single cylinder or in-line six, V-twin or boxer, road racer or full dresser, Aprilia or Zundapp—the variations are endless and reflective of the individuals riding them. There is one common factor that is present throughout the biking community, however, and that is the passion that each person brings to this incredible sport.

The motorcycling family in Ohio is large and growing steadily. Currently, there are 400,000 registered motorcycles in Ohio according to the Motorcycle Industry Council, which is a significant and growing number of intelligent folk who know a great thing when they see it. Ohio is the third largest state in motorcycle ownership according to the Council. Also, according to the MIC, the average age of an Ohio motorcyclist is thirty-eight, with one half of motorcycle owners being between the ages of thirty-five and fifty. These folks are mostly married, have a college education, and have discretionary income that they spend on their sport. In other words, this isn't a passing fad—motorcyclists aren't a fickle group that's here today and gone tomorrow.

One of the most gratifying recent developments in motorcycling is the remarkable increase in the number of female riders. Women are now becoming very much a part of the motorcycling scene and, in every sense of the word, are no longer taking a back seat to anyone. As new owners, they account for a significant

part of the recent upsurge in motorcycle sales and are as enthusiastic about their machines and what they represent as male riders. As a result of this phenomenon, there are a growing number of support groups and organizations dedicated to the female rider. I list several of these organizations in the web site appendix.

As the father of two daughters who I hope can be whoever and whatever they want to be, this illustrates still another positive step in the ability of women to live full lives of their choosing, not society's. I think it's just great when I see a woman's long hair flying in the wind behind her as she's roaring down the road on her bike.

As is true for most enthusiasts, I derive a great deal of enjoyment reading about my sport in books and magazines. Vicarious enjoyment of the motorcycle rides of others is very real—especially on a cold winter night when my own bike is hibernating in the garage, waiting for the next warm day. Coming from the Midwest, I must admit to feeling pangs of jealousy and a desire to shout out, "Hey, take a look at us!" whenever I read a never ending parade of stories in the various motorcycle magazines about wonderful mountain roads in the West or East. I guess articles about riding Ohio's roads just can't compete with such stories as riding "The Dragon," the "Cherohala Skyway" or other great Appalachian byways, or traversing 10,000-foot passes in the Rockies.

And I understand the attraction of these fabled riding destinations. I have ridden the Blue Ridge Parkway, Shenandoah's Skyline Drive, The Dragon, and many other great roads from Georgia to Maine. I've been spellbound while riding the Beartooth Mountains Highway, Going to the Sun Road in Glacier National Park, and other incredible byways of the western mountains. I've been awed by riding US2 through the vast openness of the Great Plains, and I've struggled to find the words to adequately describe to another person the magic of motorcycling around Lake Superior. These roads and destinations are wonderful, however, since most of us don't happen to live near them, we still want to ride on a regular basis. Most motorcyclists ride the areas near their homes. If you reserve your riding time for only those special trips to faraway places, you're missing out on a lot!

So I've decided to write a book extolling the joys of riding near home. We all ride primarily where we live, and the secret is to learn the best places to ride in your own locale. Having ridden across the Midwest for well over three decades, I know it has many great motorcycling roads and wonderful places to see and things to do. The purpose of this book is to share what I've learned from years of riding the length and breadth of Ohio on two wheels.

I subscribe to the belief that one rides a motorcycle for the joy of riding, and that if you can ride a lonesome, twisting, hilly, sinuous road surrounded by breathtaking mountain scenery, then that's icing on the cake. But it's still the operating and riding of a motorcycle that is the essence of the experience. Any motorcyclist knows what I mean. The sound of the engine, the visceral feel as you lean through and accelerate out of curves, the heightened invigoration and sensory awareness like the smell of freshly turned earth or newly cut hay or October leaves, the absolute feeling of freedom, the ability and opportunity to leave all else behind and immerse yourself in the motorcycling experience, and the indescribable feeling of power literally at your fingertips with a roll of the wrist. If you've never done it, take my word for it, it's great! There aren't many things in life that cause ear-to-ear grins and the desire to just shout out loud with joy as does riding a motorcycle down a great road on a beautiful summer day. Not to rub it in, but when was the last time you experienced an inner smile that turned into a full-faced grin while driving your minivan? Motorcycling is a wonderful way to replenish the psyche, which is constantly drained by the stresses and duties of everyday life.

This experience can be enjoyed almost any time and almost any place. I use the qualifier "almost" because even I will admit that I don't find enjoyment riding in large cities and busy expressways. In fact, I avoid such places when possible.

Motorcycles, like horses, are creatures of the open road. That's where they and their riders are the happiest.

This brings me back to why I would write a book highlighting the riding experiences to be had in Ohio. Simply put, it's because there are thousands of miles of wonderful motorcycling roads in Ohio, and I don't believe this fact is universally known. But to enjoy these highways and byways, one has to know where they are. In an attempt to save all of you the trouble of finding these roads for yourselves, I've written this guide.

From the beginning I've intended this book to be more than a typical tour guide that simply provide routes and destinations or a bit about how to keep the kids amused and where to eat once you arrive at a destination. In this book it's all about the journey, not the destination. I want to tell you about Ohio at the same time. There are thousands of fascinating stories, natural and manmade attractions, underappreciated historical events, and just plain interesting things to see and do and learn about while traveling across this state. I want to do more than just suggest some roads that you might enjoy riding or places that you might enjoy visiting. I want to tell you the stories of the places you're riding through, so that the land and the people who shaped it come alive, enabling you to appreciate the events and people that forged what we see around us today.

I believe that the motorcycling experience can be enhanced if you delve into the history and events that shaped the places you're visiting. Fascinating discoveries about our country are waiting out there to be discovered. All we have to do is slow down and look. I want to tell you about the Ohio that most people don't see because they're rushing by the real stories on busy highways, oblivious to all the interesting things around them. I suppose it can be said that this book has three fundamental underlying principles: first, it is the trip that counts, not the destination; second, that motorcycling and exploring the forgotten places, events, and stories of Ohio make a wonderful partnership; and third, to show you the Ohio that hasn't been blighted by the homogenous and uninspiring urban sprawl that is inexorably creeping across the landscape.

I think you will find that the tours in this book take in a high percentage of the natural and cultural wonders that are located across the length and breadth of Ohio, and this is accomplished by way of the best motorcycling roads—not the straightest or most efficient routes that a typical automobile guidebook would include. Since lodging and restaurant decisions are so personal and varied, I stay away from recommending hotels, motels, or restaurants, unless there is something especially unique about it. This is a book about exploring the state by motorcycle. It's not meant to be a guide to hotels and restaurants.

Allow me to get off the subject of motorcycles for just a bit so I can set the stage. *What is it that makes Ohio an interesting and enjoyable place to ride?*

Though almost any road can make for enjoyable motorcycling, there are certain traits that make it more appealing and keep us coming back for more. These traits are usually geographic in nature, though of course, in this modern age manmade features also figure strongly. Ohio is blessed with four basic geographic and cultural zones: the Lake Erie region, the Ohio River valley, the farmlands of the northwestern part of the state, and the Appalachian hills of the east and southeast. This book discusses riding opportunities that take advantage of all four of these regions.

We have to look back in history to find the reasons why Ohio looks like it does—both its natural geography and its manmade features. First, a few millennia ago the last Ice Age helped shape the familiar topography of the Midwest. Roughly the north half and much of southwestern Ohio was covered by the Wisconsonian glacier, which retreated about twelve thousand years ago—just a blink of the eye in geologic time. This massive ice sheet gave us the generally flat lands of northern Ohio, as well as Lake Erie itself. The Allegheny Plateau of southern Ohio escaped glaciation, and its rolling hills remain much as they have for eons.

Nature has given Ohio much in the way of beautiful land to enjoy on two wheels. Its many rivers result in meandering roads and carved river valleys that are a joy to ride through. The Karst geologic formation, underlying a large portion of Ohio, resulted in fabulous caves, tunnels, and grottos that provide fascinating underground tours through a fantasy world of crystals and mineral formations.

The farm lands of northwestern Ohio have their own charms. There are few things more relaxing than enjoying a peaceful ride down country roads on a blissful summer day witnessing the bounty of this good earth. As the candy bar advertising jingle goes, "sometimes you feel like a nut, sometimes you don't," so it is with motorcycling. Sometimes a high speed run down a curving and technically challenging road is just the ticket, but other times a relaxing laid-back ride down a peaceful road through farm country is just what the doctor ordered. In Ohio you can certainly enjoy both.

Majestic Lake Erie brings a large slice of maritime geography and culture to enjoy. Its shore is lined with fascinating attractions, such as lighthouses, old forts, monuments, beautiful parks, and scenic vistas of blue water stretching all the way to Canada. Ohio motorcyclists are fortunate indeed to be able to enjoy all that this Great Lake brings in the way of nautical attractions not usually found in the middle of a continent.

Southern Ohio is a different place altogether. Its hills and hollows serve as the setting for some of the most enjoyable motorcycling roads to be found anywhere. The natural beauty of this area will cause even the most diehard peg scraper to slow down and marvel at the wonders that Mother Nature has bestowed. One of motorcycling's oldest dilemmas is encountered here in abundance: to ride for hours on challenging roads through beautiful countryside concentrating fully on the riding or stop frequently to enjoy the fabulous views? I'll leave the answer up to you, but you will battle this inner conflict whenever you ride through Ohio's beautiful hill country.

Throughout Ohio there are wonderful riding opportunities through glacial river valleys formed millions of years ago. The 44,000 miles of creeks and rivers twist and turn across the countryside, often with roads built alongside them for our enjoyment. All one has to do is look at a map to realize that in most of Ohio the checkerboard system of roads so common in the Midwest is missing. Instead, there is a network of roads that curve across the countryside in a seemingly inefficient but highly enjoyable fashion for motorcycling. Ohio was the first state to be formed out of the new Public Domain Lands guaranteed to the United States by the Treaty of Paris following the Revolutionary War. As a result, land surveying was a cross between the rectangular system used in the rest of the Midwest and the old metes and bounds system of the East Coast, in which property lines and roads wander aimlessly across the countryside. This means that the rectangular road system wasn't instituted in much of the state as it was in neighboring states, such as Michigan and Indiana, which were admitted to the Union later. Bottom line for motorcycling is that Ohio enjoys roads that meander a great deal, following the lay of the land rather than cutting straight through it. These are the roads that bring smiles to motorcyclists' faces, no matter how much modern highway designers hold them in disdain.

So forget what California canyon carvers might say. Ohio is a wonderful place to ride and explore on a motorcycle. And it is best seen from back roads and in forgotten small towns to be really appreciated and enjoyed. This is a book about exploring the real Ohio from atop a motorcycle on back roads. I think you'll find these trips to be not only great motorcycling adventures but also learning experiences as well. You'll enhance your appreciation of the history of this fascinating state and better understand the lives of those who trod on this soil before us, while having a wonderful time motoring down thousands of miles of great biking roads.

These are not just any back roads, however. For roads to make it into this book and be recommended for motorcycle touring, they have to meet several criteria. First, they have to be paved, with the pavement in at least reasonably good condition so that a large touring bike or sport bike can navigate the road safely and without difficulty. Second, the road and area has to have some scenic appeal. Traffic on the roads has to be light, and the general touring area must have something to offer in the way of interesting scenery, history, land cover, geologic features, or other attractions. By intent, you'll notice many natural, historical, or cultural points of interest along these routes. Third, the road has to have some character: that is, curves or hills or other qualities that make it an attractive riding route. Finally, and what may be most important, is that the routes laid out in this book rely heavily on well-maintained grey line roads—state, county, and local roads with low traffic density—with major state routes or federal highways designated only when they are either necessary for a short connector stretch, are truly worthy of a good motorcycle riding label in their own right, or have a unique historical significance. Perhaps one of the most noteworthy aspects of riding the roads I've identified herein is that, unlike better known routes in the Appalachians or other high-profile destinations, you will find few tourists and RVers on the majority of the roads I recommend.

Buckeye riders are fortunate in two ways pertaining to the state's roads. Local transportation officials have obviously had a policy in place for some time to pave as many roads as possible—even most of the rural township roads have been paved. This makes motorcycle touring a real joy. The second advantage is that ODOT has gone out of its way to connect what in most states would be a mix of county primary roads into state routes. This makes following primary rural roads

much easier since the state route number remains the same even as local names for the road change. It also means fewer stop signs along these primary routes.

Over the years, all motorcyclists have taken road maps and tried to lay out enjoyable trips utilizing main highways that appear interesting on a map. I think most of us would like to avoid busy state or federal highways and find suitable local roads to use for trips, but there is too much uncertainty. Unless we know an area intimately, it just isn't possible to know where each road goes. Often, county roads are meant to serve local residents, not as long distance routes. How many times have you taken a country road while out on a ride only to have the pavement or the road itself suddenly end?

Obtaining road maps from each county road department is a major undertaking. Even when one has up-to-date and accurate maps, the many roads still have to be hooked together to create a tour across several counties. But it's just this kind of research, and a great deal of riding on back roads and knowledge of local lore, that is necessary if one wishes to organize great rides with the intent of keeping off major roads as much as feasible. I think you'll find that this book accomplishes these tasks for you.

Riding what many consider back roads may be of concern for some who fear being stranded by mechanical problems. I've found just the opposite. On major roads, many motorists are either out-of-towners themselves, who are unlikely to stop and help, or they're local folks going about their busy lives, assuming that the police will be by to help a stranger. While there is definitely less of a law enforcement presence on county and local roads, I've found that people who live or travel these roads are much more likely to stop and lend a hand than are drivers who travel busy highways and expressways.

You will find that almost all of the rides depicted in this book are great for just kicking back and relaxing. The traffic is lighter than on main roads, and the roads themselves are generally narrower and more interesting. High speed isn't what it's all about on most of these routes. Exploring the history and attractions of a region adds a whole new component to motorcycling. While we all enjoy riding open roads with great biking character through scenic grandeur, there is also much to be said about slowing down to do some exploring and viewing from a totally different perspective—that of learning about and appreciating the unique history and culture of an area. We're all familiar with the old adage that advises us to slow down and smell the roses. Well, I think an equally apt philosophy for motorcyclists is to occasionally slow down and read the inscriptions on the many granite markers and historical monuments and signs that dot Ohio's countryside.

I suppose there is a bit of a Kerouac-like romanticism and searching for the meaning of life in most motorcyclists. As was the case with Jack Kerouac in his wonderful essay, "On The Road," motorcyclists today also seek and enjoy the adventure that being on the road brings. Whether a teenager on a crotch rocket or septuagenarians on full dressers, every biker finds adventure by being on the road while at the same time satisfying a hard-to-explain need to explore beyond familiar horizons, be they physical or mental.

The fascination of traveling and seeing what's over the next hill isn't confined to modern times. The author Robert Louis Stevenson was also an inveterate traveler. He penned many verses extolling the joys of wandering, such as this one from his *Songs of Travel*:

> *Let the blow fall soon or late,*
> *Let what will be o'er me;*
> *Give the face of earth around*
> *And the road before me.*
> *Wealth I ask not, hope nor love,*
> *Nor a friend to know me;*
> *All I ask, the heaven above*
> *And the road below me.*

Being on a motorcycle on this vast continent certainly puts things in perspective for a rider, and there is something about being out there in the wind on two wheels that makes the scale of things more obvious. It helps separate the important from the trivial. Because of fewer distractions, riding affords time for reflection as well as simply losing yourself in the wide-open world. There is certainly no doubt about the fact that you can see and appreciate the world around you much better on two wheels than on four. Most riders just love to be on the road simply enjoying the ride, the companionship of good friends who share the same love of motorcycles and riding, and discovering what's over the next hill. Others might spend time deep in thought, contemplating the meaning of life. For some of us who aren't gifted musically, it's a chance to sing our favorite songs out loud without offending anyone.

Perhaps there is even a little pride involved in knowing that we can face adversities without quitting. Rain? No problem—stop to put on rain gear and keep going. Or you stop and wait out the storm under an overpass or a pavilion at a park or rest area sharing stories and small talk with other bikers who have sought similar refuge. It's all part of the experience. If we didn't want to be part of the natural setting, we'd drive a four-wheeled cocoon and be comfortable, as well as disconnected, at all times.

For me the motorcycle has been a ticket for escape and freedom for decades. I can't describe to a nonenthusiast the visceral level of enjoyment riding these machines through wide-open spaces has brought me. As any citizen of this world must do, I've spent my life working and doing all the things required of a responsible person for the sake of family and community. While some may find a fishing boat, the opera, rock climbing, or the golf course as their means of escape, for me it has been motorcycles. The adventure and happiness I've experienced aboard my faithful horses of steel is immeasurable.

All motorcyclists have some favorite local riding roads they escape to when they have an opportunity to take a quick ride. I've found it more difficult to find tours close to home—one- or two-day rides that aren't part of a longer trip to distant points. With this in mind, I've identified twenty three tours of various lengths that are within the one- to four-day category—with time figured in to enjoy the various attractions to be found on each ride. In fact, what may seem like a one-day ride in many cases is a two-day tour because the average speeds are well below the mile-a-minute rate we're all used to, and there are many sites along the way that call for exploration.

The majority of these trips are round-trip tours so that a rider doesn't just go from point A to point B, having to figure out a way back home. Over the years I've noted that many of my rides are "circular" and start and end at a common point—either home or some other base, such as a campsite or motel. With this fact in mind, I lay out round trips that include scenic and enjoyable roads for the entire distance, ending up back at the beginning without doubling back on the same road.

I will no doubt expose some "secret" riding roads of long-time Ohio residents. Unlike other "secret" places, such as a favorite trout fishing hole that can, in fact, be ruined by overfishing or a golf course that a player hopes will not become crowded by being discovered, I don't think having more motorcyclists on these great riding roads will harm the experience or make them somehow less enjoyable for current users. I've learned about some of my favorite roads by talking with other motorcyclists, often at a gas station or restaurant. I've observed that bikers like to talk about great riding roads that they've discovered, and they are generally more than happy to share that information with others they know will find similar enjoyment.

In fact, a fascinating phenomenon that only occurs when traveling on a motorcycle is the number of total strangers—people that wouldn't pay you a moment's notice if you were another car driver—who will go out of their way to talk to you about where you're from, where you are heading, how the trip is going, and so on. It's a very interesting statement on how people view us. I'm constantly amazed that folks from young kids to great-grandmothers will make it a point to talk to bikers at a gas pump or restaurant. I think even those who wouldn't get on a bike on a dare are still fascinated by the sense of adventure that motorcycles, and those crazy enough in their minds to ride them, represent.

Rides described in this book cover all parts of the state. In fact, a total of 6,697 wonderful miles are detailed in the twenty-three tours outlined herein, taking you, the reader and the rider, to innumerable fabulous places on fun-filled roads. I have little patience with travel writers who only extol the most obvious places or roads. The Hocking Hills, for instance, are fantastic and are frequently the topic of moto-journalism articles, but there are many other areas in Ohio that also deserve coverage because they, too, have great roads, attractions, and grand stories to be told. I think you'll find that I cover not only the obvious places that are already well known but the lesser known regions and roads, as well.

Besides its distinct geographic areas, Ohio also has cultural attractions, such as canals, Indian mounds, old military forts, covered bridges, and other features that offer a means of categorizing tours. Rides are grouped according to these basic geographical, historical, and cultural criteria. Another category covers the several historic roads that cross Ohio. In the same way that so many people are fascinated with U.S. Route 66 and the sense of adventure and freedom of travel that it represented, Ohio also has historic roads that for generations represented that same kind of opportunity to satisfy the wanderlust in millions of folks in the past. These roads and highways are part of our history, both as a state and nation. I think we ought to rediscover and celebrate them and keep their stories alive.

You will note that I've tried real hard to keep you off of expressways. These super highways have their place in this modern world, but I don't believe that expressways are the realm of motorcyclists. Besides, most of us have to drive them every day in our four-wheeled cages, so what's the attraction? I also avoid the interstates because I don't believe you find America along them: you find America in small towns and along country roads where friendly smiles and waves are part of the scenery. Kids on bicycles, farmers in pickup trucks, clerks at small stores or gas stations—they all have a ready smile or wave and are happy to make small talk with you, asking about your motorcycle, your trip, and your adventure.

Hurtling down an expressway at seventy miles an hour, unable to stop to enjoy the scenery, take a picture, or just stretch one's legs isn't pleasurable riding in my mind. Motorcycling is not about being assaulted by the visual blight of billboards or simply trying to arrive at a destination safely without noticing the countryside around you. And you certainly won't find adventure and exploration on expressways. The further off the beaten path you get, the more adventure and enjoyment you will find.

As Charles Kuralt said: "The Interstate Highway system is a wonderful thing. It makes it possible to go from coast to coast without seeing anything or meeting anybody. If the United States interests you, stay off the interstates."[1]

On the freeway, we are anonymous strangers in our own private world, not giving a thought to the scenery. Riding in a car with windows up, the air conditioning on, and the stereo system turned up heightens this feeling of separation. Motorcyclists, on the other hand, are always aware of the world around them. We can never isolate ourselves from our surroundings nor do we want to; rather we willingly immerse ourselves in it, which is, of course, part of the attraction. In fact, the essence of motorcycling not only includes the mechanical aspects—the leans, the power, the acceleration, the feel, and sound of the machine and so on—it involves being part of the environment around us. Motorcyclists want to be part of the real world. We know we will get cold, wet, hot, or whatever the conditions are around us, and that's fine. We accept it because the occasional discomfort is a small price to pay for the immeasurable enjoyment we receive year in and year out by riding these marvelous machines and being part of this fascinating lifestyle.

While writing about individual routes, I found myself making several references to safety issues—not things like speeding or reckless operation—those are topics you're smart enough to figure out on your own. No, I'm referring to less

[1] *A Life on the Road*. Charles Kuralt © 1990. G.P. Putnam's Sons Publisher, New York, NY.

well-known issues, such as the deer, Amish horse-drawn buggies, and agricultural equipment that share Ohio's back roads. Rather than sound like I was repeating myself, I thought I'd discuss these realities just once—so listen up!

The summer population of Ohio's state mammal, the whitetail deer, numbers about 700,000 animals, and they are located in every county. In 2004 there were 29,874 reported vehicle/deer accidents according to the Ohio Insurance Institute. This number places Ohio in fourth place nationally in the number of car and deer accidents. Only Pennsylvania, Michigan, and Illinois have more.

Ride accordingly, especially between dusk and dawn when most accidents involving wildlife occur. Also keep in mind that deer seldom travel alone. If you see one, there are almost certainly other animals nearby. This is especially true of does in the summer. If you see a female deer, chances are very good that there are a couple of fawns hiding within a few yards of mom.

Deer aren't the only problem. There are other large critters on the loose, as well as the occasional farm tractor, cow, or some other unexpected sight. The farming season and motorcycling weather coincide, of course, and that means that farm equipment will be on some of the same roads we enjoy riding. If your riding experience is primarily limited to urban areas, this reality could pose a danger if you're not cognizant of it. Also, some of the most scenic areas in Ohio have large Amish populations, and they can often be seen on primary roads in horse-drawn buggies. Give them a wide berth. Spooked horses are a danger to both the motorcyclist and buggy passengers.

Given its geographic location, Ohio has many railroad tracks crisscrossing the state. I've found that ,particularly on country roads, these crossings are often very rough. A practice of slowing way down at every crossing will pay off big dividends.

So just use basic common sense, courtesy, and intelligence, and you will enjoy safe, as well as exhilarating and enjoyable, riding. Don't cut your life's ride short—ride safely so that you'll still be enjoying motorcycling many years from now.

Many of the most desirable destinations and unique things to see and do are located in Ohio's state parks. This makes these natural and cultural wonders available to the public and protects them for future generations to see and appreciate. Whether it is a one-of-a-kind museum, historic village, lighthouse, unique geologic formation, old fort, or just a good camping spot or beach where you can relax, you won't want to miss out on the many wonders and opportunities found in Ohio's seventy-four state parks. Ohio has many dozens of local parks, campgrounds, and recreation areas, but state parks, in particular, are very popular. You should definitely make reservations if you wish to camp or reserve a cottage in one of the parks. Reservations are available at fifty-six of Ohio's state parks, and assuring a place to camp is easily accomplished by calling 1-866-OHIOPARKS or by going on line to www.ohiostateparks.org. According to the Ohio Department of Natural Resources, about fifty-five million people visit Ohio state parks each year. This is the second highest total for state park use in the country.

Ohio is one of only eight states that don't charge an entrance fee for its state parks. There is a proposal that could result in parking fees being charged in 2006 or beyond, but nothing is certain yet. These parking fees will be similar in price to what some states charge as entrance fees. So stay tuned and be ready for the possibility of shelling out a few bucks if you visit an Ohio state park in the future. Personally, I have no problem with it. I am willing to pay for the services that state parks offer and the protection they provide for irreplaceable public treasures. I take comfort in knowing that my great grandchildren will also be able to see and enjoy the wonders protected by our country's park system.

There are also six national parks and historical sites in Ohio that protect public resources. These sites include: the Cuyahoga Valley National Park south of Cleveland; Perry's Victory and International Peace Memorial at Put-In-Bay; the James A. Garfield Historic Site in Mentor; the Hopewell Culture National Historic Park near Chillicothe; the Dayton Aviation Heritage National Historic Park (at three locations in Dayton); and the William Howard Taft National Historic Site in Cincinnati.

Every group that shares a common passion stresses the need to get young people involved. That is no different in motorcycling. There is a bit of built-in tension when it comes to our machines, however, because of the very freedom and ability to get away from life's daily issues that they represent. We usually want to escape by ourselves to find that intrinsic freedom that being on the motorcycle brings. I encourage you to make motorcycling more of a family-oriented activity when possible. It can be a wonderful way to connect.

I believe those who are developmentally disabled can benefit and find great enjoyment in this activity. While this might seem a stretch, I know from personal experience that it works. My son is developmentally disabled and is also autistic and hyperactive. When he was five years old, I set him on the gas tank in front of me—I know, all the experts recommend against this, but on back roads and at very slow speeds it can be done safely. No parent would knowingly expose their child to excessive danger, but taking a youngster for a ride, assuming they have the desire, is a great way to allow them to enjoy the activity and do some bonding at the same time.

My son just loved it. At home or in public, he couldn't sit still for ten seconds and wanted to be by himself all the time due to his autism. But on the motorcycle, he sat motionless for long periods of time, soaking in the world around him and

enjoying all the sensations he was experiencing. He quickly graduated to the back of the bike and has traveled many thousands of miles throughout the Midwest with me. He enjoyed every minute of it, learned a great deal, and had many memorable experiences as a result of the trips we took. The alternative—sitting home and watching television or otherwise idling away his time—was just unacceptable in comparison.

If you have or know of a child that is able to ride and who is willing to give it a try, then provide the opportunity if you feel confident in doing so. Don't make the mistake of assuming they can't or that they don't want to—you just might be wrong on both counts.

Before hitting the road, I have just one more suggestion for you back road travelers. That is, experience not only the road, the scenery, and the local lore but the other things that make up Ohio. Food, for instance, is always high on any motorcyclist's list of priorities. Make fun and memorable eating part of the overall experience. I appreciate the convenience of fast food establishments, but it's so much more interesting when you avoid the clown, the king, and the pig-tailed girl and enjoy real food with an ethnic or local flavor. I find that eating in the many hometown restaurants that can still be found across the state adds an additional sense of discovery when on a trip, as well as allowing one to meet some wonderful small-town folks who still serve up home-cooked food. A glass of locally-produced wine or a beer from one of Ohio's microbreweries is a great way to end a fun day of riding.

Oh, one final point. I hate to admit it in this book, which after all is dedicated to motorcycle touring, but these tours make great automobile trips as well. Now if I had my way, four-wheeled vehicles would be banned from all the great riding roads identified herein any time the ground wasn't covered with snow. But if you must drive a car, these tours can make that burden a little more enjoyable.

The fine print: You'll find that each tour has a mileage chart accompanying it, with distances between certain points of the tour and a running mileage total, as well as a map that give you a picture of the route without a lot of detail. These charts and maps are meant to provide a quick overview of the trip so you know what's around the corner. They're not meant to provide mileage to the tenth-mile level of exactness. I've yet to meet the biker who needs someone to hold their hand and tell them to go exactly 8.6 miles and then turn left.

In calculating mileage for the circular tours, I had to choose a starting point and also whether to go in a clockwise or counterclockwise direction. I also had to start at one end of the straight line of historic road and Ohio River tours. You may well choose to make the trip in the opposite direction and use different starting points, so don't feel bound by the charts and maps—they're here to help you plan the trip, give you an idea of what towns and roads await you and where, and give a graphic representation of the layout and geographic location of the tours.

I have tried hard to give enough detail in the rides so that you can plot the tours on your GPS unit if you wish. In recent years I've become a big fan of GPS. If your riding style is such that you use interstate highways to travel long distances, then a GPS unit might be a waste of money. Use those dollars for other motorcycle accessories! But if you ride a lot of back roads, a GPS will not only make these adventures more fun but also safer. Glancing down frequently at a map in the plastic sleeve on your tank bag is dangerous. We all do it, but a GPS unit—mounted near eye level—offers a safer alternative. If you don't use a GPS device, I suggest purchasing a map book of Ohio counties and plotting the rides on the pages of the map book. (By the way, I don't recommend the popular DeLorme county map books. The print used to label roads is extremely small in size and impossible to read at a glance, and the differentiation between a small dirt township road and a primary paved county road is so slight as to be nondiscernable—they're all just red lines across the pages. Get a map book with each type of road shown in a different color so that you will be able to tell, in a quick glance, whether the road in question is gravel or paved, and whether it's a county, state, or federal road.)

Over the years, I've "destroyed" many county map books by tearing all the pages out so I could fold them up as needed in my tank bag and take them with me. That way I just changed to a new map as I entered a different county. This isn't necessary if one rides just main roads, but if you ride a lot of back roads, it's a county map book you need, not a state highway map. I still do this even with a GPS unit on board. The need for paper maps will never disappear in my opinion.

In an attempt to provide you with helpful information, I have provided numerous phone numbers in the appendices. These include contact information for all sheriff and highway patrol offices, plus numbers for motel chains and emergency numbers for lost or stolen credit cards. I've made every attempt to ensure up-to-date accuracy, but of course, phone numbers are not cast in concrete and do change occasionally. I also provide a lengthy list of motorcycle dealers for virtually every brand of bike out there. In the event you encounter mechanical problems on the road, you'll be able to find a nearby dealer for help. (Dealers—this resource is to help bikers, it's not meant to be the equivalent of a yellow pages listing so if I missed you, *mea culpa*.)

Enough talking! Let's do our preride checklist and saddle up! We've got some riding to do!

William M. Murphy

Discovering Ohio

T HIS SECTION, as its name not very subtly suggests, is all about discovering the great places and roads of Ohio. In this chapter we'll travel the length and breadth of this beautiful state and discover some of its best kept secrets that beg exploration, as well as its better-known attractions that are even more enjoyable when experienced from atop two wheels. Be prepared to ride on some of the best motorcycling roads in the Midwest, to learn about some of Ohio's most fascinating natural and manmade places, and discover first-hand the stories and people that make up the very fabric of this state and its culture. You can do all of this while enjoying some of the best motorcycling routes this side of the Rockies!

Castles and Caverns

THIS TOUR MAY BE THE BEST introductory ride in this book because of its location. Situated in the area just north and northwest of Columbus, it's a region that most folks wouldn't think of as prime motorcycling country. Wrong! This ride takes you through beautiful countryside on marvelous motorcycling roads and to natural and cultural attractions that are just fantastic and that should be high on everybody's list of must-see places. It goes through a remarkable landscape rich in both beauty and history.

This particular tour is also a good place to discuss some of the behind-the-scenes issues involved in crafting the rides you'll find in the book. You may be thinking, for instance, that this and some other tours have irregular jogs or shapes, and couldn't I have made them a lot easier to follow, and wouldn't it have made more sense to just use roads that make a nice neat package without the twists and turns? Well, there are two reasons why these tours take the form they do: First, I hate taking straight and boring roads and avoid them whenever possible; and second and the most important, a great deal of thought has gone into these tours. I take you down roads and to places that are not only great fun on a motorcycle, but where you can see up close and personal the natural and cultural attractions that are fundamental to the character and history of Ohio.

I purposely devised tours that take the rider down history-filled roads that started out as trails, such as the Sandusky Trail, the Bullskin Trace, Hull's Trace, and more. I planned the rides to include as many attractions as possible on each route, carefully crafting tours that take in the best attractions in the area (obviously not getting to all of them, but most!). So, when the route jogs or turns in ways that don't seem sensible, just be patient and remember there is logic behind the seeming madness and that wonderful roads and attractions await you around the next bend!

So, with the above thoughts in mind, this particular tour will make an extraordinary one- or two-day motorcycle trip with frequent stops to see the many attractions along the way. Let's fill up the gas tank (I'm serious) and begin our trip in the city of Delaware. Take US42 to the northeast corner of town, just past the YMCA Greenwood Lake Camp and turn left on Horseshoe Road. Horseshoe is an okay riding road but certainly not the best you'll experience during this trip. After

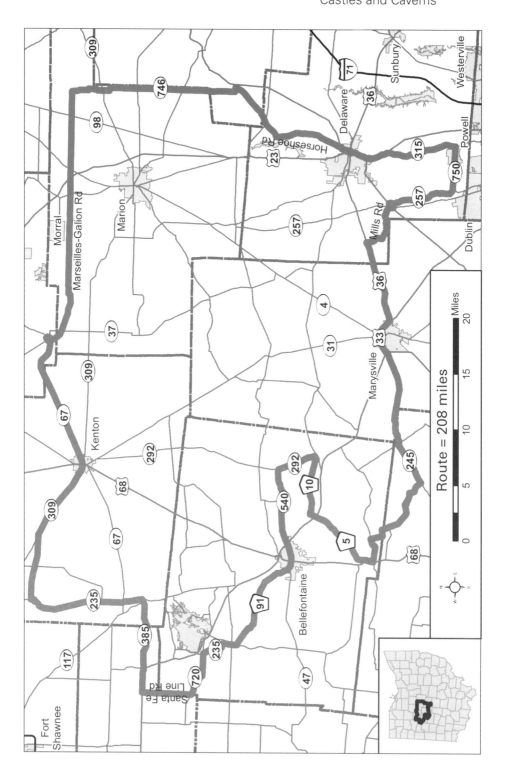

CASTLES AND CAVERNS 208 MILES		
Miles	**Destination**	**Total**
0	Delaware	0
27	Caledonia	27
27	Marseilles	54
13	Kenton	67
25	Roundhead`	92
31	Bellefontaine	123
18	Zanesfield	141
31	Marysville	172
36	Delaware	208

a few miles, it forms the east boundary of the Delaware Reservoir Wildlife Area and has enough curves and scenery to keep it interesting.

At SR229 the road angles northeast and becomes CR156, which we'll continue on for four more miles to SR746. The state road jogs west a very short distance and then continues north through land that changes from wooded to mostly farmland as you approach the small town of Caledonia (the boyhood hometown of President Warren G. Harding). SR746 ends in Caledonia, but we want to continue straight north on what is now Caledonia–Northern Road. It makes a couple of small jogs just north of town but essentially goes due north.

From the north side of Caledonia, we go less than three miles to Marseilles-Galion Road and turn west/left. Hopefully, you took my advice and topped off the tank, because from here west you're going through one of the most wide open of Ohio's various wide-open spaces. This segment due west to Marseilles is probably different than what you had in mind. It's through farm country—some of the best farmland in Ohio. In fact, it's called the Grand Prairie, and you'll do a double take thinking you've inexplicably ended up in North Dakota. But this is Ohio—a part of the state that folks who commute on expressways each day don't see. This portion of the trip, while lacking hills and serious curves, is an experience in itself and something different than the routine. It's twenty-four miles due west to the village of Marseilles, which itself is merely a wide spot in the road. Marseilles-Galion Road isn't meant for speed, tempting as it may be, and of course, keep in mind that this is farm country so don't be surprised by farm implements sharing the road with you. Just before reaching Marseilles, you join SR37 and follow it to town where you get on SR67 westbound—next stop Kenton.

One of the most famous characters in Ohio's colorful history is Simon Kenton. Explorer, frontiersman, Indian fighter, military officer, and woodsman—it's regrettable that his name and deeds aren't better known than they are. He is certainly Ohio's Daniel Boone (in fact, they were close friends, and in 1777 Kenton saved Boone's life), and while his name will be long-remembered, I don't believe the man himself gets his due respect. That's a shame because his story is a fascinating one. I know of no one today who possesses the courage Kenton had and who endured what he did. Kenton survived on pure grit, guts, and incredible tenacity. Amazingly, he survived running *nine* gauntlets while a prisoner of the Shawnee at various times (most men didn't survive the ordeal once), and he once traveled hundreds of miles through the wilderness after escaping captivity despite having received several broken bones during one of these events. He survived injuries that would have left most others in the grave. Kenton is buried in Urbana, where a life-size sculpture honors him.

The city of Kenton is as rock-solid as its namesake, located in the heart of an area with history stretching back to the late 1700s, though the town itself didn't have its beginning until 1845. Three miles west of town is where General Hull cut what was to be called Hull's Trace through the wilderness while on his way to garrison Fort Detroit in the early days of the War of 1812. It is also the location of Fort McArthur, which was built in 1812 to protect this vital supply route. (A monument marks the site—take SR309 northwest out of town and turn left on CR106).

An interesting story about the city of Kenton involves the famous cowboy crooner, Gene Autry, and his trademark silver six-shooter. The Kenton Hardware Company had once been the largest manufacturer of iron toys in the world. During the Great Depression they fell on hard times and were struggling to survive. The company's vice president believed that if they could produce a toy gun based on Gene Autry's famous revolver it would save them. The venture was so successful they couldn't keep up with demand. Today, Kenton celebrates Gene Autry Day and a wonderful mural graces the side of a downtown building at the corner of Franklin and Market Streets, along with a small park at that location. During the Civil War, Camp Simon Kenton, located at today's county fairgrounds, was a Union training camp.

We continue our trip by heading west on SR309. On the west side of Kenton is a railroad track, and six miles from this track, you'll come to where County Roads 90 and 95 intersect with 309. You want to take CR90 west to the village of Alger and SR235, heading south on 235 to the tiny village of Roundhead. If you happen to miss CR90/95, don't panic—just take SR309 to SR235 and proceed south.

Roundhead is a tiny village with quite a story to tell. It was the home of Detroit Wyandot Chief Stiahta—*aka* Roundhead. Chief Roundhead was fiercely opposed to white encroachment in the Ohio Country. He joined Tecumseh's Indian Confederacy and sided with the British during the War of 1812. Like other Native Americans allied with the British, Roundhead didn't give a damn about Great Britain and their empire, he simply believed that British enmity toward the Americans could be exploited for the Indian cause. Roundhead is most infamously known as the assassin of Wyandot Chief Leatherlips near present-day Columbus. Chief Leatherlips believed that the time had come to lay down the hatchet and try to live with the white man, and for this Tecumseh ordered him killed. Roundhead fought several battles in the War of 1812, including the Battle of River Raisin (Frenchtown) and the Battle of the Thames (Moravia) in Ontario, where he and Tecumseh were both killed. The village of Roundhead is also in the headwaters of the historic and strategically important Scioto River.

From Roundhead we proceed eight and a half miles west on SR385, past the village of New Hampshire to Santa Fe Line Road (CR17), and turn left, going four and a half miles to the tiny crossroads of Santa Fe. At this point we turn east on SR720, taking it southeast and then east four miles to SR235, where we turn right. Follow SR235 as it curves southeast past the Honda Transmission Plant and then straight south less than a mile and a half to County Road 91, where you turn left. County Road 91 goes southeast cross-country toward Bellefontaine. Just west of Bellefontaine, it joins CR130, which enters Bellefontaine as Garfield Avenue and then Sandusky Avenue through downtown. It's very simple to follow, just the road names change, not the route.

Bellefontaine is an historic and attractive city. You'll pass through the small downtown section, and I suggest parking the bike to admire the beautiful Logan County Courthouse and other buildings whose 19th-century architecture adds character to this very typical Ohio small town. In front of the courthouse is McKinley Street, which in 1891 was the first road in America to be paved with concrete.

Following Sandusky Avenue east out of Bellefontaine, it becomes SR540. Take route 540 east until it makes a T with SR292 and turn right. The area east of Bellefontaine is Ohio's high country. A stranger might expect that the hilly south of Ohio would be where one would find the highest land in the state, however that's not the case. Campbell Hill, the highest point in Ohio, is just east of Bellefontaine, and the entire region is wonderfully hilly with very nice geologic relief and beautiful scenery. Roads in this area are custom-made for motorcycling, with hills and curves aplenty dishing up top-notch riding for the most discriminating biker.

This area is physiologically different than southern Ohio because of glacial action. Glacial drift up to one hundred feet thick covers the preglacial sandstone

*Bellefontaine
Courthouse*

and limestone landscape, resulting in "softer" hills of clay and gravel as compared to the hills common in the south, where exposed bedrock is the common feature.

In a sense that gives this area the best of both worlds—the presence of high hills plus the Karst formation common in limestone regions. The first of several of the most obvious by-products of Karst geology (caverns) can be found along SR540 east of Bellefontaine at Zane Shawnee Caverns, which is open to the public for tours. Call 937-592-9592 for more information about tours.

Heading south on SR295 takes you through more wonderful countryside on the way to the village of East Liberty. The riding gets even more fun as you head

Mac-a-Cheek Castle

west out of East Liberty on CR10 along the Bristol Ridge to the town of Zanes-field. This is a grand road, and the last mile into Zanesfield, where you drop three hundred feet in elevation very quickly, is especially enjoyable. Once at Zanesfield you want to turn left, go past the very large boulder monument to Simon Kenton and Isaac Zane, and then southwest on CR5 to the town of West Liberty. Just out-side of Zanesfield, you'll notice the Mad River Ski Area on your left. County Road 5 to West Liberty makes for a very enjoyable ride. On SR68 on the north side of West Liberty, notice the historical sign for Hull's Trace and Moluntha (who was the leading Shawnee Chief who surrendered himself and his family to General Logan but was murdered by an overzealous colonel).

This area lies within Logan County, which has a rich Native American history. Many tribes hunted here and several, including the Shawnee, Wyandot, Seneca, and Mingo, established villages. Zane's Town was a Wyandot village, and Wapa-tomica, which was the capital village of the Shawnee and the Seven Tribes, was also located near present-day Zanesfield. In 1786 General Benjamin Logan led a contingent of soldiers in a concerted effort at moving the Indians out of the Ohio Country. Many atrocities followed, including the burning of entire Indian villages. You're truly riding with the ghosts of those who came before you in this fascinating part of the state.

Mac-o-Chee Castle

For such a tiny town, West Liberty has an astonishing amount of history—too much to detail in this book. A camp located immediately south of town even served as a training base for soldiers during the Spanish-American War and World War I. Today, West Liberty may be best known for two fabulous homes built after the Civil War by two very gifted brothers—Abram and Donald Piatt.

From West Liberty take SR245 east. Just outside of town you'll notice the sign for Mac-A-Cheek castle. There is also an historical marker at this site explaining the history of the Shawnee villages in the Mackachack Valley. Machachak is a Shawnee word meaning "smiling valley," and what a beautiful valley and home for generations of Native Americans this must have been!

Take Township Road 47 a very short distance to Mac-A-Cheek castle, the first of the two Piatt Castles. A mile farther east on SR245, where the road turns south, is Mac-O-Chee Castle. Both of these palatial homes are open daily, 11:00 am–5:00 pm, for self-guided or group tours. Even if you don't do the tour, it's a

wonderful stop to walk the grounds and gaze upon and appreciate these marvelous labors of love. Call 937-465-2821 or go to www.piattcastles.org for more
information on tours and events at the Piatt Castles.

Upon leaving the castles, SR245 heads south, and shortly you will see signs
for Ohio Caverns. These are the largest and perhaps the grandest of the caverns
in Ohio and make an enjoyable stop—assuming you're not claustrophobic. From
April through October, daily tours are offered from 9:00 am–5:00 pm. At this point
SR245 is running generally south and just past the Caverns is Tabor Hill, with a
cemetery and church at the peak. This spot provides a wonderful panoramic view
of this beautiful area. In fact, the entire stretch of route 245 in the Mingo area
provides fabulous scenery and motorcycling as the road dips and weaves and takes
you along for a most enjoyable ride.

Enjoy SR245 all the way east to US33, where you can skirt around Marysville,
and then continue east on US36 for seven and a half miles to Ostrander Road. Go
south on Ostrander Road a total of a mile and a half, which takes you through
the village of Ostrander and over Mill Creek, where you will come to Mills Road.
Take this enjoyable county road east as it curves alongside Mill Creek to its juncture with SR257. Follow SR257 as it turns east across the river and then about six
and a half miles south along the east shoreline of the O'Shaughnessy Reservoir to
SR750/Powell Road. The Columbia Zoo is at the northeast corner of the 257/750
intersection.

Take Powell Road east four miles through a rapidly developing area of yuppie
housing to SR315/Olentangy River Road. This Ohio Scenic Byway hugs the shore
of the Olentangy River and is a very pleasant ride. About midway to Delaware,
you'll see signs for the Olentangy Indian Caverns, located just west of SR315 on
Home Road. It's an easy intersection to spot—just look for the large 1810 Liberty Presbyterian Church on the corner. The Indian Caverns are very interesting.
There is evidence that Native Americans used the caverns for many years prior to
their discovery by white settlers in 1821. Site operators claim that Wyandot Chief
Leatherlips was assassinated in 1810 at the entrance to the caverns, though others
claim the killing took place about three miles to the south. Associated with the
caverns is Ohio Frontier Land, where a replica frontier town teaches today's visi-
tors about frontier life. Between April and October, cavern tours are offered daily
from 9:30 am–5:00 pm. Call them at 740-548-7917.

Finish the tour by taking SR315 north to the city of Delaware, a thriving city
of 30,000. Delaware derived its name from the Delaware Indians who lived in
the region in pre-Columbian times. A great time to visit Delaware is September,
when there are week-long events surrounding the Little Brown Jug harness racing
event—a very popular race that is part of the triple crown of harness racing. A hot

air balloon festival is also held each September. Perhaps more in line with your motorcycling interests is the Love America Cycle Expo & Rally—a fun motorcycle event held in mid June each year at the Delaware County Fairgrounds. Call 614-893-3311 for more info.

Delaware was the 1822 birthplace of President Rutherford B. Hayes. It was also a major player in the Underground Railroad, with nearby Africa Road a legacy of that era. It has many historic homes, and its downtown historic area is a fine place to park the bike and take a walk.

And there you have it! A fabulous ride through wonderful scenery, down roads that deserve distinction as great motorcycling routes, through locations of compelling historical significance, and to natural and manmade attractions that must be seen to be appreciated. This tour in the heart of Ohio really does have it all.

The Amish, Zoarites, and Simon Bolívar

LIKE A BEAUTIFUL QUILT, Ohio is made up of many different pieces and includes not only differing geographic areas but also diverse ethnic and cultural components. The land is rich with the culture of its native peoples and with the contributions of its various immigrant groups, from German sausage makers in Bucyrus to the Welsh iron and coal miners of Ironton. One group that has left a very definite mark on Ohio is comprised of European immigrants who came here in the earliest days of settlement seeking freedom from religious persecution. These folks were outside the accepted mainstream back in Europe but found acceptance and a new life in the Ohio wilderness. In grade school we all learned about the Pilgrims, however, there are many other religious groups who severed their Old World ties for the New World. Among these were the Mennonites, Amish, Dunkards, Zoarites, Quakers, and Moravians. These hard-working and highly principled people played a significant role in the settlement of Ohio. They were also later to become a powerful force in the abolitionist movement because of their very strong opposition to the idea of slavery.

While there are clusters of these cultural groups throughout Ohio, the east-central portion of the state has the highest concentrations. In fact the Holmes County area has the largest Amish community, not only in Ohio but in the world! This tour takes in the best of that part of Ohio where these unique religious communities settled. Keeping in mind the fundamental principle of this book—exploring the world around you on two wheels and on great motorcycling roads—I know you're going to enjoy this tour.

So just who are these peaceful, hard-working neighbors who are called Amish? According to Amish Brotherhood publications, the Amish are a conservative segment of the Anabaptists, of which the Mennonites are a part. They came from Germany and Switzerland in the 1700s to escape religious persecution. Their name derives from Jacob Amman, a leader of the group in the early 1700s.

The Amish believe the Bible teaches them to live lives of simplicity. It's not that they believe modern gadgets to be inherently evil, it's just that they believe adoption of modern ways and use of modern technology disrupts the simple, family-oriented lifestyle they cherish.

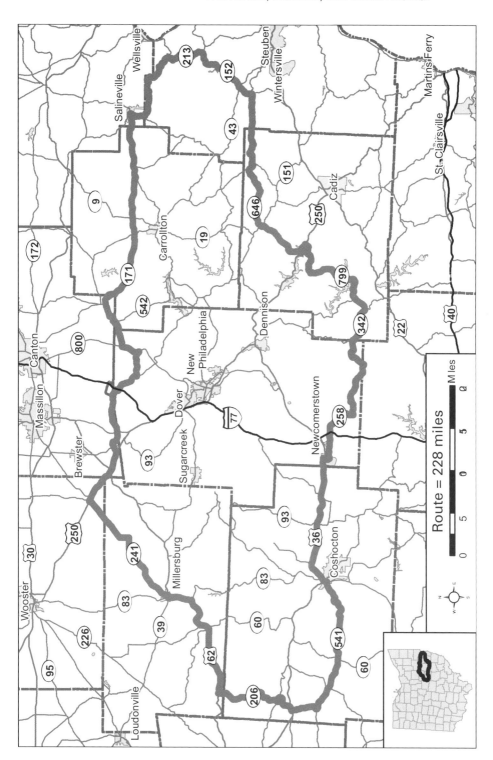

THE AMISH, THE ZOARITES, AND SIMON BOLIVAR 228 MILES		
Miles	**Destination**	**Total**
0	Coshocton	0
34	Highway US62	34
16	Millersburg	50
16	Mt. Eaton	66
18	Zoar	84
36	Salineville	120
23	Richmond	143
20	Scio	163
23	Freeport	186
25	Newcomerstown	211
17	Coshocton	228

I've always felt that the Amish hold a special place in the hearts of many Americans because they hold firmly to traditional values, such as hard work, honesty, a high quality work product, and family—values that the great majority of the general population still believe in, even if they're not always put in practice. The Amish also remind us that even in the twenty-first century people can exist just fine without the latest gadgets and distractions that most of us can't imagine living without.

We begin this marvelous tour in Coshocton, which is yet another example of Ohio's wonderful small and vibrant historic towns that also happens to be a fun place to spend some time exploring. On the north edge of town is Roscoe Village, a re-creation of the old canal town that this city once was. Here you can discover how a canal worked, see a canal boat, and visit the Johnson-Humrick House Museum, where various regional artifacts, including Native American items, are on display. A tour of the village is an enjoyable and educational diversion.

We commence the trip by going west on SR541 to New Guilford and SR206, which we follow north to Holmes County and US62, twisting and turning all the way! In Holmes County we're in the heart of Amish Country. Go east on US62, a designated Ohio Scenic Byway, taking it all the way into the county seat of Millersburg, a charming and attractive town with a character all its own. With its beautiful nineteenth century courthouse, the magnificent Victorian House, and historic

Millersburg Courthouse

Hotel Millersburg, it's a great place to stop and walk. Spending the night at Hotel Millersburg would be a special treat. They served their first guest in 1847, so they have had plenty of experience in this business! Call 330-674-1457 if you're interested. Every August Millersburg hosts a classic car show, and each September they host Motorcycle Mania—an event you won't want to miss. Call 330-674-5629 for more information on these events.

Upon departing Millersburg, go north on SR241—another Ohio Scenic Byway and good biking route—and take it through a picture-perfect landscape of farms and scenic hilly countryside to Mt. Eaton. I suspect SR241 earned its Scenic Byway title from its cultural uniqueness rather than its purely aesthetic qualities. While it's a nice enough road, there are many others that outrank it when it comes to pure scenic value and fun riding. There are lots of Amish folk in horse and buggies along this route, so don't be in a hurry. As cars pass these buggies, they cross the center line and on hills and curves you need to be watchful. Along this route there are also many shops and stores where you can part with your money. Fortunately, motorcycles really aren't compatible with shopping for wicker baskets, quilts, chairs and so on, so while it may be fun to browse, you probably won't buy much. (More money for those necessary motorcycle accessories!)

At Mt. Eaton go east on US250 for seven miles and get on SR212 at Beach City. With its many curves and hills, SR212 is a nicer riding road than 241 or 250 (which weren't bad!). Take SR212 east to Tuscarawas County and the town of Bolivar—the next recommended stop. Bolivar is very much a canal town, being the west terminus of the short-lived Sandy & Beaver Canal, which ran from Bolivar to Glasgow, PA (the canal is named after local streams, not soil and a furbearing animal). The town is named after famous South American General and freedom fighter Simon Bolívar. The town was originally called Kelleyville but was renamed in honor of Bolívar. We have to put ourselves in the minds of folks alive in the early 1800s. From the period of 1810 to 1824, Simon Bolívar defeated the Spanish colonial masters in what are now Venezuela, Columbia, Bolivia, and Ecuador. The same year that Bolivar, Ohio, was formed, the name of the country called Upper Peru was changed to its current name in honor of Bolívar. The young country of America, having won its own revolution not long before, admired such men.

Besides the canal history, the main attraction in Bolivar is the site of Fort Lauren, the only Revolutionary War fort built in Ohio. It was built in 1778 by General McIntosh as part of George Washington's plan to take the war to the British in the frontier. For decades the British had held Fort Detroit, and they were encouraging Indian attacks on settlers throughout the frontier. (The English thought the Great Lakes area so important that they refused to leave Detroit until 1796—thirteen years after they lost the Revolutionary War and signed the Treaty of Paris, which granted these lands to the new United States of America.)

The colonies couldn't afford Washington's plan to attack Detroit, so instead, the order of battle was changed to simply attacking British interests in the Lake Erie region. The placement of a fort in the middle of enemy territory certainly got the attention of the British and their Native American allies. It was repeatedly attacked, and twenty-plus American soldiers were killed and buried in the fort cemetery. The Tomb of the Unknown Patriot of the American Revolution is located at the Fort Laurens museum.

From the fort, go back to SR212 and take it southeast to the town of Zoar.

The history of Zoar is a fascinating one. In 1817 a group of Germans seeking religious freedom (a common theme in America's early immigrants) bought five thousand acres at what is now the town of Zoar. These people called themselves Zoarists, after the city of the same name in the Old Testament, which means "sanctuary from evil." They believed strongly in the separation of church and state. Once in America, they formed a communal society in 1819 called The Society of Separatists of Zoar. The commune prospered until the late 1800s and was disbanded in 1898, with assets divided among members. The many old buildings of the commune still exist.

To resume the trip, turn east/left on 2nd Street at the Zoar Hotel, go over the narrow bridge, and continue east on what becomes Mineral City–Zoar Road beyond the city limits. This road is a bit rough though certainly passable on any motorcycle. Take MC-ZR east to SR800, turning north/left on 800 just a bit to SR183, where we turn right, taking it through the village of Magnolia and on to Waynesburg. At Waynesburg get on SR171, taking it cross-country through the rolling woods and farmlands of Carroll County. State Route 171 ends at SR9, but Cobbler Road/CR71 continues straight ahead, so take it. This whole stretch is wonderful riding and beautiful countryside. Cobbler Road runs into SR39, where we turn left and continue east to the town of Salineville just across the Columbiana County line. On the east side of Salineville, you want to get on SR64 southbound. At this corner, there is a brown sign pointing south to "Brush Creek Area." This is a short but very fun road south to Monroeville, and the Monroeville–Irondale Road, on which you turn left. I'm sounding redundant, but Monroeville–Irondale Road is another cool biking road as it winds over the hills and through the woods to Irondale. It's the kind of road that makes you and your bike feel like dance partners as you float gracefully across the rural Ohio ballroom, moving to a beat created by machine, road, and scenery.

The last couple of miles into Irondale are especially nice as you wind down the steep hill to the river valley below. As you enter Irondale, you will see a blue iron bridge straight ahead of you and a road immediately before the bridge. Turn right on this road, called Creek Street/CR56, and take it to Hammondsville. This short stretch of road is very cool! It has high cliffs on one side and the river on the other as it winds south.

From Hammondsville take SR213 south through the beautiful hills and valleys that make up this entire region of the state. Tag along with SR213 to the crossroads of Knoxville and pick up SR152 and follow it southwest. I guarantee you'll love this part of the tour, and it only gets better. Just beyond the village of Richmond turn right on SR646 and follows its wonderful curves over hill and through dale into Harrison County and the town of Scio. Shortly before arriving at Scio, you'll pass through the tiny burg of New Rumley. This town's claim to fame is that it was the birthplace of General George Armstrong Custer, of Civil War and western Indian Wars fame. (The greatest fame, of course, being the Battle of the Little Big Horn where Custer and his entire troop were annihilated). A statue showing the General in all his glory is the centerpiece of a small park set aside in honor of Custer in New Rumley.

Route 646 deserves to be nominated for the motorcycling roads hall of fame. It is that wonderful. In fact, if at any time on this tour you lose the grin on your face it's because you've been pulled over for speeding. There is no other rational explanation. These roads are just great!

We depart Scio to the south on SR646/Tappan-Scio Road to US250 and Lake Tappan. Take US250 east along the shoreline less than two miles and turn right to drive over the lake on Deersville Road, following it as it curves around, eventually reaching the small village of Deersville. At the stop sign in Deersville, turn left/south onto Mallarnee Road, which becomes SR799 a few miles south. Route 799 is a designated scenic highway, and as you follow it along the rugged shoreline of Clendening Lake, you'll understand why. The scenery is just fabulous. Enjoy route 799's charms all the way to SR800, then follow 800 a short distance into the village of Freeport.

From Freeport, we work our way west for quite a distance on route 342, which will shortly join forces with SR258. I'm sorry if I'm again sounding redundant, but this road will continue to amaze and please you with its wonderful scenery, hills, curves and just plain great motorcycling ambience. These magical qualities aren't lost until just prior to arriving at Newcomerstown, located just west of I-77.

The name of Newcomerstown almost certainly brings a puzzled look to many faces when they first hear it. You're no doubt guessing that there's a story behind the name, and you'd be correct. If the town had retained its original Indian name—Gekelemukpechuk—there would really be a lot of pained expressions as people tried to pronounce it!

Gekelemukpechuk was the capital of the Delaware Indian nation. When the white folks first arrived in the 1770s, they found a prosperous and peace-loving village of a hundred log cabins ruled by Chief Netawatwes, a name that was pronounced Newcomer by the whites. Chief Netawatwes maintained peace during the Revolutionary and Indian Wars. Chief Newcomer's town had always been a large and important village, but it began to grow substantially when the canal arrived in 1827. Newcomerstown has always been strategically located. In the past it was the canal, two railroad lines, and a stagecoach road that crossed here, while today, it's two major highways. The town has stories to tell beyond those I've mentioned. Have you heard of names such as Cy Young and Woody Hayes? They were both native sons. A couple of very interesting places to visit here are the Temperance Tavern Museum, housed in an 1841 inn, and the USS Radford National Naval Museum located next door.

Coming into Newcomerstown from the southeast on route 258, you'll want to turn left onto State Street, taking it several blocks west to College Street, where you'll turn right. Going north on College Street will take you to US36, but just prior to reaching route 36, you'll pass Cy Young Park on your right. There's a monument to this baseball superhero in the park that's kind of nice to see.

Get on US36 and follow this scenic highway west to Coshocton. This road itself is by no means a slouch when it comes to pleasant riding. Sure, it is calm

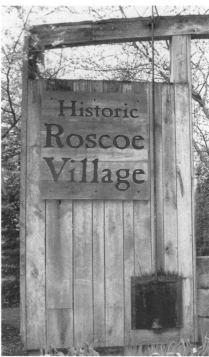

Roscoe Village is a re-creation of the old canal town at Coshocton, where you can learn how canals worked and visit the museum.

compared to the hours of fun we just had, but as you ride over forested hills next to exposed sandstone cliffs on your right and the Tuscarawas River making cameo appearances on your left, you'll have to agree that it qualifies in its own right as a fun biking road. United States Route 36 will deliver us back to Coshocton, where the Walhonding and Tuscarawas Rivers join forces and become the mighty Muskingum River, which we'll explore on another tour. When you depart route 36 at SR541, you'll be delivered to a point right across the street from Roscoe Historical Village in case you saved it for the end of the tour. The canal and canal boat are a few blocks to the east of Roscoe Village, while the various buildings and old canal locks are in the village proper. The signs will guide you on your way.

This completes a most enjoyable motorcycle tour through this part of Ohio, where thousands came to enjoy religious and economic freedom, and where the fight for freedom is honored. But beyond all that, it is plain and simply a wonderful motorcycling trip!

The Great Black Swamp

MOST FOLKS' KNOWLEDGE of the greater Toledo area is based on three things: time spent in Toledo itself, time spent at the resort and recreation areas at Marblehead and Sandusky, or by driving on I-75 or the Ohio turnpike. Certainly Toledo is an interesting place with lots of attractions. Destinations like Cedar Point and Marblehead Peninsula truly deserve their reputation as fun places, and the interstate highways are, well, efficient. But none of these activities give a true sense of north-central Ohio. This area has miles of great country roads to explore and small towns with fascinating stories to tell. I've designed this tour to take in the best of northern Ohio—the well-known places and the little-known gems that await discovery.

The area that this tour traverses is part of what was called the Great Black Swamp, which stretched south and southwest of the western Lake Erie basin. It was an inhospitable region avoided by all travelers, whether native or European. It was one of the last areas of Ohio to be explored due to miles of low swampy land that made travel extremely difficult at best. Today it's a land of fertile farms and pleasant small towns. Country roads that are a joy to ride connect towns and farms, delivering motorcyclists to attractions that add spice to the trip. I think any preconceived impressions you may have about this part of the state and what it can offer bikers will be cast aside once you've experienced the roads and many attractions that are found here.

We'll start this circular 190-mile journey in Bowling Green, proceeding straight east on SR105/Wooster Avenue out of town. If classic cars are your cup of tea, you will want to make a slight diversion to visit Snook's Dream Cars, a living museum of over twenty cars from the 1930s through 1960s. There is plenty of memorabilia, including a Texaco gas station from the 1940s. The museum is a father and son labor of love and is much more than a dusty collection of objects. All the vehicles run and, in fact, are regularly operated on the road. Snook's is located on the southeast corner of Bowling Green. Heading east out of town, turn south on Dunbridge Road just past I-75 and take it south a couple of miles to US6. The museum is at 13920 County Home Road, just north of US6 (www.snooksdreamcars.com).

Continuing on the trip, take SR105 as it meanders northeast from Bowling Green, closely following the Portage River as it tries to decide the best route to

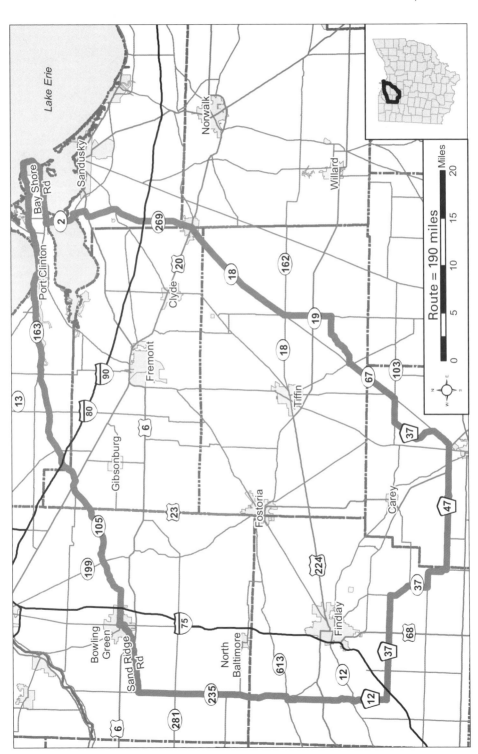

Lake Erie

Bay Shore Rd

Sandusky

Port Clinton

Norwalk

Willard

2

269

20

18

162

163

19

90

18

67

103

13

80

Fremont

Tiffin

37

6

Gibsonburg

23

Fostoria

Carey

47

105

199

224

37

Bowling Green

75

12

37

Sand Ridge Rd

North Baltimore

613

68

Findlay

37

12

235

12

6

281

Route = 190 miles

Miles
0   5   10   15   20

N
W   E
S

Snook's Dream Cars, a living museum located in Bowling Green.

Lake Erie. The stretch of road from Bowling Green to Port Clinton is truly enjoyable on a bike, having lots of curves and riverside scenery. In Oak Harbor, SR105 turns into SR163 but no turns are necessary—just follow your nose straight ahead. State Route 163 will deliver you to Port Clinton and the Marblehead Peninsula, where the maritime side of Ohio can be experienced. Follow SR163 east all the way to Marblehead Lighthouse State Park, located at the east end of the peninsula. The Marblehead Light was built in 1822 and is the oldest continuously operating light on the lakes. It opens after Memorial Day, and to top it all off you can climb the spiral staircase and really appreciate the lighthouse experience.

When ready to leave Marblehead, continue south and then west on SR163 on the south side of the peninsula. Before leaving the peninsula, consider paying the one-dollar fee and cross the Johnson Island Causeway to go to the island, which is located in Sandusky Bay off the south shore of Marblehead Peninsula. During the Civil War, Johnson Island was a large POW camp for Confederate prisoners. More than 10,000 prisoners were held there. A cemetery holds the remains of over 200 men who died on the island.

THE GREAT BLACK SWAMP 190 MILES		
Miles	**Destination**	**Total**
0	Bowling Green	0
17	Woodville	17
24	Port Clinton	41
13	Marblehead Lighthouse	54
25	Bellevue	79
14	Republic	93
28	CR47/Indian Mill	121
17	Mt. Blanchard	138
16	Rawson	154
27	Weston	181
9	Bowling Green	190

State Route 163/Bay Shore Road will take you to the Thomas A. Edison Bridge and over Sandusky Bay to the mainland. Very shortly after reaching the south shore on US2 ,you will find SR269, which you want to take south to the city of Bellevue. There are a few attractions in and near Bellevue that might interest you. High on my list is the Mad River and NKP Railroad Museum, located in town. To get to the museum, take Southwest Street (SR269) south from US20 a couple of blocks. It's a large facility with lots of rolling stock and exhibits. It's open daily from Memorial Day to Labor Day.

East of Bellevue is Lyme Village, a collection of log cabins and other preserved historic buildings, plus the Wright Mansion. If you want to visit, go east a bit to SR4 and then north a mile. They're open Tuesday–Sunday in the afternoons (419-483-4949/www.lymevillage.com for more information).

When you're ready to resume the trip, take SR18 south out of Bellevue to the small town of Republic. Just south of Bellevue, there is one more attraction you might find interesting—the Seneca Caverns. It seems odd to find a cavern in this part of Ohio because it's, well, flat! It's the last place you'd expect to find underground caverns, but that's just what you'll discover in the Karst formation found in this region. The Seneca Caverns have been a tourist attraction since 1872. The only suggestion of the existence of such a geologic phenomenon is a large limestone quarry across the road from the cavern headquarters. If you want to take an

Marblehead Lighthouse (Photo courtesy of Ohio Division of Travel and Tourism)

underground tour, turn left from SR18 onto T82 about two miles southeast of Bellevue and take it two miles to Fireside Road/Township Road 178 and the caverns. When finished, just take Fireside Road west back to SR18 and proceed south.

The next leg of the ride is straightforward—ride down SR18 to the small town of Republic. South of Republic the fun starts. The segment from Republic to Upper Sandusky actually has two possible routes depending on the rider's comfort level with narrow and twisting rural roads. In Republic, SR18 ends but SR67 continues southwest on the same alignment. If you feel that riding on one lane of blacktop on a township road isn't something you or your bike were designed for, then just continue straight on SR67 to the point on the north side of Upper Sandusky, where the trip heads west on CR47.

However, if you love a winding narrow country road, there is another option that I highly recommend. This isn't for the faint of heart, however, and it's definitely not for large groups of riders.

In the village of Republic, turn left from SR18 onto SR19 and take it due south five miles to the town of Bloomville. By the way, just south of Republic on SR19, note the really cool narrow stone railroad overpass. Built in 1900, it is quite unique. In Bloomville turn right/west at the main intersection onto CR12. County Road 12 goes straight west for two miles, then turns southwest as it twists and turns with the meanderings of Honey Creek. In this stretch the blacktop is narrow and will have some occasional dirt or small stones on it, so road racing isn't the goal, in fact, it's discouraged for reasons that will be obvious. However, it is a wonderfully enjoyable road and a fun ride. County Road 12 winds its way to the village of Melmore on SR67, then straightens out and goes straight west into Melmore for the last mile or so.

Proceeding south on SR67 close to four miles, you'll come to the town of Sycamore. In Sycamore turn west/right onto SR103 and follow it roughly three miles to CR37 and turn left. County Road 37 eventually follows the twisting headwaters of the Sandusky River and is another narrow but unique biking road as it winds through the woods and farms of this beautiful area. There are two noteworthy attractions on this route. The first is the Parker Covered Bridge, which you will

Parker Covered Bridge

find by turning left on Township Road 40. At this small intersection, you'll see a farmstead with several of the circular metal Butler buildings used for grain storage. Parker Bridge was built in 1873 and is in a very pretty setting. About a quarter mile beyond the bridge is a rural intersection that can serve as a turn-around point rather than utilizing the farm driveway just past the bridge. (I'm sure the farm residents would prefer that their driveway not be used as the place for cars and bikes to turn around after viewing the bridge.)

Back over to CR37, turn left and in about a half mile, you'll notice a monument to the great Wyandot Indian Chief Tarhe on the right side of the road, really located in the middle of nowhere. This secluded location was actually the site of the Indian village of Cranetown in the early 1800s. Chief Tarhe was a tall, slim warrior and was given the name The Crane by the French. This name stuck and was his *nom de guerre* during battles he fought against white encroachment into the Ohio country during the late 1700s. He later became a proponent for peace and was instrumental in the signing of the Treaty of Greenville in 1795. He died at this location in 1816. All signs of the Indian village are long gone.

Upon leaving the Tarhe stone, continue south on CR37 to its juncture with SR67, then turn right, taking it two miles to CR47. At this point the tour heads straight west on CR47, but you might want to make a very short side trip east to the Indian Mill State Memorial and Museum on the Sandusky River. The existing mill was built in 1861 and replaced a structure built in 1820 for the benefit of the local Wyandot Indians, rewarding them for their loyalty during the War of 1812. A note of caution: the area around the mill is quite congested with a narrow road

Chief Tarhe Monument located on the site of the Indian village of Cranetown.

and limited parking space. Unfortunately, construction of new houses in this very scenic area also adds to the congestion and detracts from the natural beauty of the river valley. It's a nice side trip if you're riding solo or in a small group, but I recommend against more than three or four bikes at a time going to the mill.

Proceed west on CR47 and, in the first three miles, you'll cross State Routes 53, 199, and US23, and then it's a ten-mile ride through open countryside to SR37 just past the village of Wharton. Five miles north on SR37, you will come to the town of Mt. Blanchard. Just north of that village, you'll cross the Blanchard River, and about three miles past the river, you'll come to CR37 (again). This time, turn left onto CR37 and take it west through nearly eleven miles of farmland to the town of Rawson. Just prior to Rawson, you'll cross over I-75 and the Dixie Highway.

Upon reaching Rawson, you'll find yourself at a stop sign at the south end of town, with the Cory-Rawson Elementary School across the street. Turn right at this corner onto what becomes CR12 and take it north about five miles to the town of Benton Ridge. Going into Benton Ridge requires an eastward jog and a left turn onto what is now SR235.

State Route 235 will be your companion for the next twenty five miles north. The tiny towns of McComb and Hoytville are the only distractions you'll encounter as you ride this lightly-traveled road north to the town of Weston. Be careful along this stretch as a fairly deep drainage ditch accompanies the road, with only narrow shoulders separating the two. Not a place to daydream and wander off the blacktop.

At the southeast corner of Weston, Sandy Ridge Road goes east, winding back to Bowling Green and the end of this nice 190-mile tour. This portion of Ohio was scoured by the Wisconsinian glacier more than 12,000 years ago, and Sandy Ridge Road quite clearly follows a ridge, or esker, of sandy soil that was deposited here by the glacier. It's not a striking feature, but if you look closely you can quite clearly distinguish the difference in the land and soil along this road as compared to nearby flat farmlands.

One final suggested stop awaits those of you who have an interest in big equipment. Just west of Bowling Green, about a mile and a half north of US6/SR105 on Liberty Hi Road (also called CR46), is the National Construction Equipment Museum. This one-of-a-kind museum is home to antique construction, mining, and other heavy equipment. It is operated by the Historical Construction Equipment Association and is a very out-of-the-ordinary place to visit. Their address is 16623 Liberty Hi (not a misspelling) Road, phone number 419-352-5616.

Well, I hope you enjoyed the trip and that you now agree there are fun and interesting roads to ride and things to see and do in this former swamp.

The Great Ohio Circle

IF YOU REALLY WANT to explore all that Ohio has to offer, with its various landforms, historical sites, and motorcycling roads, this tour does it. It's a chance to discover the Ohio that perhaps you've never fully known before. This marvelous 814-mile ride takes you through forests and farmlands, to incredibly scenic rural areas and into bustling urban landscapes, past coal mines and outlet malls, through upper-crust developments, and past examples of rural poverty that never seem to make it on the radar of the social policy makers. Even if you're a life-long Ohio native, this tour will show you things you may never have seen or known—and all of it on roads that make for mighty fine motorcycling. I think you'll agree that this is one great tour. Give yourself a few days to complete it so that you can stop regularly to explore and really learn about this great state. There are too many attractions, museums, historical sites, markers, and monuments to list. Just be ready to stop occasionally to explore the out-of-the-way and out-of-the-ordinary.

We begin our tour of discovery in Tiffin, a town of 19,000 built on the old Sandusky Road following the War of 1812. Tiffin actually began as Fort Ball, one of several forts built along this vital military supply road that followed the Sandusky River to Lake Erie and was critical to the success of campaigns in the Sandusky and Toledo areas, as well as Detroit and southern Ontario.

The first permanent settlement at Tiffin occurred shortly after the end of the war, when a tavern and inn was built near Fort Ball. The site was midway between Upper Sandusky and the lake and was one-day's travel to each destination, resulting in a logical overnight stopping place at present-day Tiffin. After statehood the settlement's name was changed to Tiffin to honor Ohio's first governor, Edward Tiffin.

Like travelers of old, we too begin our journey by going north on SR53, following the river toward the big lake. Fort Seneca—former location of another of the forts built along this trail by the future President Harrison—is the first village we encounter. Two historic markers tell the story of military action in this area. Less than three miles north of Fort Seneca, CR61 heads west to Bettsville, formed in 1838 by Mr. John Betts. The peaceful village on Wolf Creek hasn't changed a whole lot since (which, in my mind, is a very good thing). In Bettsville go across the main intersection at SR12 and a block later turn right on SR590, taking it north

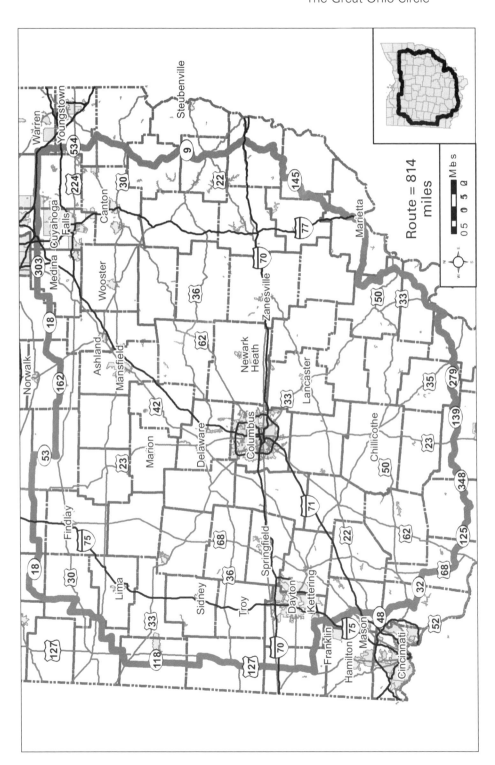

Route = 814 miles

Miles	Destination	Total
	THE GREAT OHIO CIRCLE **814 MILES**	
0	Tiffin	0
34	Cygnet/I-75	34
57	Cloverdale	91
41	Rockford	132
46	Greenville	178
26	Eaton	204
24	Germantown	228
36	Loveland	264
29	Mt. Orab	293
37	West Union	330
67	Oak Hill/Jackson Lake State Park	397
35	Chesire	432
75	Marietta	507
53	Beallsville	560
25	St. Clairsville	585
46	Carrollton	631
53	Newton Falls	684
32	Cuyahoga Valley National Park	716
42	Wellington	758
56	Tiffin	814

less than a mile where you'll turn west onto Seneca County Line Road/CR62. We'll follow this country road many miles through the farmlands and ultimately across US23 into Wood County, where our road angles southwest and becomes Cygnet Road. You'll encounter the village of West Millgrove at SR199 (preceded by a large quarry next to the road just east of the town). After leaving West Millgrove, you'll cross the East Branch of the Portage River and then continue southwest on Cygnet Road for less than a half mile when Cygnet Road angles to the right/straight west. Make the turn and follow Cygnet Road to the village of Cygnet at I-75.

Stay on Cygnet Road across the expressway, following it west to the stop sign at SR235, where you turn left to SR18. We then follow SR18 west as it makes a couple of jogs and passes through the farming towns of Deshler and Hamler on its way to Holgate.

In Holgate turn south on Wilhelm Street, which in town will be route 108 for a short distance. Follow Wilhelm southwest through town, where outside of Holgate it becomes CR16. This road then becomes CR17 and then 17A as it angles southwest to the village of Kieferville. This nice stretch of county road from Holgate to Kieferville is old SR115 and is easy to follow despite changes in county road designations.

From Kieferville we need to go southeast on SR15 about a mile and then turn straight south on SR115, taking 115 down to the town of Kalida on the Ottawa River. Turn right onto SR114 in Kalida and follow it along the river to Cloverdale, where you'll pick up SR634, which goes south to Fort Jennings. As its name suggests, Fort Jennings was yet another of the many forts built during the Indian Wars of the 1790s and the War of 1812. Fort Jennings was in place from 1812–1815 and was part of a chain of forts that protected supply lines for the theater of war that included Lake Erie and Detroit.

At this point, get on SR190 and follow it into the old canal town of Delphos. Route 190 will deliver you to 5th Street in Delphos, which is also the Lincoln Highway. Take 5th Street west to Main Street and turn south through town three blocks to 2nd Street, going west to State Street, then south to Ohio Street, which after just a couple of blocks angles southwest out of town becoming SR697. Believe me, it sounds more complicated than it is. You enter Delphos at the northeast corner and exit at the southwest corner.

While in Delphos, do yourself a favor and park the bike to do some exploring. This old canal town has some really neat history and things to see. The Miami & Erie Canal bisects the town north and south, and there are several locks that are still in very good shape for inspecting. There is a canal museum on Main Street that is also a nice stop. Snapping a picture of the mural on the side of the Delphos Herald building, which depicts Delphos during its canal heyday, is a must.

Take route 697 straight west to SR116 and turn south to the village of Venedocia where you turn west on SR709. Go exactly five miles on 709 and turn left on Mendon Road, taking it south to SR117, then right on 117 to the village of Rockford on the St. Marys River. From here we start seriously working our way south in the far western portion of the state. The surrounding landscape transitions from the open prairie of the northwest to the rolling hills of southwestern Ohio in this leg of the trip.

From Rockford go south on SR118. It'll be our road for the next thirty miles, until we arrive at the tiny village of Rossburg. In Rossburg turn east on the

Annie Oakley statue in Greenville.

Rossburg-Lightsville Road and take it four miles to US127. There's a jog midway. After going south just one mile on 127, there'll be a road going east to the town of Brock. The claim to fame for this tiny village is that Phoebe Ann Mosey is buried there. You might know her better by her stage name, Annie Oakley. Road signs point the way to the cemetery, and historical markers at the gravesite of Oakley and her husband tell the story of these two famous world travelers and Wild West Show entertainers. There is a park in downtown Greenville called Annie Oakley Park, in which a life-size bronze statue of the sharpshooter has been placed. Like so many intriguing people, Annie Oakley's story is a fascinating one. There aren't a lot of people who shook hands with both Chief Sitting Bull and Queen Elizabeth during their lifetime. You can learn much more about Annie Oakley at the Garst Museum at 205 North Broadway Street in Greenville. While there, you can also learn about Meriwether Lewis and Captain William Clark—you see, they first met in Greenville and became life-long friends. They, of course, went on to lead the Corps of Discovery to the Pacific Ocean in 1805.

United States Route 127 is our riding partner for the next fifty miles, down to the town of Camden. Along the way, notice the changing landscape from flat to rolling. You'll also pass through two very historic towns—Greenville and Eaton. The 1795 Treaty of Greenville was one of the most important events in Ohio's history. You'll learn much more about these sites in the Frontier Forts tour.

When you arrive at Camden, turn east on SR725, which will take you east all the way into Miamisburg. On the way, you'll pass through the town of Gratis, and if you wish, you can make an easy loop prior to reaching Gratis to see the Brubaker Covered Bridge. About a mile west of Gratis, you'll see Brubaker Road

Miamisburg Mound, one of the largest in the nation.

going north. Turn here and go a half mile and then turn right onto Brubaker again (it makes a ninety-degree turn here while another road goes straight north) Go east a half mile and you'll cross the bridge. Beyond the bridge you can continue east the very short distance to SR122 and south just a bit to Gratis, where you can continue your eastward journey on SR725.

Follow SR725 across the Miami River into Miamisburg. Right after crossing the river, you'll see the Dayton-Cincinnati Pike (called Main Street in town/*aka* Dixie Highway) running along the east shore of the river. If you go south just a mile or so, you'll see Mound Street (there are flashing red warning lights at this corner) and signs for the very impressive Miamisburg Mound—a conical burial mound that is approximately seventy feet high and covers one and a half acres at its base, making it one of the largest such mounds in the nation. It is both a very impressive and very humbling sight. Could we build such a structure with our bare hands today?

We're going to take the scenic Dayton-Cincinnati Pike/Dixie Highway south along the river to Franklin and SR123, where we head east. You'll pass northbound 123 first but just keep going a little farther to south SR123 and take it southeast to the city of Lebanon—a very charming city with a lot of history and attractions. If you're ready for a break, you're in luck. In Lebanon you can take a ride on the Turtle Creek Valley Railway. This hour-long ride, in either an enclosed passenger coach or an open gondola car, is great fun. They're located at 198 Broadway Street in downtown Lebanon. Call 513-398-8584 for more information. In the downtown section of Lebanon, you'll find The Golden Lamb, Ohio's oldest inn. It's

Turtle Creek Railroad Depot in Lebanon.

been in business since 1803, when the first log cabin housing the business on this site was built. The portion of the building housing the lobby was built in 1815. It would be a delightful and memorable place to spend a night or just to stop for a meal. Call them at 513-932-5065 if you're interested. Also, just in case it comes up in your next *Trivial Pursuit* game, the Lebanon area once was home to one of the country's largest Shaker communities.

In Lebanon SR123 will turn straight east and join SR48 on the east side of town. We're going to leave 123 and turn south on 48, following its circuitous route south to Loveland. This stretch of route 48 ranges from quite nice to tolerable. This area has the unfortunate fate of being the northern exurbs of Cincinnati (or is it the southern exurbs of Dayton?). In any event, the landscape is being altered from rolling hills covered with fields and woods to a checkerboard of suburban sprawl. Such development gives me no joy, but I guess this is what brings smiles to the faces of developers.

If you have patience and take a map with you showing its location, you can go see the Loveland Castle, *aka* Chateau LaRoche, located at 12025 Shore Drive in Loveland. This castle-like structure was built essentially by one man, Harry Andrews, between 1927 and 1957. It is three stories high, with four-story battle towers. It's open only on weekends. In case you want to get married there, call them at 513-683-4686 for reservations. It isn't easy to find, and you won't see any directional signs to help you, so if you wish to see it, take a map with you.

Leave Loveland on SR48 and follow it southeast to the point where it forms a T at SR132, which we take south for several more miles through the scenic rolling hills east of Cincinnati to US50. At 50 we jog east about a mile to Owensville, where we continue south on route 132. This one-mile stretch of US50 is one of the more unpleasant of the whole trip if you happen to catch it at rush hour.

Take SR132 south to route SR32 at Batavia and head east on 32 all the way to the Route 68 exit at Mt. Orab. Take US68—a nice enough riding road in its own right—south to SR125, and the fun begins in earnest! Head east on route 125 to begin a marvelous trip across southern Ohio's gorgeous landscape. There is not a bad riding road between here and far northeastern Ohio, where we turn back west to close the loop. Most of the roads we'll be on in southern and eastern Ohio are nothing short of fabulous and the landscape exquisite. About six miles east of West Union, pick up SR348 and follow it east all the way to US23. Route 348 follows several different streams, including Brush Creek and Bloody Run Creek, as it winds through the valleys these streams occupy. It makes for an absolutely delightful ride. As you enter the village of Otway from the south, you'll see the Otway covered bridge in a small park next to Route 348.

At US23 we'll continue straight across on SR728, taking it east to the village of Minford, where we pick up SR139. When you reach the village of Minford, you'll want to turn right on SR335 and take it the very short distance into town and then turn left onto Route 139. You could take Route 728 straight to 139, but there is a stop sign at that intersection that is on a very steep, small hill. On a bike, especially if you have a passenger, this would be a very tricky stop and difficult to get going again. Take the one-half mile jog south and pick up 139 in town. You will be very glad you did.

State Route 139 eventually drifts off to the north at its juncture with SR279, *aka* Dever Valley Road, which we will take as we continue east along the northern edge of the Wayne National Forest. State Route 279 is an Ohio Scenic Byway and has the extra designation of being the Welsh Byway as a result of the historic mining heritage and the role of the Welsh in this region. It will eventually deliver us through Jackson Lake State Park, over Jackson Lake itself, and through the town of Oak Hill, ultimately taking us to the village of Centerville at US35, where it ends.

At Centerville get on US35 and take it east less than four miles to the Rio Grande exit and SR325, which we'll take north just over the overpass and turn right onto SR554. If you want to visit the Bob Evans Farms and associated tourist attractions, turn south when you exit, then left onto SR588. The farm is only a mile outside of town—just follow the signs.

State Route 554 will take us east all the way to the village of Chesire on the Ohio River and SR7. You will know that you've arrived when you come over the last hill and see the cooling towers and smokestacks of the large power plant at the corner of Routes 554 and 7. Route 554 is another fabulous riding road that meanders all over the countryside as it cuts between hills and through hollows and creek bottoms. If you want roads that are straight and efficient, then this isn't your road. But if you love curves, hills, and fantastic scenery that you can wander around in all afternoon, then this road was custom-made for you!

From Chesire follow Route 7 north to Pomeroy and get on northbound US33. Take 33 north a few miles to the exit for SR681, which you'll take east to Tuppers Plains—once again ending up on Route 7. Route 681 is really great! It's newly paved and will be the smoothest blacktop you'll encounter on the entire trip. It follows the stream valleys and doesn't have a straight stretch anywhere. Valley walls and the always nearby stream follow your every move. From Tuppers Plains, turn left onto Route 7 and follow it north to SR144, turning left again. Route 144 will take you north across dynamite countryside, and the road is fantastic. I believe it may be my favorite stretch of road on this entire tour—and that's saying something!

At the village of Stewart, we pick up SR329 and continue to follow it north through the Wayne National Forest and ultimately to SR550. Turn right on 550 and ride it all the way to Marietta and, once again, Route 7, which is continually angling northeast as we're gradually working our way east.

There are just tons of interesting and fun things to do in Marietta—many of which I discuss in other rides that pass through this wonderful small city. From 2,000-year-old Indian mounds on the banks of the Muskingum River, to Campus Martius and the Ohio River Museum, plus a downtown historic area that's a joy to walk through, this town really is worth a couple hours of your time. Better yet, make it an overnight stop and do it up right.

Going east across the Muskingum River on Route 7 will deliver us to SR60, where we want to head north a short distance to the road we really want: SR821. With the traffic of Marietta behind us, let the fun begin again! Route 821 goes generally north, albeit in a very indirect way, and in the tiny town of Lower Salem, we leave this fun road and pick up SR145, another wonderful southern Ohio hill country road that goes generally northeast for many ear-to-ear grinning miles. In fact, we'll be on Route 145 all the way to SR148, which we pick up north of Beallsville. At the very high risk of sounding repetitive, you'll find 145 to be yet another in a wonderful succession of fabulous biking roads on this tour. By the way, notice the large coal mine at the intersection of Routes 145 and 148. Coal may no longer be king in Ohio but it's certainly not entirely dethroned.

Go east on SR148 just a few miles to Armstrong Mills for a north/left turn onto SR9 and the beginning of a fabulous northward ride up the east side of Ohio. A word of caution about the intersection of Routes 148 and 9: As you approach it you should slow way down. It's a tricky and potentially dangerous intersection because the turn onto Route 9 is very tight—less than ninety degrees. Once you make the turn, you'll see ahead of you a very steep and long uphill run, which is quite amazing. Route 9 is going to be our riding partner all the way up to the town of Salem. This stretch between Armstrong Mills and Salem will take you through mile after mile of beautiful countryside and a montage of green pastures and forest-covered hills. To top it all off you don't have to think about your next turn for many miles! In Ohio's hill country there are basically two types of roads—those that primarily follow the stream valleys, meandering across the countryside next to the waterway, and roads that follow the ridges and hilltops. Route 9 is one of the latter. It offers mile after mile of marvelous scenery and vistas that'll have you smiling the entire way.

There are several attractions along the way, although for the most part, it's just great riding through a scenic area on a fun biking road. In Cadiz you might want to stop to see Clark Gable's birthplace, or in Carrollton you can visit the home of the Civil War family called the Fighting McCooks. This awe-inspiring family contributed two brothers and their fifteen sons, all whom fought and five that died, fighting for the Union in the Civil War. Six of the family ended up as generals in the war.

Continue north on Route 9 through the pleasing eastern Ohio countryside, past the Lincoln Highway at Hanoverton and on up to Salem. Coming into Salem will be a shocker. After a couple hundred miles of open road and beautiful scenery, you ride through a several-block-long "tunnel" between large factory buildings. But don't despair because this sudden change of atmosphere is short-lived. Like most towns in Ohio, Salem has wonderful stories to tell about the people and events of its past. Begun in 1803, it was incorporated in 1806 by a Quaker who moved to this wilderness location from Salem, New Jersey. The name Salem was retained because of its biblical meaning, "City of Peace." Salem has a strong Quaker history, resulting in its residents being very active in the Abolitionist movement. It was known, in fact, as the headquarters of the anti-slavery movement prior to the Civil War. Some of the homes in town still have the hidden rooms and tunnels used to hide runaway slaves 150 years ago. A replica of Freedom Hall, which was the meeting house for the Quakers as well as the headquarters of the Anti-Slavery Association, has been rebuilt and is located behind the town's historical museum.

It houses many items from the Civil War era as well as a blacksmith shop with very cool old tools used in that trade, which was vital to nineteenth-century America.

If you're into drag racing, you'll certainly want to stop at Quaker City Raceway, located just three miles north of town on SR165. They host a wide variety of IHRA-sponsored, quarter-mile drag strip activities, ranging from dragsters to motorcycles and every imaginable type of event in between. Go to their website at www.quakercityraceway.com for more information and a schedule of events.

When proceeding on the trip, go west on SR14 out of Salem, angling northwest to SR534 on which we continue our northerly journey as it passes through a pretty area with nearby wildlife land and a state park. Route 534 is quite straight until you get near Newton Falls, where its reverts to the normal curvy ways of Ohio's three-digit roads, but the entire way is an enjoyable mix of rolling countryside that's a pleasure to ride through. Newton Falls is an old canal town—at one time a stop on the Pennsylvania & Ohio Canal. It was also a stop on the stagecoach run from Youngstown to points northwest and was noted for its mills. A one-lane wooden, covered bridge in town still carries traffic across the Mahoning River. The huge Ravenna Arsenal is located just west of town. The town's zip code (44444), proudly displayed on the water tower, is also quite unique—there are only a couple other towns in America in which all the digits in their zip code are the same. (Since you asked, they are the Marine Corps Institute in Arlington, VA, and Young America, MN, where you mail all those rebate forms.)

Continue north of town on 534 to just beyond the I-80 Turnpike and turn west on SR303. This road will take us west across a very large chunk of northeastern Ohio between the Cleveland and Akron metropolitan regions. Surprisingly, 303 is a decent road for motorcycling and is not as developed or traffic-laden as one might expect as it threads the needle between cities, traversing semi-urban and rural areas. It also cuts through the Cuyahoga Valley National Recreation Area, taking you near many attractions—both natural and man-made. Continuing west on SR303, you'll find slow going from I-77 west to Brunswick. Much of this stretch has an unreasonably slow 35- to 45-mile-per-hour speed limit, plus occasional stretches where traffic will begin to wear on you. It's not all bad, however, and the worst stretches of road will quickly pass. Just west of I-77 in Richfield, note the white octagonal house. Apparently, it's kind of famous as there is a marker in front of it. Follow 303 west through Valley City, location of a former railroad depot and old steam engine, stopping finally at SR83, where we turn left/south for about five miles to SR18, where we go partway through the traffic circle and commence our westerly journey toward Tiffin.

Follow Route 18 through the very nice historic town of Wellington and into Huron County and the town of Clarksfield. Route 18 makes a large northerly

This replica of Freedom Hall, the meeting house for Quakers as well as headquarters of the Anti-Slavery Association, is located behind Salem's Historical Museum.

curve just west of Clarksfield. About a mile west of town, you will see Fitchville River Road, where you will turn left. Take this enjoyable scenic road as it follows the Vermillion River south to Fitchville, where we pick up SR162, again heading west. This area west of Route 83 gets progressively better riding as the countryside opens up and the road attains a bit more character. Route 162 has smooth pavement and plenty of personality to keep you in high spirits. It's not the Appalachians, but it ain't bad, either. In the vicinity of North Fairfield, notice the several very large boulders along the road. They were deposited there by the glaciers, carried all the way from Canada no doubt. This is evidence that this part of the state was covered by the last Ice Age, which isn't true for a large chunk of Ohio.

At the small town of Republic, SR162 ends but SR18 picks up again. Take 18 straight west the final few miles to Tiffin, past the beautiful red brick buildings of Heidelberg College, and the completion of this amazing tour around the entire state.

Arrowheads and Superbikes

THIS FUN RIDE IS in the heart of Ohio, just east and northeast of Columbus. It is like two rides in one—the first through typical southeastern Ohio hill country with lots of natural attractions, and the second in the other Ohio, the one that's comprised of farmlands with the occasional small urban area. The roads you will be riding reflect this geographic difference, but rest assured, there are no roads on this trip that you won't enjoy. This ride also takes us from the ancient to the modern, leaving us marveling at both extremes.

We'll start in Newark, where man's activities in the twenty-first century collide with some of the greatest accomplishments of ancient Americans. Proceeding south on SR79, it's easy to see that Newark and Heath, immediately to the south, are showing definite signs of an expanding girth. Sprawl reaches from Newark pretty much all the way down to I-70. The Newark area is home to several of the most notable Indian mounds in Ohio, some of which are in harm's way due to development. While some are on private property and inaccessible, several are safely protected in public parks and accessible for us to walk through and marvel at the people who built them. One of the finest is the Newark Earthworks State Memorial located on SR79 in Heath, just after the limited access highway ends. Viewing this collection of 2,000-year-old earthworks that formed a series of large circles and berms is just mind-boggling when you consider that, like all the mounds and earthen forts constructed by these amazing people, the work was done by hand! Tens of thousands of cubic yards of soil were moved by men, women, and children to build these elaborate structures, and archeologists today are still trying to understand the uses and meanings of all of them. Other Indian earthworks in the area include Octagon Earthworks at North 33rd and Parkview Streets, and the Wright Earthworks at James and Waldo Streets in Newark.

Another man-made wonder in Newark of a decidedly more modern design, and one that archeologists ten thousand years from now will have fun deciphering, is the Longaberger Company basket building. This architectural wonder—a seven-story, 180,000-square-foot building in the shape of a huge basket, is the home of the Longaberger basket company. It's on SR16 just east of town. A person really shouldn't go to Newark without getting a look at this amazing structure.

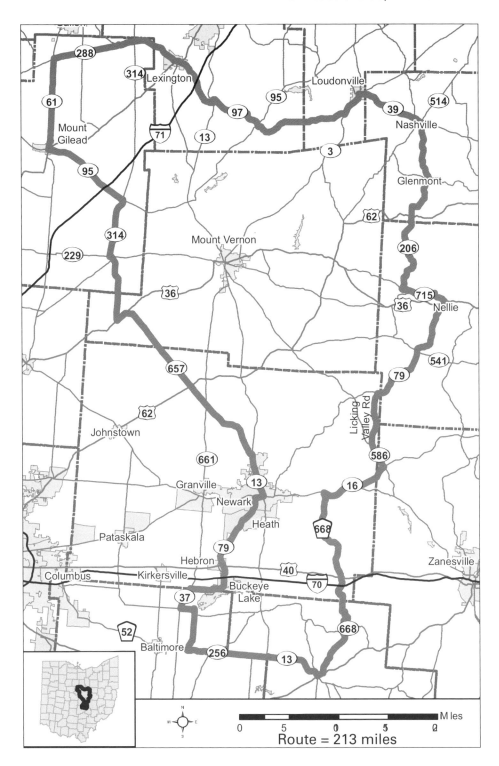

Route = 213 miles

Miles	Destination	Total
	**ARROWHEADS AND SUPERBIKES 213 MILES**	
0	Newark	0
18	Millersport/Buckeye Lake State Park	18
18	Somerset	36
15	Flint Ridge State Memorial	51
14	State Route 586	65
21	Nellie	86
19	Glenmont	105
13	Loudonville	118
29	Clear Fork Reservoir/Mid Ohio Track	147
19	Mt. Gilead	166
47	Newark	213

We depart the Newark area on SR79, taking it south to Buckeye Lake where the road swings west. Go the couple of miles to SR37 and then south three miles to SR204 (where you'll see a windbreak in the form of large pine trees) and turn left a short distance to the old canal town of Millersport. From Millersport we continue straight south on Millersport Road, paralleling the old Ohio & Erie Canal as it worked its way to the Ohio River. Stay on Millersport Road to the village of Thurston and SR256, where you turn east/left. When you enter Thurston from the north, it seems a little confusing because the road suddenly forks for the last few blocks. It really doesn't matter which fork you take—both will get you to SR256.

At this point you'll be the closest to the American Motorcyclist Association headquarters as any of these trips will take you. If you haven't been there, it's worth the trip west on SR256 to the suburban town of Pickerington, southeast of Columbus. A stroll through the AMA Museum is always enjoyable, and it's a great place to talk motorcycles with folks who share your passion and who are protecting our interests.

To resume the trip, take SR256 across pleasant countryside to the very nice small town of Somerset. State Route 13 joins 256 along the way. Somerset is a small but prosperous-looking town. In the traffic circle in the center of town is an impressive monument to the Civil War hero, General Sheridan, and the stately 1829 courthouse. Several other fine old brick buildings are also in Somerset.

This berm is part of the Newark Earthworks State Memorial, home of several of the most notable mounds in Ohio.

Leaving Somerset, head northeast and then north on SR668. We're now getting into the really fun roads for which southeastern Ohio is famous. For the entire stretch, SR668 is a collection of high hills, tight curves and grand scenery. You'll love it! Route 668 terminates at US40, just north of I-70. At this point, jog two blocks left and proceed north again on CR668, following the signs to Flint Ridge.

This ancient flint quarry is just a few miles north of US40 and is a highly recommended stop. Taking the short walk on the trail that winds through pits dug over the past 10,000 years is truly thought-provoking. The many small quarries aren't much to see by today's standards, but you have to use your imagination to truly understand that they are the result of thousands of people digging with their hands and stone tools for the last one hundred centuries. The flint found in this part of Ohio is particularly high quality and made excellent knives, spear points, and arrowheads. Aboriginal peoples came from long distances to quarry flint at this site, and the items they formed from the flint were used as barter in trade. As a result, the flint mined at Flint Ridge can be found at archeological digs around the country.

We continue north on CR668 upon leaving Flint Ridge. Six miles north—just prior to crossing the Licking River—is Brush Creek Road. If you go down this road a very short distance, you will see a parking lot for the west end of the Black Hand Gorge Nature Reserve. The area east of here has the deepest gorge in Ohio. The famous "black hand" was a petroglyph on the river cliffs, which was long ago destroyed by engineers digging a canal. There is a lengthy walking trail (five miles) along the south side of the river that goes from the west parking lot to the east lot, located near the village of Toboso.

To continue the tour, we go north past Brush Creek Road to SR16 and turn right. Even though this is a divided four-lane highway, it is quite scenic, with hillside escarpments resulting from blasting through the hills during construction. Four miles after you turn east on SR16, you'll see the exit for SR146. If you take this exit and follow the signs about two miles to the southeast, you'll come to the headquarters of the Black Hand Gorge area and the east parking lot.

If you choose to pass up the gorge, I suggest getting off here to top off your gas tank anyway—it'll be the last gas station you see until Loudonville, which is about fifty-five miles away. We will get off at the next exit and proceed north on SR586. This is where the tour really gets fun. Take 586 north to SR79, turn right and continue north on 79 all the way to the tiny village of Nellie. In Nellie we'll go right on US36 for maybe one hundred yards. Immediately after crossing the creek, make a tight left turn onto SR715 for a wonderful, but much too short, ride on one of the best riding roads in Ohio. State Route 715 twists and turns in a westerly direction and then goes over the levee of the Mohawk Dam on the Walhonding River. This stretch on and near the levee is just breathtaking, in my humble opinion. Continue on 715 through the village of Walhonding and turn north onto SR206. This route will take you to US62 and a stop sign. Although 206 ends here, straight across from you, County Road 25 continues due north—and so do we. After a mile, CR25 makes a ninety-degree right turn. Another road goes straight at this point, so you have to be sure to follow the traffic sign and turn right. (There

One of the preserved cabins in Black Hand Gorge State Nature Preserve and Natural Area.

is also a warning sign at this rural intersection, saying "dangerous intersection." I suspect that the folks taking the road that goes straight ahead assume they have the right-of-way, rather than drivers coming around the curve on CR25.) Once you make the right turn, CR25 meanders northeast and north into the village of Glenmont. This last stretch is very enjoyable, although it passes through countryside that now has more farms and less wooded land. In Glenmont go left two blocks and proceed north again on Monroe Street, which turns into CR52. Route 52 is a fun ride that goes north to Nashville on State Routes 39/60. If your bike is giving you some trouble, you might want to stop at TOMCAT Repair Shop (Tired Old Motorcycles, Cars and Trucks) in Nashville. If you feel the need for some nourishment, a stop at the Buckeye Deli across the street will take care of your hunger pangs. If you're a deer hunter, go to the rear of the seating area to admire the many dozens of deer hunting pictures tacked to the wall.

We leave Nashville via 39/60 westbound. This road gets somewhat heavy use, but it is great fun with its many dips, curves, and hills. Eventually, it arrives in Loudonville, where gas stations are once again available. Loudonville, in the Mohican River Valley resort area, is a fine town to stop and stretch your legs. We're going to go south on SR3 for just a bit and then west on SR97 through Mohican State Park and State Forest. Use caution here as this is prime recreational country and the road is patrolled quite heavily by the local gendarme. This is a beautiful area, and I definitely recommend going into the park to the Clear Fork Gorge overlook, and a bit farther west on Forest Road 51 to the orange fire tower, which is open for climbing by the public. The climb is truly "breathtaking," and the view from the top is fantastic.

If you wish, before turning onto SR97 from SR3, continue south just a short distance to a neat old grist mill.

Take SR97, with all its twists and turns and indecisive, albeit very enjoyable, ways to just southeast of Galion. Along the way you will pass through the towns of Butler, Belleville, and Lexington. It's Lexington that is of most interest to us because of its proximity to the Mid-Ohio Sports Car Course. This venue hosts the AMA Super Cycle Weekend motorcycle races each summer, generally in late July or early August. Its layout makes it a fabulous place to watch the races, and throughout the race event, you can see and even test the latest models at manufacturer displays, and of course, spend lots of money at dozens of vendors selling motorcycle accessories and riding gear. Mid-Ohio is also the venue for the annual Vintage Motorcycle Days sponsored by AMA. This event is an absolute feast for those who ride, own, or just love to look at old bikes.

A new program at the track is Sportbike Track Time. For a fee you, too, can learn to ride the track the way the experts do. Mid-Ohio instructors make it very easy to improve your motorcycling skills on a newly-paved track and in a safe environment. The course includes classroom lessons and at least twenty minutes out of each hour on the track itself. There are levels catering to riders from novice to skilled. What's more, alterations to your street bike are fairly minimal. Call them at 888-390-4020 or go to www.sportbiketracktime.com for more information and enrollment.

The race track is just west of Lexington and south of SR97, where it passes the Clear Fork Reservoir. Many thousands of us have camped on the shore of Clear Fork Reservoir while attending events at Mid-Ohio.

Not too far west of the race course, you will come to SR288 where a left turn is in order. Follow 288, which unlike SR97 lives its life on the straight and narrow, to SR61, turning south and proceeding to Mt. Gilead. This is yet another cool, small Ohio town that gives small-town America a good name. It was the home of President Warren G. Harding. In the center of town is the Victory Memorial Shaft—a monument that was a gift from the federal government following World War I—and is the only one of its type in the nation. The monument was bestowed on Morrow County for purchasing more war bonds during World War I per capita than any other county in the nation.

The fire tower in Mohican State Park is open for climbing, offering a truly fantastic view from its top.

Take SR95 southeast out of Mt. Gilead to Chesterville and SR314, which we will follow south to Centerburg and US36. Go east/left on US36 just a mile to SR657, which delivers us all the way back to Newark, after joining SR13 for the last few miles.

The entire stretch of this trip from Galion down to Newark is very pleasant, though not as dramatic as the area north of Somerset. This is rolling farm country, but because we stick to the roads less traveled, traffic is light and the riding is easy.

Ohio: Top to Bottom

THERE ARE SEVERAL ROADS that traverse Ohio from east to west or north to south, but for the most part these roads weren't made for enjoyable motorcycling. While they have enjoyable stretches, to ride them end-to-end would involve much more in the way of heavy stop-and-go traffic than enjoyable highway riding. Examples include US Routes 20, 23, and 42, Ohio Routes 3 and 4 (these roads being some of the primary pre-expressway highways in the state), and of course, the several expressways that now crisscross the state. There are two state routes that go from the north to south, however, that are, for the most part, enjoyable and very interesting roads to ride. These are State Routes 93 and 60. Interestingly, while they traverse the east-central part of the state, they cross each other in Zanesville and head off in different diagonal directions. Route 93 runs between Ironton and Cleveland, while SR60 runs between Marietta and Vermillion. These roads really allow you to experience all that Ohio has to offer: from the flat, Lake Erie plain in the north to the Appalachian highlands further south.

Route 60 offers up loads of things to see and do all along the way, starting with the Great Lakes Museum in Vermillion to the many must-see attractions in Marietta. Route 60 is a river road for most of its length, meaning that it has all the character and charm of a road that closely follows a river. Heading south from Lake Erie it begins following the curves of the Vermillion River south of the Ohio Turnpike and becomes a very nice, if not exactly heart-pounding, ride through pleasant countryside. The first city of any size heading south through the Firelands is New London, a town that received its name from early residents who relocated here from New London, Connecticut. The ride and surroundings improve as one heads south, becoming very nice as you approach Loudonville. In fact, from the point where route 60 turns southeast of Loudonville until it hits route 36 near Coshocton, Route 60 is just an absolute blast. There may be a hundred-yard stretch that doesn't have either a vertical or horizontal curve, but I don't think so!

Things tame down as Zanesville draws near, and the ride through the city is much like any other small urban area—grin and bear it, it doesn't last long. South of Zanesville (Ohio's capital from 1810–1812), Route 60 follows the Muskingum River all the way to Marietta. All along this stretch are remnants of the locks and dams that made the Muskingum River a major water transport artery. Riding next

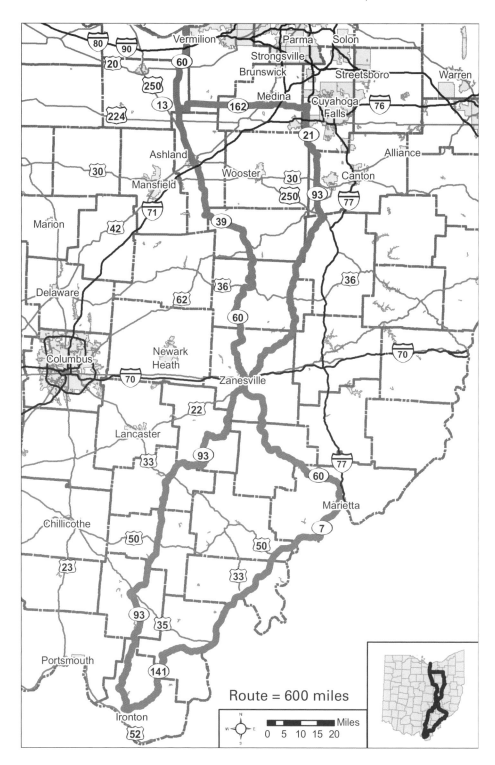

Route = 600 miles

The W.P. Snyder, Jr., *one of the last remaining examples of a steam towboat. This one plied the Monongahela and Ohio Rivers, pushing barges loaded with coal.*

to the water makes for a pleasant ride, even though traffic does seem to pick up in the stretch between Zanesville and Marietta.

A few miles south of Zanesville is a town called Duncan Falls. This name isn't the result of a waterfall or rapids, as one would expect, rather it's the spot where Mr. Duncan, a white trapper, fell after being shot by Indians. He earned this fate by shooting Indians whom he thought were stealing game from his traps. A shallow area on the river where he was found is still called Dead Man's Ripple.

A bit farther south, we enter an area that was a major coal mining region. In an industry where coal mine disasters are all too commonplace, an amazing success story from 150 years ago still reinforces the hopes of mine rescuers. In 1856 a local mine collapsed and four miners were feared dead. A rescue effort was undertaken, and fourteen long days later, the miners were found alive!

Route 60 continues to be an enjoyable ride south along the historic Muskingum River all the way to the Ohio River. Because it tightly follows the east shore of the river for the majority of the way to Marietta, it is in the river flood plain and hills aren't a common occurrence. An old river like the Muskingum has also straightened itself out and doesn't have the many tight curves and kinks that a tributary stream would have, so the road gently curves as it follows the

Miles	Destination	Total
OHIO, TOP TO BOTTOM 600 MILES		
Miles	Destination	Total
STATE ROUTE 60		
0	Vermillion	0
25	New London	25
16	Ashland	41
18	Loudonville	59
35	Warsaw	94
34	Zanesville/I-70	128
27	McConnellsville	155
35	Marietta	190
STATE ROUTES 7 & 141		
46	Pomeroy	236
21	Gallipolis	257
44	Ironton	301
STATE ROUTE 93		
31	Oak Hill	332
20	Wellston	352
33	Logan	385
24	New Lexington	409
25	Zanesville	434
34	West Lafayette	468
49	Canal Fulton	517
STATE ROUTES 21 & 162		
58	New London	575
25	Vermillion	600

path that the Muskingum River has carved for itself over the last 12,000 or so years. Just take your time and soak up all the scenery, attractions, and history that you'll find along this very nice biking road. There are a variety of historical signs and small parks that tell the story of various events, people, or places along the river. Ashland and Zanesville are the only two "large" cities that Route 60 goes through as it knits together the various pieces of Ohio between Lake Erie and the Ohio River.

Because of its strategic location at the intersection of major highways, several of the tours in this book pass through Marietta. I talk about the charms of this town in other rides, so I hope at some point you'll take the time to visit the natural and cultural attractions to be found here. I think a stop at Mound Cemetery, on Fifth Street, is a must. The large Conus Mound surrounded by circular moats and rings, is in the center of this old cemetery and is both very impressive and humbling in its subtle magnificence. The monument and rows of flags in honor of the many Revolutionary War soldiers buried in this cemetery is also something everyone should see. With its ancient Native American mounds, Revolutionary War graves, and headstones of the earliest settlers to this region, this cemetery really tells the stories about the long and fascinating history of this region.

When you're ready to leave Marietta, head west on Route 7 to Route 141, taking these fine biking roads over to Ironton and Route 93, which we'll follow back north.

On the many miles between Ironton and Oak Hill in southern Ohio, Route 93 is just a delight. Winding and rolling its way through the rugged forested sandstone hills of the Appalachian foothills, this road offers up great riding in large volume. Surrounding the town of Oak Hill is Jefferson Township. In the mid 1800s, the word Jefferson was used to identify iron made from local furnaces. It had a reputation for excellent quality, and furnaces in Jefferson Township and other nearby mills produced the iron that made cannons for the Union Army and built the ironclad Union warship, the *Monitor*. Nearby salt springs and mines have also played a major role in the history of this area for many centuries. In fact, when Daniel Boone was captured by the Shawnee, he was forced to make salt for them at a nearby salt spring during his captivity. Coal also reigned over the economy in this region for many decades.

North of Oak Hill, the countryside opens up a bit as agricultural uses predominate. Orchards in particular are becoming more commonplace in this part of the state. The character of the road changes little, however, as you continue north, at times wandering about in a seemingly aimless fashion, through miles of scenic landscape on a wonderful asphalt surface. In northern Vinton County, a very short side trip from SR93 to view the Cox Covered Bridge is worth a few minutes of your time. Watch for Woodgeard Road to the bridge. Once you leave the bustle of Zanesville behind you, the road once again becomes a very enjoyable ride through rolling farmland and woods as it winds its way north in its trademark indecisive manner. It's not until you arrive at Brewster that the road

Mound Cemetery is a must-see when visiting Marietta. It holds a Revolutionary War momument, headstones of the area's earliest settlers, and ancient Native American mounds.

begins to take its transportation efficiency role seriously as it straightens out for the remaining few miles north to Canal Fulton. While SR93 doesn't quite make it all the way to the shores of Lake Erie, you probably wouldn't want to ride it through the Cleveland metropolitan area anyway. To close the figure-eight loop, take Erie Street northwest in Canal Fulton through Clinton to SR21. Follow Route 21 north about eleven miles to SR162 (Sharon–Copley Road) and take it across the countryside west to New London and SR60.

SR60/93 makes a wonderful two- or three-day/600-mile loop through central Ohio, allowing the rider to really discover the great variety of landscapes, marvelous natural and man-made attractions, and fascinating history that is Ohio.

Riding Through History

THIS JUST MAY well be my favorite section of the book. It combines the pleasures of motorcycling on roads that are plain and simply a great deal of fun to ride, with the excitement of discovering places and events that are worthy of a great movie or book in their own right. How could a person not be swept up in the drama of events such as the Indian Wars, the War of 1812, sieges on wilderness forts, major battles upon which the fate of a young nation turned, magnificent structures built by mysterious lost races, and in following the paths of men and women whose very lives defined adventure and courage? This section will take you across the state to places where you can rediscover things that have unfortunately been nearly forgotten in our modern lives. I hope that by exploring the places and events written about in this section, you'll come to appreciate the many marvelous stories that exist across the length and breadth of Ohio that await the curious and interested person. All of this while having a blast riding your faithful steel steed down fantastic motorcycling roads. Could it possibly get any better than this?

A cabin located at Fort St. Clair.

On the Trail of Mad Anthony

NORTHWESTERN OHIO gets a bad rap. Far too many people criticize it as an area where one cannot find enjoyable motorcycling opportunities. How wrong they are! This area is filled with natural and cultural attractions, fascinating history, nice scenery, and roads that are a delight to ride. I suspect that the bad reputation by bikers for this corner of the state is because they have only seen it from the Ohio Turnpike or I-75. Not to nag, but you really do have to get off the expressways to see the wonderful roads and places that are all around us.

I named this tour in honor of General Anthony Wayne, nicknamed Mad Anthony by his loyal troops. Wayne is a national hero. He served the nation extremely well in the Revolutionary War, and when President Washington needed a military leader upon whose shoulders he could place the future of the Northwest Territory, he turned again to Wayne. The late eighteenth century was a very turbulent time on the frontier. Indian wars were raging, prompted in significant part by the urging and materiel support provided by the British, who did not want to lose the interior portion of the continent, whatever the outcome of the American War of Independence. Two military campaigns in 1790 and 1791, led by Generals Harmar and St. Clair, were disastrous. In fact, with a seventy percent casualty rate, the November 1791 battle fought near present-day Fort Recovery was the worst battle in American history for the proportion of soldiers killed or wounded. A very large contingent of warriors led by Shawnee Chief Blue Jacket and Little Turtle, Chief of the Miami tribe, completely routed the poorly led and equipped force under St. Clair. With over 700 killed, it was also the worst defeat for the American Army during the entire Indian Wars period. Custer's loss pales in comparison.

Seeing the hard-won western lands slipping away, Washington called on Anthony Wayne, whom he knew as a brave and capable officer during the Revolution, and Wayne didn't disappoint him.

I start this tour in Maumee, with the first stop just a few miles down US24 at the Battle of Fallen Timbers Monument. This important battle was fought in August 1794 in an area near the Maumee River that had recently been leveled by a tornado. Wayne's victory, followed by refusal of the British to provide further aid to the Indians, was a major development and led the way to the Treaty of Greenville a year later. The opening of the Ohio territory to settlement and

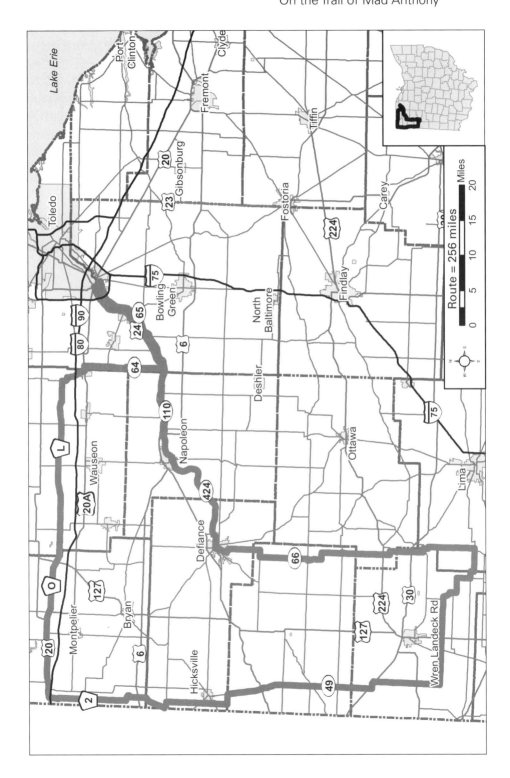

Battle of Fallen Timbers Monument.

statehood occurred just nine years later. Wayne spent many months turning a large group of volunteers into a disciplined army. He wasn't going to repeat the tragic mistakes of earlier campaigns, where undisciplined, poorly-equipped and poorly-trained volunteers were routed by highly motivated Indians. In fact, General Wayne made it a point to train his men to fight the way the enemy fought and to abandon the European approach to battles. Wayne, like all American officers of the day, had been trained by British officers in the science of war, but he saw that such tactics were of no value in the Ohio wilderness.

Once back on US24, head southwest along this scenic riverside road. The first town you'll pass through is Waterville. There is a very enjoyable train ride that departs from Waterville, called the Blue Bird, that will take you on a fifteen-mile trip along the river. This train can be found at the Toledo, Lake Erie & Western Railway and Museum, located at 49 North Sixth Street in Waterville. Call them at 419-887-2177 or go to www.tlew.org for schedules and more information. Leaving Waterville, we continue west on US24 to Providence Metropark. If you have a desire to experience life as it was in a canal town 150 years ago, this is an interesting and fun stop to make. Take a ride down the Miami and Erie Canal on *The Volunteer*—a canal boat pulled by mules through original locks that were used by thousands of farmers and travelers in a very different age. Be sure to check out the water-powered mill and other attractions, as well. The tiny town of Providence is also where we turn north from US24 onto Providence Road, taking it through the village of Neapolis. After a few miles you will hook up with SR64, proceeding straight north. This general area is quite pretty, being located near the Maumee State Forest and the large Oak Openings Preserve.

ON THE TRAIL OF MAD ANTHONY 256 MILES		
Miles	Destination	Total
0	Maumee	0
16	Providence	16
12	Swanton	28
34	Kunkle	62
15.5	Columbia	77.5
11.5	Fish Creek Jog/CR60	89
16.5	Defiance/Paulding County Line Road	105.5
22.5	US30	128
11	Wren–Landeck Road	139
19	SR81/Converse	158
13	Delphos	171
34	Defiance	205
18	Napoleon	223
33	Perrysburg/Maumee	256

This entire portion of Ohio was part of the Great Black Swamp, an impenetrable vast swampland that stymied exploration and settlement of northwestern Ohio for many years. Draining of the swamp in the nineteenth century resulted in the productive farmlands that are evident as we ride through this area.

State Route 64 makes a jog on US20/SR2 and then north through the town of Swanton and beyond. Just slightly more than a mile north of the Ohio Turnpike is County Road K. This rural road marks an historic line on the map. You see, to the east of here the road is called Old State Line Road. This is the line that all the fuss was about in the early 1830s when Ohio and Michigan almost went to war—and it had nothing whatsoever to do with football! An early survey showed this line to be the northern boundary of Ohio, meaning that the mouth of the Maumee River and Toledo would be in the Michigan Territory. Governor Lucas was having none of it and gave his name to the piece of land in contention, creating Lucas County. Because Ohio was already a state and Michigan wasn't, Congress favored the Ohio argument, giving Michigan the west half of its Upper Peninsula in return for losing the Toledo Strip.

Just a mile farther north and after making a jog on SR64, you will see County Road L. Turn left/west onto this quiet county road, which will treat you to wonderful countryside and a very relaxing and enjoyable ride across northern Ohio for nearly fifty miles. Now, a person could take nearby I-80 or US20, which parallel CR-L, but why would you want to? County Road L is a scenic road with lots of character, few cars, and virtually no trucks. The occasional stop sign is a small price to pay to avoid stoplights, diesel exhaust, idiotic drivers, and congestion on US20 or the mind-numbing monotony of the Turnpike.

County Road L curves and becomes CR-O just past US127. A couple of miles beyond 127, roughly one mile east of the tiny burg of Kunkle, is the Jacob Young log house. This unique, two-story cabin was built in 1845 and is a state historical site. It isn't generally open to the public, but appointments can be made by calling 419-485-8200. County Road O joins US20 just beyond the St. Joseph River crossing, and from there, it's about eleven miles farther west to the tiny village of Columbia, where we head south.

Before arriving at Columbia, US20 crosses SR49. For a nice side trip, you can ride north for three miles, then turn right onto CR-R to 4.75 Road on the west side of Nettle Lake (Ohio's largest natural lake). Turn left and go about a mile beyond the boat ramp to find the Nettle Lake Hopewell Indian Mounds. The land where the mounds are located is owned by the Williams County Historical Society (419-485-8200), and the site is open May through October.

Whether you visit the Mounds or not, you should get to Columbia via US20. At the west edge of this tiny town is 1.50 Road where we turn south over the Turnpike and beyond. Two miles south of the Turnpike, 1.50 Road takes a slight jog east and then continues south as 2.0 Road. Enjoy a very nice ride about eleven miles south on 2.0 Road, at which point it forms a T at Fish Creek on C-60 Road. Jog left on C-60, following it over the creek and then back west a bit until you see 2.50 Road going straight south again—this is the one you want. In less than three miles, 2.50 Road jogs to the southwest, becoming Concle Road, which follows the St. Joseph River and delivers you to SR249 about three miles later. Turn left on SR249, taking it just one mile to Casebeer-Miller Road, turning right. Follow C-M road almost ten miles straight south, under a very cool old railroad viaduct just northwest of Hicksville, to the Defiance-Paulding County Line Road and follow this road east a mile and a half to SR49. State Route 49 will be our host for the next approximately 30 miles until the intersection with US224.

This stretch of road takes you through open lands that mark the eastern edge of the great prairie that stretches hundreds of miles to the west. I find roads such as these wonderful places to just relax and enjoy the more subtle side of motorcycling; listening to the music of the engine, absorbing the smells and sights around

This cannon is located at Fort Defiance, which was built on the confluence of the Auglaize and Maumee RIvers.

me, and just soaking it all in. On technical roads with lots of curves and hills, a rider is too busy with the mechanics of operating the machine to kick back and relax. Roads that curve and climb are wonderful, but on this road, you can really enjoy those other qualities that make motorcycling special.

When you reach US224, SR49 turns to the west. We, however, want to cross US224 and continue straight ahead on what is called Convoy-Heller Road. Taking Convoy-Heller Road south for three and a half miles takes us to Wren-Landeck Road, where we turn east/left, and follow it twelve miles to its juncture with SR116. Turn right onto 116 and follow it six miles to the crossroads of Converse at SR81. Head east on SR81, and after five miles, you'll come to SR66 heading north—that's the road we want. SR66 will be our guide all the way for the thirty-six-mile ride north to the city of Defiance.

Delphos is the first recommended stop on the trip north. The Miami and Erie Canal is well preserved in Delphos, and there is a Canal Commission Museum downtown that is a very interesting stop. The museum is open only irregularly, so call them at 419-695-7737 for specific days and times. A large mural depicting activities along the canal during its heyday is painted on the side of the Delphos Herald building in town. Delphos is also the hometown of author Zane Grey, where his boyhood home still stands.

Proceeding north again on SR66 will deliver you to the historic city of Defiance. You'll probably be ready for a break at this point, and I highly recommend that Defiance be a place where you do some exploring on foot. The Auglaize and Tiffin Rivers join the mighty Maumee in Defiance, making it an historically important and strategic location. It was here, at the confluence of the Maumee and Auglaize

Rivers, that General Wayne had Fort Defiance built in 1794. Fort Defiance was the last of several forts built by General Wayne as his army traveled north from Fort Washington (present-day Cincinnati) to ensure that he had a safe logistical route for supplies and strategic operations. The name of the fort allegedly resulted when General Wayne was supposed to have said "I defy the English, Indians, and all the devils of hell to take it." The fort was completed on August 17, 1794, and just three days later Wayne marched his army down the Maumee and defeated the Indian confederation near Fort Miami, a British fort where the Indians had massed. This victory at Fallen Timbers broke the back of the Indian resistance, made all the more final when the British at Fort Miami refused to provide further military or other aid to the Indians. This victory also temporarily stymied the aspirations of several European powers that still had hopes of making the area between the Ohio River and the Mississippi River part of their empire.

Unfortunately, the site of Fort Defiance isn't as well marked as it should be. As you go north on SR66 in Defiance, immediately prior to crossing the Maumee River you come to Fort Street on your right. The monument is on, logically enough, Fort Street just past the library at the point where the two rivers meet. Near the site of Fort Defiance is Fort Winchester, a War of 1812 fort.

Three miles west of Defiance on US24, you will find AuGlaize Village, a reconstructed nineteenth-century village with museums that cover topics as diverse as farming, military history, and model railroading (419-782-7255).

Continuing the ride, immediately after crossing the Maumee River, SR424 will go to the right on the banks of the Maumee. It would be hard to exaggerate describing 424 as an absolutely wonderful motorcycling road. It twists and turns along the river shoreline, and to make it even more interesting, it hugs the Miami and Erie Canal for many miles. It is one of the nicest motorcycling roads in northwestern Ohio. The first mile, while still in Defiance, is very interesting and I recommend a slow speed through here so you can stop if you wish to read the several stone monuments that line the shore, including a stone marking the birthplace of Chief Pontiac, a chair-shaped stone that Chief Blue Jacket used as a chair during meetings, and a marker noting the location of Johnny Appleseed's first nursery. Independence Dam and lock 13 on the Miami and Erie Canal are at a riverside park just a bit farther east on 424. This fascinating area is just chock-a-block full of interesting history. You will be tempted to do this run twice—the first time to view all the attractions along the way, and the second to concentrate totally on the great motorcycling to be had along this scenic and winding byway!

Follow 424 into Napoleon and at the main downtown intersection, with the beautiful Henry County Courthouse on your left and the bridge over the Maumee and SR108 to your right, cross over the river. As soon as you get over the bridge,

Fort Meigs was ordered to be built by General (later President) William Henry Harrison during the War of 1812.

SR110 will head east again on the shoreline. Turn left onto SR110 and cruise it all the way to Grand Rapids, where it becomes route 65. This entire stretch is a state scenic byway and makes for wonderful riding. Grand Rapids is a wonderful small town, and you really should park you bike and see what it has to offer.

Take SR65 all the way to Perrysburg, where I strongly suggest a stop at Fort Meigs, the famous War of 1812 fort built by General William Henry Harrison (later President Harrison) to protect the northwest from British invasion. Harrison built the fort in 1813 after the terrible American loss and subsequent massacre at Frenchtown (Monroe, Michigan). It withstood attacks in May and July of 1813. In the July attack 1,000 Indian warriors under Tecumseh and 2,000 British and Canadian soldiers under Colonel Proctor inflicted serious damage on the American units, but in the end failed to defeat them. After the unsuccessful July attack, the British regrouped and moved back to the Canadian side of the Detroit River, where Harrison and his army pursued them, fighting the pivotal Battle of the Thames in October 1813 in which Tecumseh was killed and the British routed.

Fort Meigs was one of the largest wooden forts ever built and has been reconstructed. It has a large visitor center in addition to the fort itself. Many brave men died at Fort Meigs, and its importance to the Great Lakes region and all of America, for that matter, can't be overstated. The fort and the brave men who served there deserve a few minutes of our time today. The days and hours that the fort is open depends on the time of year, so call them at 419-874-4121 for their schedule when you plan a visit.

Upon leaving Fort Meigs, head east on 65 into Perrysburg to complete this wonderful trip through an area rich in natural beauty, cultural attractions, and tons of history.

Frontier Forts

AS PROMISED, EACH RIDE in this book offers up something unique and special. The one common element, of course, is the quality of the motorcycling side of the venture, but there's always something more—something that makes the tour more than just another motorcycle trip.

I personally find this trip one of the most interesting. It might be that the history of the period before Ohio became a state, when it was literally the flashpoint of western expansion, has always fascinated me. What more could anyone who loves adventure ask for: Machiavellian political alliances; major battles, military tactics and operations (the good, the bad, and the ugly); the bravery of individuals who played a major role in the formation of the nation; outposts on the frontier where soldiers spent long lonely hours in miserable conditions, carving trails through the wilderness on which to move entire armies; treaties that opened up a new nation; and so much more. This part of Ohio is filled with the stories of a nation being built, perhaps not to the same degree as Boston and Philadelphia, but the impact that events in western Ohio had on our country should not be underestimated. And if that's not enough, it really is an enjoyable motorcycle trip.

The western portion of Ohio has four routes along which forts were built in support of two major military actions. The first is a string of forts, from present-day Cincinnati north along the west side of the state, that were built during the 1790–1795 Indian Wars. The second group of forts is actually three routes extending north and south—one in line with Defiance, which followed the Auglaize River; an overland route extending from Kenton north to the Maumee river near Toledo; and the third north from Upper Sandusky, following the Sandusky River to Lake Erie. These forts were indispensable in securing supply lines and moving troops north to the fight.

On this trip, we'll look at forts that include the Indian War fortifications, as well as some of the western War of 1812 forts. (Other forts from both periods are covered in other tours in the book.)

We start our journey through history in Spencerville, located straight west of Lima at the juncture of State Routes 117 and 66. Spencerville is a canal town, and the Miami & Erie Canal is always nearby as we proceed south on 66. Canal Locks 15 and 16 are located in Spencerville on South and North Canal Streets,

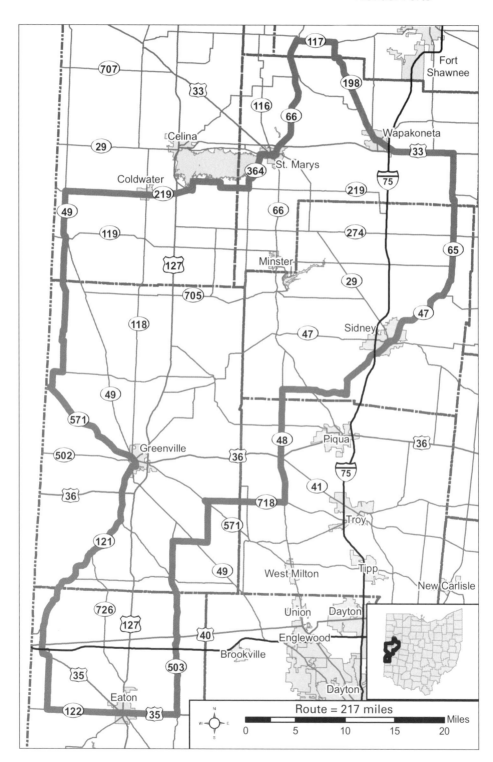

respectively. Just south of Spencerville is Deep Cut Park. A high piece of land, which is a watershed divide between two river systems, required digging through fifty feet of rock and hard clay for more than five hundred feet in order to accommodate the canal's need for level stretches between locks. This was one of the most difficult portions of the entire canal to construct. Not that the men digging through the hill had any complaints; after all, they were paid thirty cents per day and could have a shot of whiskey at the end of each day.

Located farther south on SR66 are Lock 14 and the forty-acre pond that supplied water for the canal. On South Street in the town of St. Marys, look for Memorial Park where you'll find the *Belle of St. Marys*—a seventy-six-foot-long canal packet boat replica. This nice park sits astride the canal and the St. Marys River. From St. Marys we need to go west on SR29 for perhaps a mile to Route 703, which we take west toward the lake, where we take a south/left turn onto Route 304. The feeder canal that fed water from the St. Marys impoundment to the canal runs parallel to 703. All along Ohio's canal system, there were impoundments that served as water sources for the canals, ensuring that there would always be the right depth of water in the canal, regardless of rainfall. Grand Lake St. Marys was the largest of these water supply reservoirs.

Ride Route 304 along the east shore of the lake to Route 219, then turn right and follow 219 west along the lake's south shore. As you ride along the shoreline of this impoundment, you gain an appreciation for just how large it is. Until the construction of Hoover Dam and the creation of Lake Mead, Grand Lake St. Marys was the largest man-made lake in the world at 13,500 acres. Grand Lake St. Marys is so large that it boasts three lighthouses—a rarity for an inland lake.

State Route 219 will take you through Coldwater (which formerly had the name of Buzzard's Glory until someone changed it to the plain vanilla name of Coldwater) and then west all the way to Route 49, where we turn and head south less than five miles to Fort Recovery—our first frontier fort. Fort Recovery's importance to the entire Northwest Territory can hardly be overstated. It didn't start out that way, however. In 1791, in response to demands from settlers on the frontier to do something about Indian attacks, President Washington commissioned General Arthur St. Clair, the first governor of the Northwest Territory, to reaise an army and attack the Indians in their strongholds in what is now western Ohio and eastern Indiana. An officer with experience in two wars, St. Clair and his

Miles	Destination	Total
	FRONTIER FORTS **217 MILES**	
0	Spencerville	0
30	Coldwater	30
13	Fort Recovery	43
28	Greenville	71
21	New Paris	92
15	Fort St. Clair State Park	107
20	Ithaca	127
19	Pleasant Hill	146
18	Lockington	164
36	Wapakoneta	200
11	Fort Amanda	211
6	Spencerville	217

army hacked a trail north from Fort Washington (Cincinnati) and arrived at the Wabash River at what is now Fort Recovery with a tired, hungry, and cold army in November of 1791. Disgruntled soldiers set up camp for the night without establishing defensive positions, and early the next morning, the camp was attacked by between one thousand and fifteen hundred warriors. It was a deadly rout, with nine hundred to twelve hundred soldiers—almost the entire fighting force—dead or dying within one hour. In proportion to the size of the unit, this was the worst defeat in the history of the American army. Just one year earlier, General Harmar had also suffered a serious defeat near present-day Fort Wayne.

Enter General Anthony Wayne into the picture. General Wayne earned the title "Mad Anthony" from his men during Revolutionary War battles in which he displayed his impressive courage and military skills. Wayne was selected by President Washington to succeed where others failed. Mad Anthony led a force of over two thousand well-trained and equipped soldiers north to meet the enemy. Along the way, he built a string of forts, which he believed would protect the vital logistical needs of the army as well as securing the area he passed through by manning the forts with soldiers. Wayne had Fort Recovery built in 1793 on the site of St. Clair's disastrous defeat. General Wayne had a penchant

Fort Recovery was built by General Anthony Wayne on the site of General Arthur St. Clair's disastrous defeat.

for attributing names to places that represented his confidence and intent to succeed. He named his new stockade Fort Recovery because he fully intended to recover what had been lost by St. Clair. On June 30, 1794, a confederated force of over two thousand warriors attacked Wayne's army at the fort, which had a garrison of only two hundred and fifty surviving soldiers inside as a result of a deadly attack the day before on troops stationed outside the fort. A two-day battle ensued, but within the protection of the fort, Wayne's men were able to fight off the attackers, who gave up the fight at the end of the second day.

I think Americans have long been fascinated by the castles of medieval Europe and the idea of defenders in the castle fighting off attackers. Well, wooden forts were America's castles. Across the early landscape of America, from the Atlantic to Pacific Oceans, soldiers secured the peace through the use of these wilderness stockades, enduring countless attacks and sieges.

To get to the reconstructed fort and visitor center in the town of Fort Recovery, turn right onto Boundary Street when Route 49 makes a left turn. You can see the blockhouse of the fort as soon as you make the turn. Upon leaving the Fort, continue east on Route 49 a couple of blocks, where you will come to a park and a very large obelisk monument honoring the soldiers involved in St. Clair's defeat.

It's an impressive structure. An oak tree has been planted here in memory of the many Native Americans who also died during these hostile times.

Upon leaving this monument, turn right at the stop sign onto Route 119/Butler Street and take it back west four blocks to the stop light at Wayne Street and turn left. Wayne Street transforms into Union City Road beyond the corporation limits. We'll follow this road many miles. South of Route 705, it becomes Hill-grove–Fort Recovery Road and takes us all the way south nearly to Union City. Hillgrove–Fort Recovery Road makes a short west jog at Ellis Road (at the stop sign a large red barn that you can't miss is in front of you), and one mile farther south it makes a short jog east again to the same alignment. At Route 47 turn right and follow the road around the curve to Union City and Route 571. At this point, you'll actually be about one block inside Indiana. Turn left onto Indiana Route 32 and then almost immediately turn left again onto Ohio Route 571, and it will take us to our next major attraction, Greenville, a wonderfully historic small town with fascinating stories to tell.

Depending on your interests, there are several places in Greenville that are worth a look. First is the Garst Museum, located just north of 571 on Broadway Street (Route 118) on the west side of Greenville as you come into town. Instead of turning right on Broadway and taking it into town, turn left and the museum is just one block to the north. This museum houses the largest collection of Annie Oakley memorabilia as well as many 1795 Treaty of Greenville artifacts. Also found there are historical items related to Lowell Thomas, the famous World War II CBS radio broadcaster. Lowell Thomas was born just north of Greenville. Shortly after entering town on 571/Broadway Street, you will cross the famous Greenville Creek, upon whose banks much history was made. Just after crossing the creek, turn left at Water Street (at the Episcopal Church) and a model of the Greenville Fort is a few blocks down. In 1793 on his way north, General Wayne constructed a large log fortification on Greenville Creek in what was to become Greenville. At this location, a coalition of Indian chiefs from thirteen tribes met Wayne and his aide-de-camp and future president, William Henry Harrison, on August 3, 1795, to sign the Treaty of Greenville (also called the Wyandot Peace and Friendship Treaty). In a symbolic move, William Harrison returned to the remains of Fort Greenville in 1814 to sign a final treaty with local Indians, and he returned to Greenville in 1840 while campaigning for the presidency. What I find fascinating, in an "it's a small world" sort of way, is that Meriwether Lewis was stationed in Greenville and was at the 1795 treaty signing. He was later assigned to a unit commanded by Captain William Clark, and as they say, the rest is history. In the large city park that lies along Memorial Drive off Water Street, there are several monuments marking the history of this site. Unfortunately, they're

Replica of Greenville Fort.

scattered about this large park and there is limited or no parking space near some of them. This is too bad as the story of historical events in Greenville needs to be better told.

Interestingly, Tecumseh and his brother, The Prophet, established an encampment just west of the fort in demonstration of their opposition to the treaty. From this camp, they hunted and lived as always. This place is preserved today as the Shawnee Prairie Preserve, located on Route 502 on the west edge of Greenville.

There are other attractions in Greenville that might interest you depending on your age and particular interests. Darke County's most famous native daughter is Annie Oakley (born Phoebe Ann Mosey in the small town of Willowdell just northwest of Greenville). The idea of a sharp-shooting frontierswoman who went on to a life of travel and fame has always fascinated me. There is a life-size bronze statue of her in the small Annie Oakley Memorial Park just past the courthouse.

Downtown Greenville comprises a large historic area with many nineteenth-century commercial buildings still in use. More than 80 buildings are on the National Register of Historic Places.

When you've seen all you wish to see in nineteenth-century Greenville, jump on your twenty-first century motorcycle and head south on Route 121 for a short ride down to the town of Fort Jefferson. As any military logistician can tell you, protecting the supply line is critical in military maneuvers. This was especially true in a wilderness setting through what was enemy-held territory. With this in mind,

The Whispering Oak, located in Fort St. Clair State Park, is the site where six soldiers were buried over two centuries ago.

General St. Clair built several forts and outposts along his route north from Fort Washington. Fort Jefferson, named in honor of then Secretary of State Thomas Jefferson, served this purpose from 1790–1796. An impressive twenty-foot-high field stone monument marks the location of this fort in a small park one block west of Route 121. Turn right at the main intersection in this tiny town. Signs in the park tell the story of battles and troop movements. There is also an interesting sign telling of an underground tunnel found years later while studying the fort's location.

Continue south on Route 121 as it winds and curves southwest to the town of New Paris. This is a scenic and fun stretch of road that I know you'll enjoy. Continue straight south through New Paris on what is now Route 320. Take this road over the I-70 expressway a very short distance to Eaton Road/320 and turn left. Go east on Eaton less than one mile and turn south/right onto Wolverton Road. This turn is just prior to the entry ramp connecting I-70 and US35.

Follow Wolverton Road straight south five miles to Route 122, turning left toward the town of Eaton. Just west of Eaton is Fort St. Clair State Park—our next stop. Fort St. Clair, built in 1792, was the first fort north of Fort Washington and, as such, was an important supply depot and troop garrison during the

Indian Wars. A beautiful twelve-acre park, much of it left in its virgin condition to reflect what was there in 1792, protects the location of the fort and a November 6, 1792, skirmish in which six Kentucky militiamen were killed. I highly recommend a stop at this site. It is very moving, with the site of the fort and battlefield well marked in the exact manner it appeared over two hundred years ago. Most fascinating is the Whispering Oak—a tree that was there on November 6, 1792, and under which the six soldiers were buried. The tree and the six gravesites that this giant oak has watched over during all these years of change are there today, just as they have been for over two centuries.

The city of Eaton is the county seat for Preble County. The names given to both jurisdictions by the original settlers are modern reminders of the very turbulent times our nation experienced in its infancy. The War of Independence was finally over at great cost, the Indian Wars were a major ongoing concern, Great Britain still occupied American land and was harassing our merchant marine, and to top it off, American ships were being captured and sailors by the hundreds were being killed, captured, or sold into slavery by the Barbary pirates of North Africa. For centuries European powers paid "tribute" to the rulers of current-day Libya and other North African states to ensure free passage through the Mediterranean and eastern Atlantic. America paid this protection money for a few years and then decided to take military action to stop the piracy. Commodore Edward Preble led the young US Navy into action against the well-entrenched naval forces of these states, and William Eaton led a 500-mile march across the desert to capture a coastal stronghold of the pirates. Thus, the words "To the shores of Tripoli" were added to the Marine Corps Hymn, and early Ohioans added the names of these early American heroes to the Ohio landscape.

Before leaving Eaton, be sure to go to the city park to see one of only six "double-barrel" covered bridges left in the country. Turn right from Route 122 on the west edge of town just after crossing the bridge over Seven Mile Creek. The Roberts Covered Bridge is the oldest covered bridge in Ohio and was moved to the park to ensure its survival. It's a very cool sight.

We leave Eaton by going east on US35 to West Alexandria, where we turn left/north onto Route 503. Follow 503 north beyond Lewisburg (where you can see the Dixon Branch Covered Bridge in the local park) and on north to the miniature town of Ithaca. In Ithaca Route 503 turns northwest, but we want to continue north, so we'll turn right at the stoplight onto Cross Street/Route 722, then left a couple of blocks later onto Pearl Street when Route 722 turns right, and finally left on Arcanum-Ithaca Road, which will run due north to the town of Arcanum. Believe me, Ithaca is so small that I think I've named almost all the streets in town, so this jog is very easy.

This "double-barrel" covered bridge is located in Eaton's city park.

In Arcanum, turn right at the first stop sign on the south side of town onto Alternate Route 49, which is South Street within the city limits. Take Alternate 49 east, across Route 49, and on to the village of Pitsburg (a town only slightly larger than Ithaca). In Pitsburg we're going to turn left/north onto Gettysburg–Pittsburg Road, which will take us through the rich farmlands of Darke County. Very shortly after you cross SR571, you will turn right onto CR51/Greenville–Pleasant Hill Road. Follow this road east and eventually it becomes SR718 and will lead you over the Stillwater River and into the village of Pleasant Hill. The town of Pleasant Hill is little more than a crossroads village, but smack in the middle of the main intersection, there is a very cool Civil War monument. Be cautious here as the crossroad doesn't stop and it's easy to assume that it is a four-way stop given the layout of the corner.

From Pleasant Hill go north on Route 48. This road is very enjoyable to ride and will follow the river north to Covington and then follow Trotters Creek north beyond town. About six miles north of US36 in Covington, you'll come to CR-111/Fessler–Buxton Road (one mile north of the Miami/Shelby county line). Turn right onto Fessler–Buxton and take it east through some nice countryside

The locks at Lockington were the most extensive on the Miami & Erie Canal.

on a good biking road to two historical and fun attractions. Just prior to reaching Lockington on Fessler–Buxton Road, you'll see Hardin Road heading off to your right (a cemetery is at this three-way stop intersection). Hardin Road will take you to the Piqua Historical Center, which holds Native American artifacts, original farm buildings, a mile-long restored section of the canal, the *General Harrison* canal boat, and lots of other nice attractions. It's only a couple miles south of Fessler–Buxton Road and is a very enjoyable stop. A very short distance beyond the historical center on Hardin Road, there are some roadside monuments and historical signs that you ought to visit. They explain the fascinating history of the Indian village of Pickawillany, early battles between the French, English and Indians at this site, and a general history of this very historic location.

Back on Fessler–Buxton Road, turn east/right and take it the short distance into Lockington to see the locks on the old Miami & Ohio Canal. Just prior to getting to Lockington, the road will curve right by the dam and take you into the village.

The Lockington Locks are right in town and easily accessible. These locks were the most extensive on the Miami & Erie Canal and are in remarkably good condition to this day—a must see, in my mind. There are no museums or places to visit. You simply walk along the original locks as they angle through town.

Fessler–Buxton Road makes a T in the village of Lockington at Lockport Trail. Turn left here and take it north a mile and a half to Fair Road (also locally called Infirmary Pike), which angles off to the northeast. We'll follow this angling road all

Bonyconnellan Castle is located in Sidney. It sits at the top of the hill as you drive into downtown on Walnut Street.

the way into the city of Sidney, where a very short stretch east on Route 29 will take us to Route 47, which is our road. Fair Road is easy to follow as it angles into the southwest corner of Sidney. Near downtown, there is a fork intersection where a decision has to be made—choose the left fork onto Walnut Street. Go north on Walnut a block or two to the main drag through town and turn right, go to the courthouse and turn left on the street just past the courthouse, go north one block and then turn right onto east Route 47. Just follow the signs—it's easier than it sounds.

Backtracking just a few blocks—as you come into downtown on Walnut Street look straight ahead of you up the hill, where you will see a castle. It's an old home called Bonyconnellan, and if you go straight ahead for a two-block detour, you can ride by it. It's an unusual Kodak Moment.

Once on eastbound 47, you'll ride this enjoyable and scenic stretch of road along the Great Miami River through Port Jefferson and then to the intersection of Route 65. Ride Route 65 north all the way to US33, turning left onto 33 and heading toward Tranquility Base (Wapakoneta, the hometown of moon-walking astronaut Neil Armstrong).

Wapakoneta is the home of the Neil Armstrong Air and Space Museum.

As you approach Wapakoneta from the east, you'll notice a road angling northwest off Route 33 into town. This is just east of the I-75 expressway. The road is called Wapak–Fisher Road, and once in town it becomes Bellefontaine Street. There's a brown tourist sign at this corner pointing to the Neil Armstrong Air and Space Museum. Take this road and just after you cross I-75 you'll see the museum, with its cool moon-like dome on your right, behind all the fast food restaurants and chain hotels. This is a really enjoyable stop. Maybe not all of us can remember where we were on July 20, 1969, when Neil Armstrong took those incredible footsteps on the moon, but we can all enjoy this museum that chronicles the space age and the science of flight. There are a few exhibits outside, but the best awaits you inside the museum. I find it ironic that the town that came to symbolize the space age had its beginnings less than two hundred years earlier as a gathering place for virtually all of the major Native American chiefs and warriors of the late eighteenth century. It was Shawnee Chiefs Blue Jacket and Black Hoof that formed a village here and gave this town its unique name. I made it a point to design this tour to take in this museum because I believe the same kind of courage that was needed to explore the frontier of space was required by the early settlers and soldiers who conquered the frontier that was to become Ohio.

General Anthony Wayne and Neil Armstrong share many of the important qualities that set courageous people like this apart from most of us.

From the space center, continue going into town on Bellefontaine Street to the stop sign on the edge of downtown. Turn right onto Water Street and one block later turn left on Auglaize Street, taking this main downtown street west. At the last stoplight on the west side of town, turn right onto Route 198. We'll follow this road northwest to our next stop—Fort Amanda—at the Auglaize/Van Wert County line. Fort Amanda is War of 1812 vintage. It was one of a string of forts that was built to prosecute that war in the western Lake Erie basin, the Michigan Territory, and southwestern Ontario. Other forts in this logistical and garrison chain included Fort Jennings, Fort Winchester (in Defiance), Fort Brown (near Melrose), and Fort Meigs. Fort Amanda is a very highly recommended stop. It doesn't look very impressive from the road, but once you start exploring the site, you'll find it fascinating. A trail follows the high bank of the Auglaize River past a cemetery in which seventy five flags fly over the graves of unknown soldiers who died here during the war. Historic signs explain events that shaped the state and nation. A grave marker I found fascinating was one for a certain Captain E. Dawson. According to the inscription, he was "murdered by Indians, October 1812." Walking the trail beyond the cemetery takes you to a very impressive 50-foot granite monument that marks the location where Fort Amanda stood on the banks of the Auglaize River.

We complete this remarkable journey through a very important chapter of our history by taking Route 198 north to Route 117, following it west back to the canal town of Spencerville. I suspect if we could have learned history from atop a motorcycle while in high school many of us would be much more knowledgeable about the fascinating historical stories of our country than we are.

Virginia Military District

THOUGH ALL OF OHIO shares some common history, it is noteworthy that different sections of the state have unique historical experiences. The Virginia Military District of southwestern Ohio, for instance, has a history quite different than southeastern or northwestern Ohio.

The colony (and later state) of Virginia had claims on extensive tracts of land in the west. It relinquished its claim on much of this land following the Revolutionary War, but by 1787, at the time of the Northwest Ordinance, it still retained land in present-day Ohio bounded by the Ohio River on the south, the Little Miami River on the west, and the Scioto River on the east and north. Because Virginia, like all of the colonies, was nearly bankrupt following the War, it used this land as payment to its Revolutionary War veterans. Continental Scrip, issued by the Continental Congress as currency during the War had become worthless, and land was the one commodity that the new nation had in abundance. Virginia War veterans were qualified to receive what even then must have seemed like a tremendous amount of land: Brigadier Generals received fifteen thousand acres; lower level officers received proportionately less land according to their rank; and enlisted men received one hundred acres[1]—enough to clear for a farm and a good life in a new land.

This action had its complicating issues, however. For instance, the 1787 Northwest Ordinance forbade slavery in this territory, so Virginians had to decide whether to turn their back on several generations of family history and start anew in Ohio or retain their old traditions in Virginia. Also, even though this area was subject to the new Public Lands Survey System, many Virginians brought with them their tried and true method of land surveying and subdividing. Confusion and litigation exists to this day on some properties in this region.

Interestingly, this portion of the state doesn't celebrate its historical roots in the same way that the northeast portion of Ohio remembers its Connecticut connection. In the northeast corner of the state you can't turn around without seeing a reference to the Western Reserve or Firelands. While doing research, I stopped

---

[1] *Land of Promise: The Story of the Northwest Territory,* Walter Havighurst, © 1946, The Macmillan Company, New York.

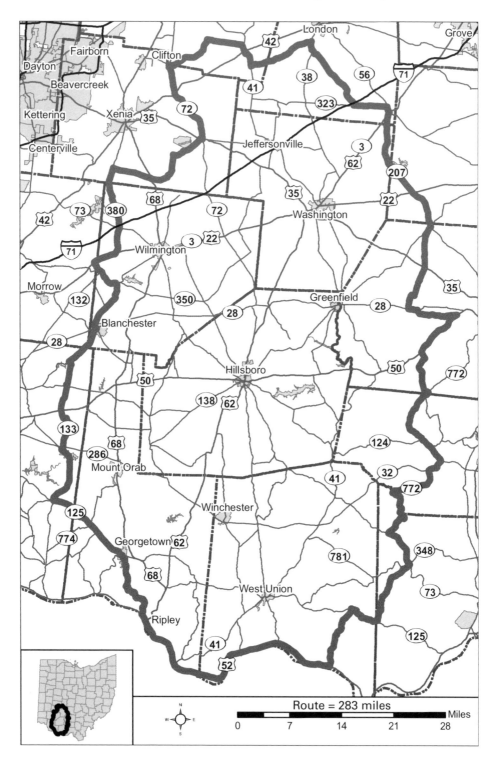

Route = 283 miles

Miles
0   7   14   21   28

Rankin House in Ripley was a prominent stop along the Underground Railroad. (Photo courtesy of Ohio Division of Travel and Tourism)

at two libraries in towns with strong connections to the historic Virginia Military District, and neither had any books or other materials on the topic. It seems that Ohio's Virginia connection may become lost in time. A quick crosscheck shows that eighteen towns in the District have names common with Virginia towns. (Forty-eight Ohio towns have the same name as those in Virginia. Some are no doubt coincidental, but I suspect it shows the movement of settlers from the east, who like their Connecticut counterparts, wanted to give their new community the same name as their colonial home town.) On this trip you will see a number of horse farms that have a certain Virginia look to them; coincidental or planned? I'll let you decide.

This is truly a beautiful part of the state and is chock-full of great motorcycling roads, scenery, interesting history, and various attractions. We'll start our journey at the same place many of the original settlers did, on the Ohio River in the small history-filled town of Ripley. This is a very logical place to begin

VIRGINIA MILITARY DISTRICT 283 MILES		
Miles	Destination	Total
0	Ripley	0
23	Bethel	23
27	Blanchester	50
23	Caesar Creek State Park	73
25	Cedarville	98
44	Mt. Sterling	142
25	Frankfort	167
26	Nipgen	193
30	Rarden	223
20	Blue Creek	243
9	US51/Rome	252
31	Ripley	283

our Virginia Military District tour, since Ripley had its beginnings in 1812 when Colonel James Poage, a Virginian, received 1,000 acres at this site in payment for his military service. The village Poage started was initially called Staunton but was changed to Ripley in 1816 in honor of General Eleazar Ripley, a commander in the War of 1812.

Ripley is remembered as a major point on the beginning of the Underground Railroad. For thousands of slaves seeking freedom, it was the Ohio River and hiding places in Ripley where their perilous journey on the Freedom Trail began. The entire town is a National Historic District, and a monument at the foot of Main Street commemorates the efforts of local residents and abolitionists. There are several existing homes in Ripley that were major stations on the railroad, including the John P. Parker House, a National Historic Landmark located at 330 North Front Street in town, and the Rankin House outside of town on Liberty Hill. This is a very enjoyable ride today on the twisting road going to the top of Liberty Hill and the Rankin House, with its commanding view of the valley and river spread out below it. I definitely recommend this short side trip.

This area was a major player in tobacco production, and today, the Ohio Tobacco Museum is in a house built in the 1850s located at 703 south Second Street next to the old tobacco warehouses. Ripley hosts the annual Ohio

Bullskin Trace Monument.

Tobacco Festival every August, which includes lots of events, including an antique car show. The Ripley Museum, with artifacts of this area going back many years, is also located in an 1850s home in town.

We leave Ripley by going northwest to Georgetown on old Route 68, located just to the west of Ripley. This is a really enjoyable and scenic road that twists and turns its way through forested hollows and over stone hills, following a cascading stream almost all the way.

If you enjoy antique machinery shows, be sure to check out the Ohio Valley Antique Machinery Show, which Georgetown hosts each August. Call 513-734-6272 or 937-379-1281 for more information.

Georgetown was the boyhood home of President Ulysses S. Grant, and the schoolhouse he attended is located at 508 South Water Street in town, two blocks south of SR125.

We'll continue our journey northwest on SR125 just outside of town. This road is cut through two hills, resulting in bedrock cliffs on both sides of the road, giving it a very Appalachian look. Closer to Bethel the road becomes a bit straighter and flatter, and the countryside changes from woods to mostly farmland. In Bethel turn right on SR133 (the intersection has a stop light and gas station). We'll stay on SR133 all the way north to just beyond Blanchester. On the way, you'll ride through the historic village of Williamsburg. With its heritage dating back to 1796, it's the oldest community in the county and was once the county seat. Early each June the town celebrates an Olde Williamsburgh Festival, which includes a car show and motorcycle ride. Check it out by calling 513-724-6107.

State Route 133 is a very nice ride all along its length. The road is on an historic trail called the Bullskin Trace, an old Indian trail later used by settlers and as a track for the Underground Railroad. The Trace went from the Ohio River to the British fort at Detroit. As you ride down Route 133 in the area of Felicity and Bethel, you are riding on historic ground. Along this very same road, Simon Kenton, in 1778, ran through a gauntlet of Shawnee warriors who

A man taps a tree to collect maple sap at Caesar Creek State Park.

lined the road. He survived the gauntlet, and despite his injuries, kept right on running, outpacing the Shawnee and continuing until he hit the Ohio River. In the tiny village of Edonton, there is a monument and plaque marking the Bullskin Trace placed there many years ago by the Daughters of the American Revolution. For a long time a slightly improved version of the Trace was called the Old Xenia Road.

Once you arrive in Edonton, you have to stop and make a right turn. I recommend parking at the old school at the corner and walking down the road to the right for a hundred yards or so to view the monument and plaque marking the Trace. There really isn't a good place to park right in front of it.

Beyond Edonton continue on SR133 through Blanchester until 133 makes a hard left. At this point, stay on SR730, which goes straight ahead to SR350, then left into Clarksville. In Clarksville turn right on Clarksville Road (it's the corner where SR132 heads south). Go north on Clarksville Road and in about a quarter mile you jog left, and about a half mile farther, take the right fork continuing north to US22 and SR380. Continue on SR380 north past Caesar Creek State Park and the village of New Burlington to Pogue Corners and Spring Valley–Paintersville Road. Turn right on SV–PR and take it to US68, where after a very short jog to the right, the road continues east to the village of Paintersville. Out of Paintersville, we head northeast and then north on Paintersville–New Jasper Road along Painters Run

Clifton Mill, built in 1802, is located on the south edge of Clifton.

Creek. After just three miles turn right/east on Waynesville-Jamestown Road and take it into the city of Jamestown.

From Jamestown, ride northwest again on SR72 through Cedarville and ultimately to the town of Clifton on the Little Miami River, where we will want to spend some time. This entire stretch of SR72 is a nice ride—nothing extraordinary but certainly very pleasant. The tiny village of Clifton and other nearby attractions are definitely worthy of some of your time. In Clifton, I highly recommend stopping at the 1802 Clifton Mill on Water Street at the south edge of town. Explore the mill and its grounds, including an old wooden covered bridge over the Little Miami River. At this point, the river carved a gorge about twenty feet into the bedrock. I also found the old storefronts along Water Street to be fascinating—they could serve as the stage set for an old western movie. West of town is the John Bryan State Park, with the Clifton Gorge and the 1886 Glen Helen Bridge being prime attractions. The State Park is a great place to park your bike and stretch your legs in a gorgeous setting—walking along the top of the gorge while watching and listening to the water cascade over the rocks far below you.

We continue the trip by turning right on North River Road in Clifton—located just one block north of Water Street and the mill. Take North River Road east and northeast to its intersection with Old Springfield Road, where a right turn will take you to SR41 and into the small town of South Charleston. In case you might be interested, there is a small railroad museum on the south side of town. There isn't much there—an old depot, a log cabin, and two cabooses.

From the main downtown intersection of US42 and SR41, you should follow 41 south two and a half miles to Xenia–London Road/County Road 12 and turn left, taking it to SR38 where a right turn is required. Going across Xenia–London Road (also known as Old Xenia Road) is a very nice ride. This is wide-open, big sky country with very light traffic. Many years ago, this was the main road between Xenia and London, and riding it reminds one why Sunday afternoon drives were so popular years ago. This and other original roads that connected towns together evolved from the days of people traveling on horseback. They meandered across the high ground and connected the scattered settlers together on a trail that eventually gets you to the large towns at either end.

Near the east end of Xenia–London Road, there is a very large radar dome. About one mile past the dome, turn south on SR38 one mile to the crossroads village of Newport. Just past the fire station on the south side of Newport, turn left onto Danville Road. It will make a jog out of town and then straighten out. After less than a mile, turn left onto Yankeetown–Chenoweth Road and follow it all the way to just past I-71, turning left onto SR323. You will have this road pretty much to yourself as traffic is normally very light and the riding very pleasant. Take Route 323 east to SR56 and then south to Mt. Sterling. From Mt. Sterling take SR207 south through a very nice area, which takes you past Deer Creek State Park and Deer Creek Lake and on to the town of Clarksburg. There are several places along Route 207 where one can turn into the state park to take a walk or just admire the view of the lake and woods.

Go one block beyond the main intersection in Clarksburg (SR138 and 207) and turn right from SR207 onto Wheat Alley, then almost immediately left onto Frankfort–Clarksburg Road south to Frankfort. In Frankfort, jog one block left/east on High Street to Main Street and continue south on what becomes Davis Hill Road south of town. Follow Davis Hill Road south, through the tiny burg of Roxabell, where it makes a short jog west and then continues south to SR28 as Little Creek Road.

The town of Frankfort sits on the line that divides northern Ohio from the hilly and wooded south. From Frankfort, you can see forested bedrock hills ahead of you. It's clear that the open farm country we've been riding through north of here has met its match and Mother Nature has won, as usual.

An old gas station located in Clifton.

Go east 1.3 miles on SR28 to Owl Creek Road, turning right and following it to US50. The intersection for Owl Creek Road is easy to spot because it's at the bottom of a hill and just past the water tower. Turn right onto US50 and take it just a tad over seven miles to Jones Levee Road and turn left (there's an old barn at this corner). Take Jones Levee Road one mile, then turn right on Spargusville Road. Take this very enjoyable road south until it ends at Potts Hill/Nipgen Road and turn left—going the short distance to Route 772 where we turn right.

Follow SR772 one and a half miles west, and when it turns south, just keep going straight west on what becomes Morgans Fork Road (follow the sign to Pike Lake Park). We follow this road as it, in turn, follows Morgan Creek. It's a fun road and will surely make you feel that you're in the heart of Appalachia. The county even installs road signs that already have bullet holes in them so they'll be accepted. (Just kidding!) The folks who live in this area might not have a lot of money but they certainly have a lot of heart and soul. I doubt if there is anywhere else on the planet that they'd rather live. Morgans Fork Road ultimately joins SR772 again at its south end.

Route 772 will be our companion for many exhilarating miles. It is a wonderful riding road, taking you over hills and through valleys, and more than enough curves to keep even the most aggressive riders smiling. Route 772 will end at the town of Rarden, where we'll turn left onto SR73 and follow it east to Otway. In Otway turn right onto SR348, and immediately after you do, you will notice the Otway Covered Bridge crossing Scioto Brush Creek. You can take the small gravel lane to cross the stream rather than the new concrete bridge on Route 348, if you wish, and thus drive across the covered bridge.

We will be on 348 for only a couple of miles when we turn left onto Rocky Fork Road. This absolutely marvelous road follows Rocky Fork Creek, sometimes on the east side, sometimes on the west, but no matter what side of the creek it's on, I guarantee that it'll have you smiling the entire way. Rocky Fork Road ends at SR125, where a right turn is called for. Follow 125—another wonderful road—as it corkscrews west to the village of Blue Creek. Coming into Blue Creek from the east on 125 will have you coming down a long twisting hill, and when you finally reach the bottom, you'll be at Blue Creek Road where we turn left so the fun can continue. Blue Creek Road, as its name suggests, follows Blue Creek south all the way to US52. Like all the roads south of Frankfort, this one is also just great!

Turn right onto US52 and enjoy this delightful river road as it follows the wanderings of the Ohio River on its way west. On the way back to Ripley, you will pass through the town of Manchester, which was the first town settled in the Virginia Military District. The river road is just great as it serves up majestic views of the river on the left and forested hills on the right. It really doesn't get much better than this!

And that does it. This trip certainly taxes the use of superlatives, but they're all earned. It's a marvelous trip through history and scenery, knitted together with fabulous motorcycling roads.

Native American Heritage Tour

ALL OF THE twenty-three tours in this book take you to wonderful places on great motorcycling roads. That's a winning combination by any definition. This particular tour has wonderful places to see, fabulous riding roads, and scenery that are worth the trip all by itself. However, it has something more: this trip makes a person think. It will make you mull over the past in a way many of us seldom do. It may even make you seem a bit small and insignificant as you consider the amazing feats accomplished by people hundreds of years ago, working without the aid of anything more sophisticated than their hands.

This trip will take you to no less than seven fabulous earthen structures built by the hands of thousands of people for reasons we still cannot completely fathom. We will also visit the location where one of Ohio's great Indian Chiefs gave a truly eloquent speech in the cause of peace. Like every other ride in the book, this is accomplished via the best motorcycling roads available—no expedient expressways allowed.

So, who were these amazing early Americans who obviously lived in these locales long enough to construct such marvelous structures? Earthworks such as Fort Ancient and the Serpent Effigy Mound were not built by a wandering tribe of hunter-gatherers that happened to stay put for a few weeks. No, the civilizations that left us these wonders, which I like to think of as Ohio's Anasazi, were sophisticated residents of this land for centuries. Scientists have been able to broadly classify the time periods of major construction at these sites. The oldest of the three major groups we'll encounter on this trip, the Adena, were active for roughly one thousand years, fading away about the time of the birth of Christ. The Hopewell culture was active from about 200 BC to 500 AD, and the Fort Ancient people from around 900 to 1750 AD. Don't get too tied up in the names of these civilizations—they're simply categories applied by archeologists to differentiate them by time. The Hopewell civilization, for instance, derives its name from Captain Mordecai Hopewell, on whose farm the first mound in that area was excavated. What I find amazing is that the artifacts found in Hopewell-era mounds include copper from Isle Royale in Lake Superior to conch shells and fossil shark teeth from distant oceans. It just confirms a point I make elsewhere that Native Americans were wide-ranging travelers who traded and traveled just like modern-day Americans.

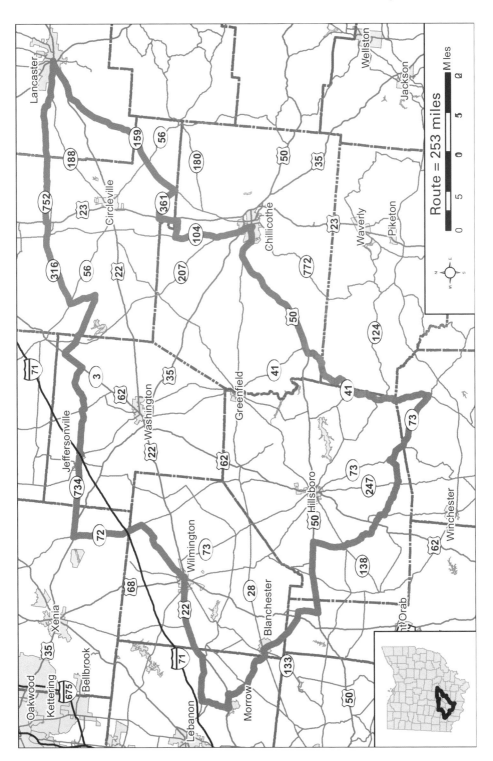

The classification name of Adena is from a large tract of land owned by Ohio Governor and former Senator Thomas Worthington's estate near Chillicothe. He named his estate Adena which, in ancient Hebrew, apparently meant "places remarkable for the delightfulness of their situations."[1] It's easy to see why a word was invented to summarize all that. By the way, the landscape view depicted on the Great Seal of the State of Ohio is of the sun rising over Mount Logan as seen looking east across the Scioto River from Worthington's Adena estate.

We start this two-wheeled exploration of Ohio's native peoples in Lancaster. This attractive town is located on the western edge of the eastern Ohio hill country. The surrounding countryside is very scenic, which makes it a fun biking region. If you happen to be in Lancaster on the first weekend in June, be sure to attend the large antique car and motorcycle show. It has been a fixture at the Fairfield County Fairgrounds for over 40 years. Later each June is the Earth Angel Super Cruise—an annual event featuring old and unusual cars, motorcycles, and more. If it has an internal combustion engine, you'll probably see it at this event (along with major entertainers and singing groups). For more information, call the Angel Foundation at 614-833-2645. It's all about helping sick children get a new lease on life. Lancaster was also the childhood home of General William Tecumseh Sherman, the Civil War general whose famous, or infamous, 1864 March to the Sea guaranteed his place in history. The Sherman House Museum is located at 307 Main Street and is open afternoons during the warm months.

Proceed west on US22, then take SR159 southwest to where it splits off from Route 22. This stretch of road is very pleasant, but we're saving the best for later. Our first stop on the tour is at the village of Tarlton. Here we turn right onto Redding Street at the intersection with the old brick building. Just a mile north of Tarlton is the earthworks called the Tarlton Cross because of its shape. It's located in a small park open to the public. You have to cross the very pretty Salt Creek on a foot bridge and then climb a hill in a picturesque setting to get to the earthwork, but it's well worth the walk. The mound looks amazingly similar to a Celtic cross with a round circle where the two arms intersect. This is the only cross-shaped mound known to exist and, interestingly, the arms are oriented north/south and east/west. There are also some conical mounds and a very unusual stone mound located in the 17-acre park. By the way, exercise caution when pulling into this park. For reasons that only the person who ordered them installed could understand why there are four speed bumps in the driveway, including one that's right on the edge of the street. It causes a real jolt if you pull into the drive at even a

[1]*Indian Mounds of the Middle Ohio Valley*, Susan L. Woodward and Jerry N. McDonald, © 2002, The McDonald & Woodward Publishing Company, Blacksburg, VA.

Miles	Destination	Total
	**NATIVE AMERICAN HERITAGE TOUR 253 MILES**	
0	Lancaster	0
16	Cross Mound Park/Tarlton	16
23	Mound City National Monument	39
19	Seip Mound/Bainbridge	58
14	Fort Hill	72
14	Serpent Mound State Memorial	86
38	St. Martin	124
24	Fort Ancient State Park	148
15	Wilmington	163
19	Jamestown	182
28	Deer Creek State Park	210
23	South Bloomfield	233
20	Lancaster	253

normal speed. In a car, they're an annoyance but on a bike the speed bump on the edge of the road could cause more serious problems if entering too fast.

From Tarlton we continue southwest on 159 to just north of the town of Kingston, where we turn right onto Route 361. We'll be on 361 just a short distance, but just prior to reaching US23, where the road heads straight west and just after crossing a stream, there is a small park with several monuments to noteworthy Indians and whites of the late eighteenth century. At this location in 1774, a huge elm tree existed, called the Logan Elm, under which Chief Logan of the Mingo tribe gave his eloquent speech seeking peaceful relations between the natives and white settlers who were beginning to encroach on the native's hunting lands. The elm tree survived until 1964 when it finally succumbed to Dutch Elm disease, which killed millions of elm trees across America in the 1950s and 1960s. Its measurements made it one of the largest known elm trees in America.

Continue west on 361 to US23, go south on 23 about a mile, then veer off to the right taking Orr Road south a couple miles, turning right onto Kellenberger Road/CR278 and heading west. Kellenberger Road will take you over the Scioto River and its wide flood plain to SR104, where we turn south towards Chillicothe.

Adena Mansion has been refurbished and was reopened to the public in 2003.

Coming into town, you will see the Mound City Group National Monument and the Hopewell Culture National Historical Park. I really hope that you will stop to check out this amazing park and museum. It offers a real insight into the lives and contributions of these remarkable people. For me, just seeing these magnificent mounds and earthworks and the handmade artifacts they contain, is a haunting and humbling experience.

A bit farther south on 104 is the Adena State Memorial. The house and other buildings on the estate, as well as the grounds themselves, were just refurbished and re-opened to the public in 2003. It's a very enjoyable stop and there's even a pull-off on the winding narrow road going up to the hilltop mansion that offers a view east to Mt. Logan—the scene memorialized on the Great Seal of Ohio.

From Chillicothe we head west on US50. For the first few miles west of Chillicothe, you will see typical urban sprawl ugliness, but be patient. After SR28 splits off US50, it becomes a very nice road west through the Paint Valley all the way to the village of Bainbridge. Two miles east of Bainbridge, immediately west of the Paint Valley High School, you will encounter the Seip Mound, a Hopewellian group of earthworks built well over a thousand years ago. Clearing and farming damaged several of the geometric formations on the site, but the impressive main central mound and an earthen wall remain. The mound is two hundred and forty feet long, one hundred and thirty feet wide and thirty feet high. Posts on site mark the locations of ancient buildings that once existed within the earthworks. This is another very cool site that will have you asking yourself how, and why, did they do this?

We haven't discussed motorcycling conditions much yet, but believe me they get better as we go along. They're certainly not bad in the area leading to Bainbridge, but when we turn south on SR41 just west of Bainbridge and proceed through a wonderfully hilly mix of forest and farmlands, it will keep a smile on your face. This area is remarkably scenic, and the roads are custom-made for motorcycling, with a mixture of sweeping curves that allow high speed coupled with very tight dips and curves that'll satisfy the most eager peg scraper.

Our next stop on this Native American heritage ride is at the Fort Hill State Memorial, a mile off of Route 41 just south of where SR753 intersects our road. It is difficult coming up with the right words to give proper due to this earthwork. The Fort Hill structure contains one of the best-preserved hilltop earthen enclosures in the country. The earthworks is a very impressive mile-and-a-half-long loop that encloses 48 acres! It is also at the top of a very high series of hills, not on flat ground like some other ancient structures. The whole site is set in a very scenic area and is a great place to take a walk to stretch your legs. You don't want to pass it by.

Leaving Fort Hill continue south on 41 until you intersect SR73 at the village of Locust Grove. By the way, by now you've earned some dessert, and the ice cream stand at the corner of Routes 41 and 73 is just what you were looking for on a hot afternoon. Give your clutch hand a rest and let your bike's brakes cool down while you treat yourself to a tasty snack.

Go west on 73 and very soon you will encounter what is perhaps the most famous Indian earthworks of the all—Serpent Mound, which is protected in the Serpent Mound State Memorial. It is the largest of all effigy mounds in America. This quarter-mile-long serpentine mound is on a bluff high above Brush Creek. The mound is almost as high as a person and averages twenty feet wide at the base. It is truly an impressive structure. A viewing stand allows a person to view the mound from above, giving a much more striking perspective of just how large and finely sculpted this earthwork is. A large museum is also located at the site, although it's open only during the summer.

This structure means many things to different people. It has been interpreted as representing everything from the biblical snake that tempted Eve with the apple (an egg-shaped object at the serpent's mouth adds to this theory) to new

Serpent Mound, an ancient Native American site found in northern Adams County, is the largest effigy mound in the United States.

age ideas about alien civilizations and lost races. I think it's great that we'll never really know. The builders are probably still chuckling as to the unsolvable enigma they left behind. What is especially profound about all this is the commonality between ancient civilizations. Egypt, Ireland, England, Africa, Central America, South America, North America—it doesn't matter. Ancient peoples almost universally created massive structures to honor their dead kings and to prepare for an afterlife—pretty amazing!

Back on the road, continue west on Route 73 to the burg of Belfast. At this point, 73 makes a hard turn to the north, but we want to turn left and go south onto 785, taking it south and continuing with it as it curves west over to Fairfax. This road becomes County Road 3/Ridge Road after you cross Route 247 at Fairfax.

I think that you will agree that 73 is just a delightful motorcycling road, and the county roads that we're going to take to get us up to US50 west of Hillsboro certainly continue that fine tradition. Follow Ridge Road west to Sugar Tree Ridge and Route 136, and then go north about a mile on 136 and then turn left on Sorg Road (which is still CR3). County Road 3/Sorg Road will go west, then turn northwest with the name changing to Danville Road as you approach Route 138 and the village of Danville. In Danville, we have to turn right on 138 for just a couple of blocks and then turn left again on Danville Road, which is CR6 west of the village. This road goes west a very short distance, then turns straight north, taking us to US50.

Go nine miles west on US50 to SR251 and turn right. Follow 251 less than three miles through the village of St. Martin to Route 123 and turn left. Route 123

One of the sites at Fort Ancient State Memorial.

will take you northwest through the town of Blanchester and then all the way to US22. Route 123 will continually amaze you with its fun biking antics. Just when you think it's about to mellow out, more tight curves and hills jump out at you. Make a left turn onto Route 22/123 following it into Morrow, where 123 continues north over the Little Miami River with its busy canoe liveries. About three miles north of Morrow, Route 123 swings west, but we want to continue right straight ahead (north) to Route 350. There is a white barn with a metal roof at the corner where Route 123 turns west, but we proceed straight north.

We'll go east on 350 just about three miles to where it crosses the Little Miami River again. Just beyond the river, you will find the fabulous Fort Ancient earthworks and museum. What an amazing three miles this is! Almost immediately after turning east onto 350 you will see a sign stating in so many words that unless you're driving a standard-sized vehicle don't proceed any farther. Route 350 descends down a long very steep hill with hairpin curves that'll have your knuckles white and your brakes cooking. This is a fabulous run but one where speed is not wise.

I've used up my supply of adequate words and therefore am at a loss when trying to describe Fort Ancient. The Fort Ancient earthwork has eighteen thousand feet of high earthen walls and is perched on a hillside above a gorge on the Little Miami River overlooking the surrounding lands. The role of Fort Ancient in the lives of the builders seems obvious. Perched three hundred feet above the river and protected on three sides by ravines, with a series of parallel berms and what appear to have been moats likely filled with water, it has all the markings of a well-thought-out defensive fortification. What makes this series of structures unique is that stone piles are included that go beyond traditional burial mounds. One of the stone piles has been shown to serve as the base point for taking celestial readings. When viewed from this spot, sunlight coming through gaps in the earthen wall line up exactly for major seasonal events such as the equinoxes and solstices. This celestial and calendar information was no doubt used by the ancients for things such as planting of crops and ceremonies. The museum has nine thousand square feet of display space for artifacts and interactive exhibits that document fifteen thousand years of native peoples and their cultures, lifestyles, and tools. The museum is open Wednesday through Sunday during summer months. Call them at 513-932-4421 for more information.

We leave Fort Ancient on 350, taking it east to US22, which we follow into the city of Wilmington. Follow the one-way eastbound US22 most of the way through Wilmington where you'll see huge white grain silos followed by a railroad track. Just prior to the tracks, turn left onto Wall Street, which goes north a few blocks and then angles to the northeast as Prairie Road. Take Prairie Road six miles to where it forms a T at Sabina Road and turn right. It'll make a ninety-degree turn to the east after a short distance, but just follow the road around the curve and take it to Route 72. Ride SR72 north to Jamestown and turn right on Route 734, taking it east nine miles to Jeffersonville. Follow Route 734/41 east through town and just beyond the I-71 expressway, Route 734 will once again continue east. Follow it east to Route 38, turn right a very short distance and make a left turn onto Myers Road/CR112. Go east on Myers Road and after a couple of miles, it will dip southeast and become Harrison Road, which will ultimately reach US62 at Madison Mills.

Turn left/north on US62 and take it almost three miles to Cooks–Yankeetown Road and make a right turn. This road will become Yankeetown Pike when you cross the Pickaway County line and enter Deer Creek State Park. Take Yankeetown Pike east six and a half miles from Route 62, through Deer Creek Park, to Five Points Road and turn left. At the intersection of Yankeetown and Five Points Road, you'll be under the electrical wires of a line of large steel power line towers. Take Five Points Road (*aka* CR21) three and a half miles to Route 316 and turn right. Follow 316 east, eventually crossing the Scioto River and terminating at US23.

The entire area between Fort Ancient and US23 is a series of pleasant roads through mostly open countryside. It's a very relaxing ride not nearly as intense as some of the roads previously taken on this tour. But let's face it—we need a break, right? If we rode only on roads that caused us unending grins, where we constantly scraped various parts of the motorcycle on the asphalt, we'd soon be worn out and seeking a respite. So kick back and relax—you've earned it.

Go north on 23 a very short distance and turn right onto SR752. Very shortly after starting east on 752 from US23, you will pass on the north side of Ashville. This town has a couple of things that might interest you. The first is the nation's oldest stop light. It is housed in the town museum but is brought out to reign over the Fourth of July celebration each year. The second is the Scioto Valley Railroad Station and Museum.

Continue east on 752 and when it ends at Route 674, continue straight ahead on Royalton Road. This road gets progressively better the farther east you go and ultimately joins Route 188, where we will turn left. Route 188 back to Lancaster is a very enjoyable finish for this fun and educational ride. I think you'll agree that these ancient Americans who left us so many awe-inspiring sites were very amazing people!

Colonel Crawford & Johnny Appleseed

IN THE ANNALS of Ohio history, three names stand out more than any others in the north-central part of the state: Simon Kenton, Colonel William Crawford, and John Chapman, who has gone down in American folklore as Johnny Appleseed. Kenton is discussed in another section in the book. In this trip, we'll use the motorcycle as the means to explore the lives of Colonel Crawford and Johnny Appleseed. Their lives could hardly have been more different: one a warrior and the other a peace-loving gentle man, but their legacies were equally durable. Colonel Crawford is unfortunately best remembered for his failed military mission and terrible death, and Johnny Appleseed as an entrepreneurial and brave soul who was a friend of Indian and settler alike and always a welcome sight in frontier Ohio. Both men have become part of Americana and their lives are celebrated with monuments and as namesakes for everything from banks to schools. The geographic area encompassed by this tour is where these two men left their mark on Ohio.

We'll begin the ride in Mt. Vernon, the seat of government for the county of Knox. Mt. Vernon was founded in 1805 on the banks of the Kokosing River. It was named in honor of President Washington's Virginia home. Young entrepreneur John Chapman owned several lots in this new town for the purpose of developing a nursery for apple trees. Born in 1774 in Massachusetts, Chapman had already begun his travels in the western frontier eight years prior to purchasing land in Mt. Vernon. Apples were a staple fruit in the lives of early Americans, and Chapman reasoned that settlers would soon be moving west and that there should be apple nurseries in place already to address the need for this critical source of nutrition. Using seeds and grafts from existing stock, he planted trees in cleared plots in western Pennsylvania, Ohio, and Indiana. He was then able to give or sell seedlings to new settlers.

Chapman was both a simple, peace-loving man and very much the rugged individualist and woodsman. He lived on his own in the woods, befriending both settler and Indian. One of his deeds is celebrated in a song titled appropriately enough "The Johnny Appleseed Song." During the War of 1812, Indians allied with the British attacked Mansfield and laid siege to the town. Their intent was to burn it and kill or take captive the occupants, as had been the practice across

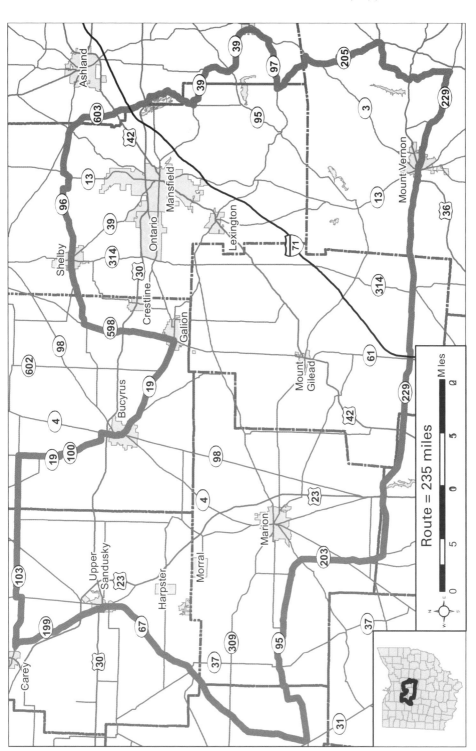

the new frontier. Chapman ran or rode (depending on which version you believe) twenty-six miles to Mt. Vernon to warn a garrison of troops who then went to the relief of Mansfield.

From Mt. Vernon, we head west cross-country on SR229 all the way to US23. This is open countryside, a mixture of farms and some woods, until you get to the Delaware Wildlife Area adjacent to Delaware Lake, just east of US23. State Route 229 ends at US23, but we continue west on the same alignment, which becomes Norton Road. Take this road less than six miles farther west to SR203, where a right turn is made. Follow 203 straight through Prospect where it picks up the name of LaRue–Prospect Road. State Route 203/LaRue–Prospect Road runs north out of Prospect, and about eight miles north of town, Route 203 turns west and then north again. At this point LaRue–Prospect Road heads straight west through the Big Island Wildlife Area. This is the route to take as it follows along the north side of the Scioto River, which is at its headwater phase in this locale. The LaRue–Prospect Road goes straight west through the village of LaRue at its only stoplight. West of town the road is known as CR200 which will take us southwest to the village of Mt. Victory. In between LaRue and Mt. Victory, there are a couple of things to watch for, however. First, just west of LaRue, there is a very rough set of railroad tracks, so slow down. Just past these tracks, you need to make a left turn on Marion–Hardin Road. Follow Marion–Hardin a half mile or less, cross the same railroad track again, and you'll see a small green sign pointing to the right for Mt. Victory. Take this road (CR230) west toward Mt. Victory, and on the east side of Mt. Victory, you will notice Wheeler Street heading to the right—take it. This street becomes CR209 once north of town. Take CR209 north to the Scioto River where it angles to the northeast as CR265.

This angling road is actually part of the original Sandusky Trail, an old Indian, military, and frontier trail. The point where the trail crossed the Scioto River was called the Indian Ford and was an important gathering place for the Shawnee. At the stop sign just south of the river, notice the large two-story brick building on the northwest corner. This private residence was the Wheeler Tavern. Built in 1835, it played an active role in the life of residents in this area for many decades. Remain on SR265 to the small town of Marseilles, where we pick up SR67 and continue northwest to Upper Sandusky.

The entire area that I have just described is a very pleasant mix of rolling countryside with a nice blend of farms and wooded land. The roads are gently curving and have enough character to earn the rank of very enjoyable. The area north of the Scioto River also has a significant Amish population. Traffic is light throughout this area, especially on the county roads that we traverse. Shortly after

COLONEL CRAWFORD & JOHNNY APPLESEED 235 MILES		
Miles	Destination	Total
0	Mt. Vernon	0
25	Ashely	25
15	Prospect	40
19	LaRue	59
23	Marseilles	82
20	Crawford	102
32	Bucyrus	134
16	Leesville	150
49	Loudonville	199
21	Danville	220
15	Mt. Vernon	235

crossing the Scioto River, you'll cross an invisible but important natural border—the watershed divide separating the Ohio River and Lake Erie watersheds.

Take SR67 into downtown Upper Sandusky, jog west three blocks on Wyandot Avenue, and then proceed north on SR199. Upper Sandusky, located on the upper reaches of the Sandusky River, is the county seat of Wyandot County. Downtown is a nice place to walk to view the impressive courthouse and other historic buildings. This area saw the last of the native tribes depart from Ohio when the local Wyandot Indians left for Kansas in 1843.

Proceed north on SR199 to the crossroads of Crawford to begin our exploration of Colonel Crawford's story. In Crawford, there is a small park with a monument and sign that explains the Crawford saga. If you feel a bit adventurous, turn right onto Township Road 29 at the church in Crawford, taking it a half mile east to another historical marker. If you really feel adventurous, take the gravel lane a half mile north from that sign to a monument to Crawford placed in a cemetery by local citizens.

The story of how Colonel Crawford came to be in this part of Ohio in 1782 is a long one, but the critical element was probably that he was a friend of General George Washington and agreed to take on one last mission at the end of the Revolutionary War. Crawford's military career was a long and distinguished one. Like most career military men of the time, he served as an officer under the British during the

French and Indian War and the Pontiac Uprising. He also served with Washington during the Revolutionary War and had been asked by the General to lead a western campaign against the Indian allies of the British in the area north of the Ohio River. These Indians, at the urging of the British, had been attacking settlers in the frontier west of the Alleghenies. Crawford's assignment turned sour and led to his capture and gruesome execution by the Wyandot Indians.

Like almost every event in life, this one did not occur in a vacuum. There were several circumstances and conditions that led to its occurrence. I've touched on the first—his relationship with General Washington, who at the end of the War of Independence saw a chance to both exact revenge on the Indians who allied with the British and supported them during the Revolution, and who also saw this campaign as the beginning of the end to the so-called "Indian Problem" in the western territories. The Indians, between their British connection and their continued resistance to white settlement, were at the receiving end of a great deal of distrust and hostility. However, that alone doesn't account for Crawford's treatment upon his capture. It took another incident, a very sad chapter in our country's story, to lead to this event.

In 1772, one David Zeisberger, a Moravian missionary, started the oldest settlement in Ohio called Gnadenhutten, which meant tents of grace, located east of here. Four hundred local Indians were converted to Christianity here and lived peaceful lives engaged in farming near that village. With the beginning of the Revolutionary War, both sides began to distrust these Indians. The British and their Indian allies assumed they were spies for the Americans, and the local settlers assumed that, like other Indians in that area, they were on the side of the British and were making attacks on frontier settlements. The truth is that these peaceful converts were simply trying to live their lives as farmers, uninterested in either side. In the fall of 1781, Wyandot Indians, under orders of the British, rounded up the Moravian Delaware and moved them west to a bleak plain near Upper Sandusky called Captive's Town. With food running out in the spring of 1782, they were allowed to return to Gnadenhutten to gather corn left in the fields. Enter Colonel Williamson of the Pennsylvania Militia into the picture. Williamson and his men were in the region hunting Indians that they believed were allied with the British and responsible for attacks on local settlers. They came across the Delaware harvesting corn in the field. Absolute in their belief that these Delaware were the enemy, Williamson's men rounded up the Indians, put them in two cabins at Gnadenhutten and commenced killing them in cold blood—a total of 96 innocents, including 39 children. This is truly a dark day in our history. Two young boys survived to tell the story, which enraged Indians throughout the region.

Thus it was in June 1782 that Crawford encountered a war party that was waiting for him. Unknown to his troop, they had been under surveillance for days, and when they arrived at the grassy prairie west of present-day Galion, the Indians attacked and routed Crawford's unit in the Battle of the Olentangy. Crawford became separated from his retreating army and was captured near Leesville. He was transported to where the village of Crawford stands today and was executed in a manner that still evokes revulsion for its brutality. Clearly, he paid the price for the misdeeds of others.

Upon paying your respects to Colonel Crawford, continue north a bit on SR199 to SR103, just east of Carey, and head east. While still near Carey, you might be interested in taking a brief detour to the Indian Trail Caverns, located four miles west of Carey on SR568. These caverns are especially renowned for the treasure trove of archeological artifacts found in them. They are only open on weekend afternoons. The Carey area is where a great deal of mining for dolomite limestone occurs. You can see some of the limestone processing activity on Routes 199 and 103.

Back on the tour, head east on SR103 almost nineteen miles to SR19 and turn right. Use caution when you reach the intersection with SR100—you have to stop but it isn't well marked. We'll take SR19 south through Bucyrus and to the town of Galion. This entire area is a nice ride, with light traffic and open countryside. Riding south on Route 19 you will pass through a village called Brokensword. Allegedly, this name is in reference to Colonel Crawford's act of deliberately breaking his own sword just prior to capture so that it couldn't be used against him by his captors. SR19 will take you into Bucyrus, county seat for Crawford County, and a very nice small city.

If you happen to be in Bucyrus in mid-August, you're in luck because you can take part in the annual Bucyrus Bratwurst Festival in the Bratwurst Capital of America. In mid-September each year, a motorcycle show and swap meet is held at the fairgrounds. Downtown Bucyrus is a nice place to park and walk. A beautiful mural celebrating Bucyrus's claim as the "Crossroads of America" is painted in a stunning 3D effect on the side of a building in the downtown square. Like many cities of this size in Ohio, Bucyrus has a healthy and vibrant downtown, just like the good old days. When riding through small towns such as Bucyrus (or Van Wert, Coshocton, Marietta, Lebanon, and so on), I'm constantly amazed at the remarkable architecture and quality of the houses and public buildings built a century or more ago. In the age of no power tools and little money, people built magnificent houses and buildings whose quality and style have survived the generations and continue to impress today. I just don't think the cookie-cutter houses and stores we've built since World War II will be the target of such awe and respect a hundred years hence.

OHIO HISTORICAL MARKER

CLEAR FORK GORGE
A Feature of Ohio's Forests

Clear Fork Gorge was formed when glacial meltwater cut through the sandstone bedrock that forms its steep walls fourteen to twenty-four thousand years ago. The gorge is one thousand feet wide and over three hundred feet deep. Its seclusion has preserved a rare forest community that includes native white pine and towering eastern hemlock. A National Natural Landmark, the gorge displays a wide variety of other tree species more common throughout the state, with sycamore on the bottomlands, beech, ash, and tulip farther up the slops, and oak and maple on the ridges above. The gorge has changed little since pioneer legend Johnny Appleseed tended his apple orchards nearby.

THE OHIO BICENTENNIAL COMMISSION
THE INTERNATIONAL PAPER COMPANY FOUNDATION
THE OHIO HISTORICAL SOCIETY
2003   7-70

Clear Fork Gorge is the deepest in Ohio.

Heading southeast out of Bucyrus on SR19 you will see the monument marking the site of the ill-fated Battle of the Olentangy where Crawford and his men were routed, and a sign marking the site of the ancient Indian village of Secciaum. This was a village that was recognized by all Indians as neutral ground where they could meet for council and trade.

From Galion we will go north on SR598, with the next stop being Leesville and a monument marking the spot where Colonel Crawford was captured. To get to the monument, turn right on Leesville Road (at the main intersection in town, a small general store on one corner and a large old white vacant building on the other). Take Leesville Road about a half mile east, and just after crossing the river, you'll see the monument on the right.

Leaving Leesville continue north on 598 to SR96 and turn east. Follow 96 east to the crossroads of Olivesburg and SR603. Route 603 is a marvelous ride through wonderful scenery, history, and hills that will have you floating over them as if on a magic carpet. We're now entering Johnny Appleseed's realm. The first hint of Mr. Chapman is in Miffin, where a large sign is painted on the side of a building advertising the annual Johnny Appleseed outdoor theater. The site of the theater is two miles south of town at a beautiful wooded site on a hillside. Just south of this location you'll see the Charles Mill Dam and park. In this park is a historic marker that provides information about Indian attacks in the area and Johnny

Little Lyon Falls in Mohican State Park is a picturesque waterfall. (Photo courtesy of Ohio Division of Travel and Tourism)

Appleseed's role in these events, especially as it relates to the Copus Massacre, which occurred just a mile south of that point.

Continuing south on 603 for a mile will take you to Township Road 1225, where a sign points the way to the Copus Monument. Unless you're riding a V-Strom or Ulysses, I highly recommend you not try to ride this unimproved dirt road to the monument. There isn't much to see anyway, and the road is rough and narrow.

Enjoy Route 603's curves as it heads south through beautiful countryside to SR39 and into Loudonville. On the west side of town, SR39 is also Mt. Vernon Street, and we'll just stay on this street after SR39 heads east. Mt. Vernon Street will arc to the southwest and join SR3 just southwest of Loudonville (turn right at the log cabin in the small park). We will be on SR3 for just about one mile when we reach SR97 going west through Mohican State Park and State Forest. State Route 97 is a real nice stretch of road, and I recommend spending some time in the park, at a minimum to view the spectacular Clear Fork Gorge, Ohio's deepest, in the western portion of the park. A little farther west on Forest Road 51, you will find a fire tower that can be climbed for fabulous views of the park and Mohican River Valley.

Just beyond the western park boundary, you will find McCurdy Road/CR3275, which we take south/left. This corner is at the top of a small hill that you come to rather quickly—watch for a house with beige siding and a metal shed of the same color, located right at our corner. Make sure that no one is tailgating you because the turn is just over the crest of the hill. After a stretch of curving road, CR3275 heads east and Township Road 3475 goes straight ahead at the curve. We want the township road that will take us to CR959 which, in turn, will deliver us to a stop sign where we turn right on Ravin Road/CR75. This will take us to SR3 near the village of Jelloway. We will be on SR3 for only a very short stretch through Jelloway to SR205 (at the corner with the white Methodist Church building). Turn left on this scenic road to the village of Danville. Route 205 is a wonderful riding road. Though not a really technical road, it's just great fun. If the road isn't going over the many hills it's hanging off the edge of them, making for excellent riding. In Danville you'll be heading straight south on US62. In the center of town you will see Rambo Street going west (at the last stop light, with St. Luke Catholic Church at the corner). Rambo turns into Howard–Danville Road/CR9 west of town, which is the road you want. Take it southwest to the village of Howard and at the T go left/east on US36 for a very short distance and then right on Howard Street, which then becomes Pipesville Road/CR35 outside of town. There is a sign for Hidden Hills Golf Course where you turn onto Pipesville Road from Route 36. Take this fun road down to SR229 and head west, taking it all the way back to

Mt. Vernon. I may sound like a broken record, but the motorcycling entertainment just keeps continuing almost all the way into Mt. Vernon.

Mt. Vernon is a wonderful place to spend time. It seems like a very elegant town, what with its stately historic homes (mansions may be a better word to use in many instances), its wonderful public square and park downtown, its very impressive public buildings, churches, and stores. It is another nice place to park and walk about, exploring some more of Ohio's great places.

Well, that's the story of Colonel Crawford and Johnny Appleseed, and this wraps up another ride through marvelous places on great roads. Thanks for the memories.

Connecticut Yankees in Ohio

THE HISTORY OF OHIO'S formation as a state is fascinating. If you were to look at a late eighteenth-century map of this area, you would see that most of the state was claimed by Virginia, Connecticut, and several companies that owned huge tracts of land in what was to become Ohio. Add to this the fact that Native Americans had not relinquished their claim to much of the region and you have a recipe for a very out-of-the-ordinary beginning of statehood, to say the least. Connecticut had long claimed a swath of land straight west of its boundaries (roughly between the forty-first and forty-second parallels), which took in northern Ohio from Lake Erie south to approximately Youngstown and Akron and west to near Sandusky. The Colony of Connecticut claimed title to the lands extending west from Pennsylvania one hundred and twenty miles, by virtue of grants from King James to the Plymouth Council in November 1630. A final grant was confirmed by King Charles II on April 25, 1662, and primarily based upon this action, Connecticut claimed title to what was called the Connecticut Western Reserve. In 1786 Connecticut turned over its western holdings to the new federal government in exchange for federal assumption of that state's Revolutionary War debt. For some time afterward, northeastern Ohio was called New Connecticut by natives. The term Western Reserve is, of course, widely used to this day in northeast Ohio.

What has all this got to do with motorcycling? A lot, actually, because the influence of these early circumstances can still be seen and rediscovered today, making for very enjoyable motorcycling trips through a land shaped by its history. We all enjoy touring New England because of its quaint villages, covered bridges, unique architecture, and other qualities that make it somewhat different than other parts of the country. Well, a bit of New England exists right here in Ohio. Many places in northeast Ohio still noticeably reflect their Connecticut roots. Whether it is white, steepled churches, covered bridges, or trademark village squares, there are many remnants of the Yankee influence in this unique part of Ohio. All one has to do is look at the names of Western Reserve communities: Andover and Avon, Berlin and Bristol, New Haven and Norwalk, Windham and Warren, to mention just a few of the many Ohio communities that Yankee settlers gave the same names of their previous Connecticut home towns.

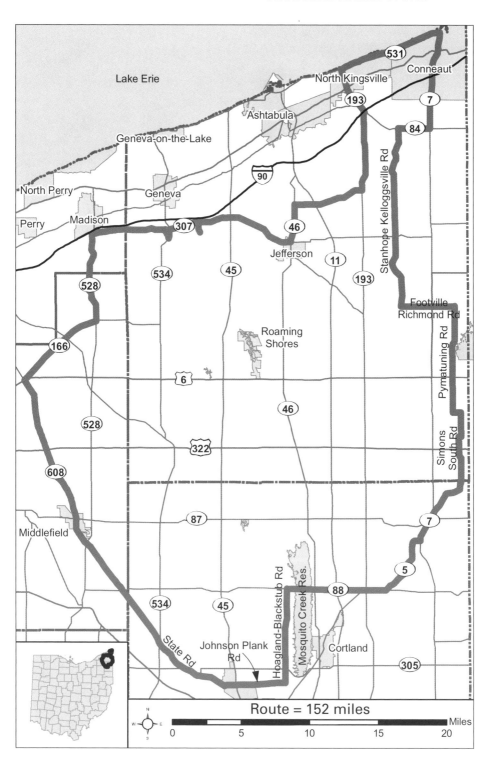

Route = 152 miles

Root Road Covered Bridge near Kellogsville.

Northeastern Ohio and Ashtabula County, in particular, are famous for their covered bridges. Because so many of northeastern Ohio's first settlers were New England natives, I suspect they brought this method of bridge building with them. Ashtabula County, with sixteen beautiful covered bridges, has a festival celebrating this unique architectural style each October. We'll visit some of these bridges on our tour.

We begin our trip traveling south from Conneaut on SR7, taking it south of I-90 to SR84, on which we go west a couple of miles to State Road and the village of Kelloggsville. Turn south on State Road and go through Kelloggsville, where the road becomes Stanhope–Kelloggsville Road. This is a more enjoyable road going south than nearby parallel Route 7, plus there are three covered bridges that are close enough that you can make very short side trips to view them if you wish.

The first is the Root Road covered bridge, located just a couple of miles south of Kelloggsville. It is on a gravel road but it's only a hundred yards or so east of Stanhope–Kelloggsville Road. About five miles farther south is the Graham Road covered bridge. Graham Road is paved, and because of that, a new bridge was constructed to handle the additional traffic. The covered bridge was moved into a pocket park right next to the new bridge. It's about a half mile east of Stanhope–

Miles	Destination	Total
	CONNECTICUT YANKEES IN OHIO	
	152 MILES	
0	Conneaut	0
9	Kelloggsville	9
20	Pymatuning State Park	29
26	Mecca/Mosquito Creek Reservoir	55
30	Middlefield	85
11	Rock Creek Road	96
14	State Route 307	110
6	Harpersfield Covered Bridge	116
4	Mechanicsville Covered Bridge	120
6	Jefferson/Route 46	126
17	Lake Erie/State Route 531	143
9	Conneaut	152

Kelloggsville Road. Two miles farther south is the Caine Road bridge. This classic covered bridge is on a gravel road that doesn't see a lot of traffic. Unfortunately, it's about a half mile east of our pavement, and Caine Road is a bit rough and muddy when wet, so you'll have to decide for yourself if you want to go see it.

Remain on Stanhope–Kelloggsville Road until you hit the stop sign at Footville–Richmond Road. Head left/east, crossing SR7, and turn right when you hit the T at Pymatuning Lake Road. Follow Pymatuning Lake Road past the lake and state park of the same name down to US322 at the south end of the reservoir. Near the southern portion of Pymatuning Lake, its namesake road will jog eastward to the lakeshore and then jog away from the shore a bit—just follow the pavement as it makes these jogs. You really can't get lost.

South of US322 we continue straight across on Simons Road to the county line, where a short westerly jog is made, then head south again. We go south only a very short distance beyond the county line, however, and then turn right on Kinsman–Pymatuning Road, which angles southwest to the village of Kinsman. You'll find yourself enjoying the good motorcycling qualities of this road. Ride past the Bronzwood Golf Course and in a short distance, you'll arrive at Route 7 where you make a left turn. SR5 will join Route 7 in Kinsman. Stay on Route 5 and take it southwest several more miles to Route 88. Head west on Route 88 to the traffic circle in Mecca on the east shore of Mosquito Lake. Note the tavern with the old motorcycle on the roof—presumably a good place to stop for lunch. Take the fun ride across Mosquito Lake on Route 88 to the first road west of the lake, which is Hoagland–Blackstub Road. Follow this road south again about seven miles to Johnson Plank Road. Take Johnson Plank Road, which becomes Champion Road, past the golf courses and through the upscale burg of Champion Heights to State Road and make a right turn.

State Road will be our guide across about seventeen miles of scenic countryside to the Amish village of Middlefield located on SR608. This entire section of Old State Road is very historic. Its began in 1807 as a trail cut through the wilderness, connecting the new cities of Youngstown and Warren with Lake Erie. We will continue northwest on Route 608 (which is part of the historic Old State Road that we have been on), taking it to SR166, where we start back east. Ride Route 166 northeast to SR528, turn left and go north to Route 307, located just north of the golf course and park on the beautiful Grand River.

This part of the state is developing an impressive nursery and vineyard business. You will see many wineries and nurseries all through this area. The microclimate of cool summers and warmer winters, as well as less likelihood of spring freezes due to the moderating influence of Lake Erie, create ideal conditions for vineyards and orchards. This same kind of specialized agriculture can be found near all the Great Lakes except Superior.

About two miles after you turn east on 307, you will reach the County Line Road and see a sign pointing north to the Unionville Tavern. I highly recommend a two-mile side trip to go see this historic tavern. It had its start in 1798 and grew as travelers on the Indian trail that became the Buffalo–Cleveland Trail increased. The trail became a major route and is known today as SR84. The tavern has a wonderful history and has gone by several different names, including Yankee Inn, over the two centuries it has been around. It was an active gathering place for social events during the Civil War, and rumor has it runaway slaves were hid there on their way to freedom. It is still a functioning inn.

About three miles east of the County Line Road, take a right on Harpersfield Road to the very impressive Harpersfield Covered Bridge. It's a fun, short ride from 307 to the bridge, and I recommend stopping at the park at the foot of the bridge for pictures. This is a choice spot for fishermen, and you will see many of them fishing from the bridge walkway. After crossing the bridge, you can loop back to 307 via State Road to Route 534, where a left turn will take you back north to Route 307. Just a few miles farther east is the Mechanicsville Covered Bridge, again located on the Grand River just south of Route 307. The Mechanicsville

Be sure to follow the sign to the historic Unionville Tavern.

Covered Bridge is still in place, but a new bridge has been built next to it. The covered bridge is still functional but is used mainly by tourists now. If you drop down off 307 the mile or so south to see it, I suggest backtracking on the same road back to Route 307.

Head east on Route 307 toward the town of Jefferson. Just west of Jefferson, Doyle Road goes to the left. A mile north of 307 on Doyle is the Doyle Road Covered Bridge. This is another of what I call "the real thing," a bridge that still carries traffic over Mill Creek. It's a very nice bridge in a pretty setting. The road beyond the bridge is gravel but is paved up to the bridge, making it easy to visit and then backtrack to 307.

In Jefferson turn north on SR46 and take it about three miles north to Griggs Road. There is a bowling alley on 46 just south of Griggs. Follow Griggs Road through this pretty countryside until it terminates at SR193. Turn left on 193 and ride it north until you hit the blue waters of Lake Erie and SR531. The countryside through which Griggs Road and SR193 traverse is a pleasant mix of farms and wooded land, with some vineyards and orchards taking root. It's a pleasant laid-back portion of this tour.

Go east along the Erie coastline back to Conneaut, completing this very enjoyable trip through the home of Ohio's own Connecticut Yankees.

The Firelands

NOW THAT YOU'RE familiar with the role that Connecticut played in Ohio's history, we can explore another facet of that story. At the western end of the Western Reserve is an area called the Fire Lands. This name was the result of a scorched-earth tactic of the British and their newfound ally—Benedict Arnold. During the Revolutionary War, Arnold led a campaign in Connecticut in which entire villages were burned. After the war, victims of Benedict Arnold's traitorous campaign were given land in the Fire Lands region as compensation—thus its name. The Fire Lands are essentially Erie and Huron Counties. On this trip, you'll notice several communities with a clear New England or Connecticut flavor, including common names such as New Haven, Plymouth, Norwalk, New London, and Milan. Several townships on this ride also have names from the colonies, such as Lyme, New Haven, Greenwich, Norwich, and others.

As the military might say, there are no high-value targets on this tour. There aren't any really famous attractions or unforgettable sights. It is a more sedate tour through a land very much touched by history.

We begin our tour, the shortest of the various trips outlined in this book, in Vermillion. Before heading south on Route 60, I recommend that you go north on this street, which in town is Main Street, to visit the Great Lakes Maritime Museum. It's an enjoyable stop.

We'll head south on SR60 to just south of the town of Wakeman. Between Vermillion and I-80 the road is fairly blah—the typical semi-urban road with traffic and congestion—but south of the turnpike it gets significantly better, and the roads stay that way for the remainder of the tour. About a mile and a half south of US20 in Wakeman, SR60 takes a right curve, however, you should follow Chenango Road, which heads essentially straight south ahead of you. Turn on to Chenango and take it twelve miles south to Townline Road. This stretch has very light traffic and a pleasantly rolling landscape that makes for pleasurable riding. A few miles south of SR18, you will see a sign indicating the road curves right— this is for another road—you just want to continue straight south on Chenango. Shortly beyond this sign, you'll cross the Conrail railroad tracks, then SR162 and one mile farther is Townline Road, where a right turn is needed. Go just one mile west on Townline to Route 60 and proceed south again. This places you one mile

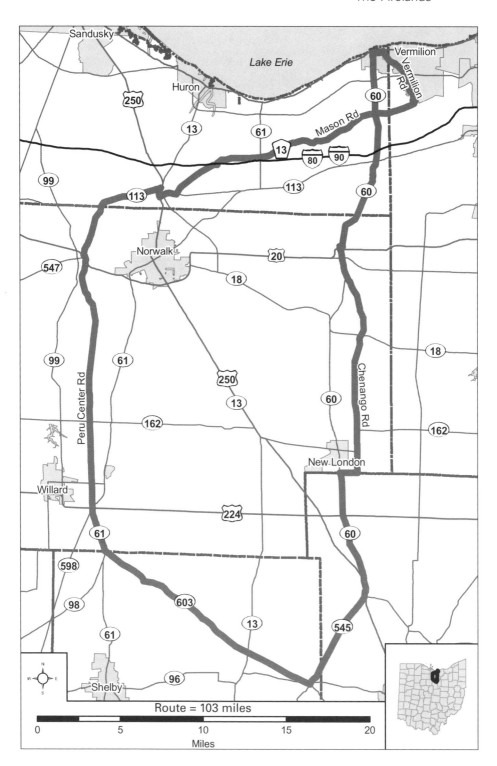

Route = 103 miles

0	5	10	15	20

Miles

The Inland Seas Maritime Museum in Vermillion.

south of New London. The scenery and countryside is very nice south of Town-line on Chenango Road, but unless you're on a GS or KLR, be sure to make the turn over to Route 60! The road is stone and very rough south of Townline.

Follow SR60 south into the town of Savannah, where it will join US250 just north of town. In Savannah follow the signs and get on SR545, taking it southwest to Olivesburg. There are a number of Amish farms in this stretch of road. State Route 545 is a very nice riding road, though the scenery is unfortunately spoiled by an excess of suburban houses built on land that should be farms and open field. Even though the view is spoiled somewhat, the road is still enjoyable riding. About midway between Savannah and Olivesburg, notice the one-room Amish schoolhouse on the west side of the road. During the school year, you'll see bug-gies parked outside the school like so many minivans at other schools.

In Olivesburg get on SR603 and take it northwest to Plymouth. Route 603 is one of the rougher state routes in Ohio. The state normally does a good job of keeping the numbered state routes in decent shape, but the paperwork for 603 must have gotten misplaced. Having said this, they'll probably repave it in the next couple of months, and you'll be asking yourself what I was smoking when I said this was a rough road. The tiny burg of Rome is located about halfway between Olivesburg and Plymouth. Notice the Rome Presbyterian Church Revo-lutionary War Cemetery. I would bet there are some folks buried in that cemetery whose homes were burned in Connecticut and who were later offered land in the

	THE FIRELANDS 103 MILES		
Miles	Destination		Total
0	Vermillion		0
12	Wakeman		12
22	Savannah		34
22	Plymouth		56
18	Monroeville		74
29	Vermillion		103

Western Reserve Fire Lands. Now, we are safely and happily riding through all this history on our modern motorcycles.

In Plymouth get on SR61 and proceed north a bit to New Haven, where you'll pick up SR598. Route 598 will end just a few miles farther north at Route 162, but we continue straight north across 162 on what is now Peru Center Road—this will be our host all the way to Monroeville. Peru Center is an entertaining road with light traffic that pleasantly dips and curves across the countryside, which you should find enjoyable. At Monroeville, you will pick up US20 on the east edge of town and take it through this small village. Just past the stop light in town, you will see a school warning sign, and straight ahead of you at the corner of US20 and Broad Street, there will be a stately old red brick house of the type so common in rural Ohio. Turn right on Broad Street and then turn immediately left again on what will be Peru Center Road resuming its journey. Take it north to SR113. The stretch north of Monroeville is really neat—a twisting road perched high above the West Branch of the Huron River.

Ride SR113 east to US250, where you have to take a short right/south jog to Milan to pick up 113 eastbound again. This charming town is a nice place to take a break. Milan looks as much like a New England village as any you will find in Massachusetts or Connecticut. Its town square and New England-style town hall are wonderful. There are a couple of historical signs in the square and a sculpture to Thomas Edison, who just happened to have been born in Milan.

From downtown Milan, go east just about a mile on SR113 to River Road and turn left. At the northwest corner of this intersection is a large abandoned old farmhouse and barn. Go down River Road about a half mile to Jeffries Road and turn right. Follow Jeffries across the I-80 Turnpike, where you will almost immediately turn right/east onto Mason Road. This road winds peacefully across

Besides being the birthplace of Thomas Edison, Milan is an attractive, New England-style town.

eastern Erie County into northwest Lorain County, where it's called North Ridge Road. Though there is nothing spectacular in this stretch of county roadway, it is a very pleasant ride through nice countryside that still retains much of its rural charms.

About three miles east of Route 60, North Ridge Road very quickly gets interesting. As the road approaches the Vermillion River, it makes several major curves and drops quickly from the highlands to the river valley. At one point, as you make a very sharp curve, a spectacular stone cliff appears ahead of you that forms a valley wall carved over the millennia by the river. It's quite a sight and quite a stretch of road.

After you cross the river and start climbing uphill again, you will see Vermillion Road—make a left turn onto it. Follow Vermillion Road, which in turn, follows the Vermillion River Valley northward into the city of Vermillion where the river enters Lake Erie. As the river ends its journey through this historic landscape, so do we.

Appalachia

B Y THIS POINT, I hope there are no remaining doubters who question Ohio's motorcycling credentials. Good biking is found throughout the state. However, I also have no doubt that, if a poll were taken, Ohio's south-central and south-eastern regions would be the hands-down winners. This area is often referred to as the Appalachian region, and in fact, the historic and cultural roots of this part of the state are more closely connected with Kentucky and West Virginia than they are to New England or the Great Lakes.

For the motorcyclist, this part of Ohio is nothing short of fantastic. I don't believe there is a straight or flat road in the region. The scenery is a wonderful mix of forests and farms with underlying hills and bedrock escarpments. Very often, a rider will have a cascading stream for company, as both the roads and rivers follow valleys carved out of the highlands over the millennia. Waterfalls, caves, rivers, stone outcroppings, and hills are the norm, not the occasional surprise. Country roads follow hollows and river valleys, where tiny villages have been mostly out of sight for generations. Cultural wonders, such as Indian mounds and relics left behind by early settlers, abound and leave the visitor awestruck in wonder.

This is an amazing part of the state, and I try to take it all in with these three tours through the heart of Appalachia.

Cedar Falls located in Hocking Hills State Park.

The Serpent

I CALL THIS RIDE in the heart of southeastern Ohio's hill country the serpent for two reasons: first, there is virtually not a mile of road in this 204-mile tour that's straight, and second, because I believe that the stretch of Route 26 from Marietta all the way to Bethesda should be hereafter officially labeled as The Serpent. If Route 129 in Tennessee and North Carolina can be designated The Dragon, then Route 26 deserves a title every bit as descriptive to satisfactorily describe its incredible motorcycling credentials.

If hilly and curvy roads, beautiful scenery, light traffic, and mile after mile of pure motorcycling delight interest you, then you will love this ride. If you prefer roads that are multilane and straight, be forewarned, this ride is not for you.

We begin our ride in the capital city of southeast Ohio—Marietta. This is fitting because Marietta's story and its own charms and attractions are up to the task of being good enough to be included in this tour. Given its strategic location and landscape, Marietta is mentioned in several other rides because many roads pass through it. If you don't live nearby, I really do recommend arriving at Marietta a day early to explore and see and do the many things they offer. This will allow you to get an early start the next morning on The Serpent.

We begin this ride by heading east from Marietta on Route 26, and the fun begins almost as quickly as you turn off of Route 7 onto 26. There isn't much more that I can say about Route 26 except that it is just a tremendous biking road that dips, twists, and weaves, turning in every direction possible as it makes its way northeast through the Wayne National Forest. All that dipping and weaving and floating like a butterfly will have you feeling like Muhammad Ali on a motorcycle! Be alert though. This road isn't your typical laid-back motorcycle ride. You'll earn those grins and shouts of joy as you work your clutch and brake like a Formula 1 racer on dipping and rising, decreasing-radius curves. Route 26 eventually joins up with Route 800 for a bit just south of Woodsville, but 800 parts company north of town and once again Route 26 is our riding host for many more entertaining miles north. Route 26 is officially labeled as the Covered Bridge Scenic Byway. This is a bit of a misnomer. There are some covered bridges along the route, and two are

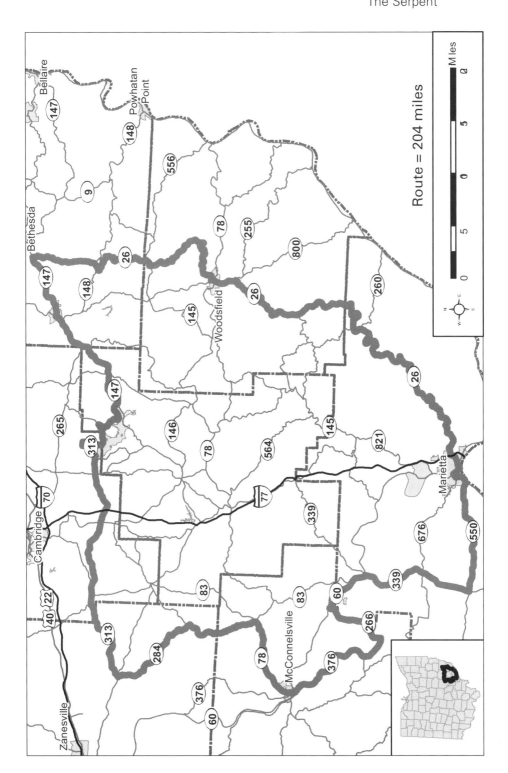

Knowlton Covered Bridge.

Hune Covered Bridge.

Miles	Destination	Total
	THE SERPENT **204 MILES**	
0	Marietta	0
48	Woodsfield	48
25	Bethesda	73
22	Kennonsburg	95
32	Chandlersville	127
27	McConnellsville	154
25	Beverly	179
25	Marietta	204

visible from 26. There aren't signs pointing out any others, though maps show a couple more.

Route 26 officially ends at SR148, but Old Route 26 continues straight north across 148 to the town of Bethesda. In Bethesda, turn left onto Route 147 and take it southwest all the way to Seneca Lake, where we get on Route 313 and continue west on the north shore of Seneca Lake. Route 313 is a really enjoyable ride because it tightly follows the shoreline of this large impoundment. Besides the enjoyment of a road with great biking character, there is wonderful scenery thrown in at no extra cost in this stretch. Once past the lake, 313 continues west—though definitely not straight west—to Route 284 at Chandlersville. Turn south on 284 and, improbable as it may seem, the ride gets even better. Route 284 follows the ridge tops and for mile after mile you're treated to magnificent scenery and beautiful vistas. Just south of the ghost town of High Hill, you will enter a large piece of land called The Wilds. This is North America's largest private conservation center and it looks like something out of South Dakota—only much greener! Rare and endangered species from around the world graze on the thousands of acres that make up this reserve and research center. Yes, those really are buffalo grazing on the distant hillsides, but buffalo are not all you will see here. Exotic animals, such as giraffes, rhinos, deer, elk, and antelope, also roam this land. All of this area was once huge, open-pit coal mines, and the land has been reclaimed into these open fields and young forests. This is, or was, coal country. From the 1940s through the 1980s, coal was mined here in great quantities. There are thousands of acres of land that have been reclaimed all along Route 284.

This huge drag-line shovel is located in Miner's Heritage Park just outside of McConnellsville.

Follow Route 284 south to Route 83, which then joins Route 78 very quickly. Turn right onto 78—yet one more wonderful motorcycling road—and head toward McConnellsville. Just before getting to town, you'll notice a large Miner's Heritage Park on 78. It is definitely worth a stop, if only to see the huge, though by today's standards miniscule, drag line shovel on display there. There are some interpretive displays that tell the coal-mining story in this part of Ohio.

Once in McConnellsville, head south on Route 376 and take this scenic Route south along the Muskingum River, which is shaped like a large "U" in this area. At the bottom of the U is what is called Big Bottom, a name derived from the large area of very fertile bottomlands in the river's flood plain here. At this location, Route 376 changes designation to become Route 266, but it's the same road. Our reason for taking this particular road is to visit a monument to the Big Bottom Massacre. On January 2, 1791, twelve settlers were killed by a war party of Wyandot and Delaware Indians who attacked their outpost. These families had moved north from the settlement at Marietta despite warnings about Indian hostilities in the area. Deadly skirmishes continued in the Ohio territory for the next three years. It was only after General Wayne's victory at the Battle of Fallen Timbers that a few years of peace arrived on the frontier.

Take Route 266 north along the river to its juncture with Route 60. At this point, the road resumes its southerly journey. You will be on Route 60 until the town of Beverly, at which point we pick up Route 339 and continue south to Barlow. In Beverly, you will find Lock 4 on the Muskingum River navigation system. At this site, you'll also see a historical marker telling the story of the *Buckeye Belle* disaster. Deadly boiler explosions were fairly common on early steamboats, and there were many major disasters in which numerous people were killed when a steamship blew up beneath them. In 1852, an explosion destroyed the *Buckeye Belle* at this location, killing twenty-four and injuring many more.

In the stretch of Route 60 between Beverly and Barlow, there are three covered bridges. From north to south, they are Harra, Bell, and Mill Branch, which is in Barlow. All of them are very close to Route 339, and even though the Bell Bridge is the only one that still carries traffic, they are all worth the short trip to see.

In Barlow, turn east on Route 550 and take this last biking road of the tour back to Marietta and the completion of this wonderful ride.

Hocking Hills Tour

THE HOCKING HILLS region of southern Ohio is known far and wide for its marvelous natural beauty. Some of the most striking natural wonders in the state are to be found in Hocking Hills State Park and State Forest. No tour guide of Ohio would be complete without a section on this beautiful area. This 242-mile ride not only takes in the best of the parklands but also includes the beautiful landscape for miles around. As with other rides in this region, it is based on roads that serve two purposes: they take you to the many natural attractions that dot the region, and they comprise some of the very best biking roads you will find anywhere. So check your tires to make sure you haven't worn them out from all the peg-scraping we've already done on other rides and get ready for yet one more absolutely wonderful tour on Ohio's fabulous motorcycling roads.

We begin the ride in the small but interesting village of Somerset, located in western Perry County. Leaving Somerset eastbound on SR13 will mean less than two miles of uninspiring riding until the fun really begins. Just southeast of Somerset, we'll get on Route 669 and take this fun road through an increasingly hillier and more wooded countryside as we wind and twist our way east. In fact, just when you're sure the riding couldn't get much better, we arrive at Route 555. The triple nickel is known far and wide as one of the great motorcycling roads in Appalachia. We pick it up at Deavertown and head south for the very best of what 555 has to offer. This road is, plain and simple, a great motorcycling byway as you'll find out for yourself if you haven't already experienced its charms.

Upon finally arriving at the village of Bartlett, get on Route 550 and turn west so the fun can continue. Route 550 meanders west, first to the tiny burg of Sharpsburg where it turns southward, then ultimately meeting Route 329 at Amesville—the small town with the library made out of coonskins. Actually, the library was originally built in 1804 with funds derived from the sale of raccoon furs—a unique fundraiser, you have to admit. I suspect Davy Crockett was a major customer.

At this point, we pick up 329, which wanders generally northwest to the village of Trimble. In Trimble turn onto Route 13 and take it south as it follows Sunday Creek for just a couple of miles to Route 685, which in turn delivers us to SR78 and the town of Nelsonville shortly thereafter. Nelsonville is situated on the shore of the Hocking River and has US33 as its main street. Nelsonville is home to

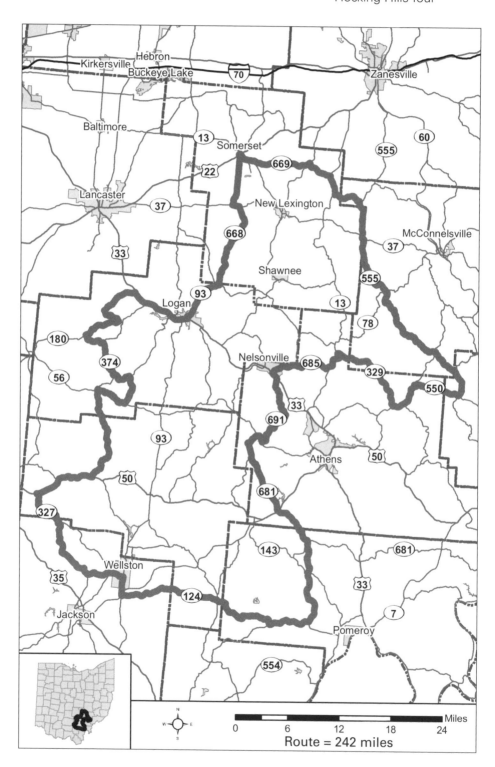

Buckeye Furnace near Wellston.

the Hocking Valley Scenic Railroad, and if you take a very short detour on Route 33 to the north end of town, you will see the railroad and lots of rolling stock on display. While there you might want to visit the Rocky Boots outdoor gear store—it's the building with the large mural of a bighorn sheep on the side. Rocky Boots is headquartered in Nelsonville.

To continue the trip we head south on Route 33 and take it along the river just a mile or so and turn right on Route 691. You no doubt have noticed that the primary roads on this tour are Ohio's famous triple-digit routes, renowned for their character and beauty. Ride 691 south through the southern portion of the Wayne National Forest. You'll enjoy its wonderful qualities all the way to Route 56. Turn right onto Route 56 and take it just a short distance, turning left onto Route 356.

Follow 356 through the very scenic Zaleski State Forest and Waterloo Wildlife Research Center, and ultimately to Ohio Route 681, where a left turn is needed. Take 681 southeast to Albany and beyond.

A little more than five miles south of Albany, Route 681 makes a ninety-degree turn to the east, and Route 692 continues straight ahead. Stay on 692 as it goes south to Pageville. On the south side of Pageville, Route 692 turns west, however,

HOCKING HILLS TOUR 242 MILES		
Miles	Destination	Total
0	Somerset	0
42	Chesterhill	42
27	Trimble	69
10	Nelsonville	79
22	Albany	101
16	Rutland	117
28	Wellston	145
26	Allensville	171
12	South Bloomingdale	183
36	Logan	219
23	Somerset	242

we want to go east and then south on Route 684. Take 684 south and at Harrison-ville (at the Route 684/143 intersection) continue straight south on what becomes CR3. I suspect this road was once part of Route 684. It's on the same alignment and has the same look and feel as a state road. In any event, just keep heading straight south on this very pleasant road all the way to Rutland.

In Rutland turn right and start your westward journey on Route 124. This is yet another wonderful road that will have you singing its praises every time you and your buddies share stories about great rides. It'll be your companion all the way west almost to Wellston. As you approach Wellston, you'll see signs for the Buckeye Furnace State Memorial. This site is definitely worth the six-mile, round-trip detour. A complete iron smelting furnace is located in the park, which is an amazing sight to see.

Buckeye Furnace is a charcoal-fired iron blast furnace of the kind that were common throughout southern Ohio in the mid to late 1800s. This furnace was built in 1852 and was in use until 1894. It's all there—the casting shed, the origi-nal stack, the charging loft where the raw materials of limestone, iron ore, and charcoal were loaded into the furnace, and the engine house which held a steam-powered compressor. If you have any interest in how things work or how things were made, this park is really an enjoyable experience. The park itself is open

A waterfall spills over a cliff and creates an unforgettable scene at Rock House in Hocking Hills State Park. (Photo courtesy of Ohio Division of Travel and Tourism)

year-round, though the museum is open only during the normal, warm weather tourist season.

Continue west on Route 124 until you arrive at Route 327 just south of Wellston. Head right on 327, taking it into town and an intersection with Route 93. Go west on 93 (this is actually south 93, which is running east and west in this stretch of road) to Coaltown. Once in Coaltown, Route 93 turns south, but we're going to continue west on Main Street two blocks to Sour Run Road and turn right. After about one mile, Sour Run Road makes a ninety-degree turn west and goes northwest to intersect with Raysville Road at the tiny village of Leo (an old red barn marks the corner). What brings us to this crossroads are the Leo Petroglyphs—figures carved into the bedrock by Native Americans at some point in the unrecorded past; perhaps the same incredible people who built the earthen mounds around the state. When you turn north onto Raysville Road from Sour Run Road, you'll almost immediately have to turn left onto Park Road if you want to see the petroglyphs. It's not a spectacular sight, but just knowing that a person took the time to carve these effigies in this rock many hundreds of years ago is kind of cool. By the way, to help you locate Park Road, you can also look for the sign at this corner that reads "Backwoods Bike Shop" with the classic V-Twin engine displayed on the sign. To continue the ride, go north on Raysville Road several miles until it intersects with Route 327. Shortly after you leave the village of Leo, Raysville Road forms the left fork at a point where two roads diverge. Raysville Road continues north to Route 327. Just before reaching 327, Raysville Road makes a couple of sharp turns and crosses a railroad track just prior to the highway. It's an entertaining road all the way. Turn left/west on Route 327 and take it the short distance to Route 50.

Go right/east on US50 almost eight miles to the village of Allensville and turn left on Goose Creek Road. (To help find this intersection—there's a car dealer on one corner and a large, white two-story building on another.) This road wanders uncertainly but generally north to the town of South Bloomingville and Route 56. We're going to turn right on 56 and follow its many curves southeast to Hocking Hills State Park and SR 374, which takes us north into the main portion of the park.

Once in the park you have a smorgasbord of delights to choose from. Follow the signs for the various attractions or stop at the park headquarters to get brochures. Whatever you choose to see, I certainly wouldn't be in too much of a hurry in this beautiful piece of God's Country. Ash Cave, the beautiful Cedar Falls, Old Man's Cave, spectacular Cockles Hollow—these and many more mar-

Ash Cave Falls in Hocking Hills State Park.

velous sites are here for your enjoyment. There are plenty of camping and other lodging possibilities in this area should you want to extend your fun another day.

When you get a call on your cell phone from your boss demanding to know where you are and you realize that you really have to move on and leave this beautiful area, continue north on 374 and follow its indirect ways to Route 33 east into downtown Logan. Almost all the attractions in this area are along Route 374. At one point, it joins Route 180 for a while and then continues on alone to Route 33.

Once in Logan follow Route 93 north out of town to Route 668 on which we turn left/north. Route 668 will guide us all the way north to our starting point of Somerset, carrying us across even more beautiful countryside and offering many miles of great motorcycling along the way. The road loses its curves for the last few miles to Somerset, but a series of enjoyable and very scenic roller-coaster hills more than makes up for the straight alignment.

Now that you've completed the journey, I think you'll agree that The Hocking Hills deserve all the praise bestowed on this unique region by two- and four-wheel tourists alike. I suspect you'll also feel that if there are motorcycling roads in Heaven they'll look amazingly similar to these!

The Circleville Circle

THIS DAY-LONG tour takes you through southern Ohio's farms and hills, forests and stream valleys, and through small towns and cities that all have their own charms and stories. It's a ride that is great for experiencing the mellower side of motor-cycling—some wonderful roads and scenery coupled with laid back stretches where you can just relax and soak in everything around you without worrying about how you're going to handle the next hairpin curve (although you will have plenty of them on this tour, it's just that unlike some of the rides in this book, this tour does offer you the occasional chance to relax and enjoy the scenery).

We begin our trip in the historic town of Circleville. The founders of Circleville must have been stunned when they discovered the extensive Indian earthworks that were there when the first settlers arrived. The city derived its name from two great concentric circular earthworks connected to a square earthen enclosure on the plain where they built the town. In fact, the original village was laid out in a circular pattern to match the earthworks, and the old octagonal courthouse was situated in a circular park looking out over the space enclosed by the mounds, with each side of the courthouse facing a street that radiated out like spokes on a wheel. In the 1850s, townspeople found the radial and circular system of streets to be inconvenient, and the layout of the city was changed to a more standard rectangular pattern.

Circleville is a great destination during fall color touring because it hosts what is called the greatest free show on earth. The main theme of this event, held the third weekend of October, is pumpkins. Yes, it's a Halloween extravaganza like none you've ever seen.

We begin the trip by heading west out of town on US22, going four and a half miles west of US23 to SR138 and turning left. Route 138 will be our fun and companionable riding partner for many miles as we travel southwest to the town of Greenfield. This is another of those small towns with lots of history to explore. There is a cluster of historic buildings at the southeast corner of town, which is right where Route 138 deposits us. Built in 1821, Smith's Tannery is the oldest of these buildings. Across the street is the Travellers Rest Inn, built just a few years later. These buildings were stops on the Underground Railroad, and Greenfield was a very active abolitionist community. The Greenfield historical museum is

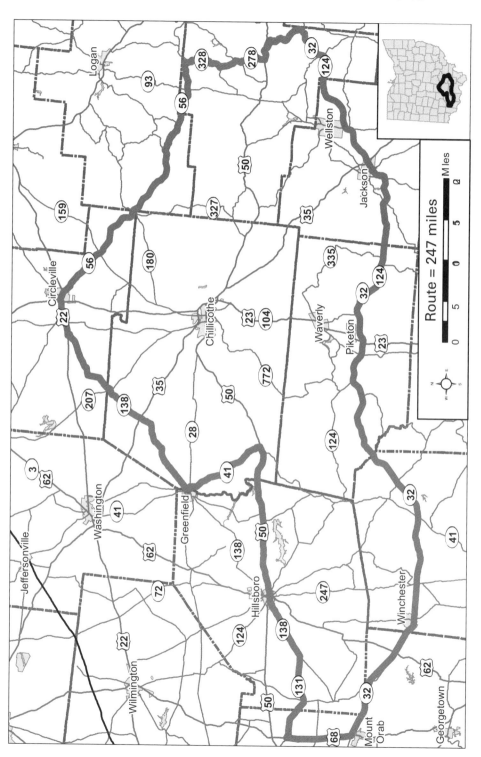

Route = 247 miles

People gather to see the Circleville Pumpkin Show's King Pumpkin, which weighed a whopping 1353 pounds. (Photo courtesy of Ohio Division of Travel and Tourism)

also located adjacent to these two buildings. Even the old Greenfield High School is of special historic and architectural interest. It's located a couple of blocks to the west and a block north, where you'll also find the 1874 Shilo Baptist Church.

On the east side of Greenfield, Route 138 intersects with Route 28/41. Turn left a very short distance and Route 41 will continue south. Turn right onto 41 and make your way through the increasingly scenic countryside on a marvelous riding road all the way south to Bainbridge. Leaving Greenfield heading south, the hills of southern Ohio suddenly appear on the horizon, giving you a hint at the enjoyable ride that awaits you.

It might sound funny, ridiculous even, but one unusual stop on this tour is the Harris Dental Museum in Bainbridge. Before you laugh this off, it's actually quite an interesting stop, though some of the old dental tools may leave you squirming. If nothing else, it will certainly make you appreciate modern dentistry! Bainbridge is known as the cradle of dentistry because the country's first dental school was started here in 1828 by John M. Harris, M.D. It makes you wonder what sort of folks worked on people's teeth before that time. Does the local blacksmith come to mind?

THE CIRCLEVILLE TOUR 247 MILES		
Miles	**Destination**	**Total**
0	Circleville	0
33	Greenfield	33
31	Hillsboro	64
28	Mt. Orab/Appalachian Highway	92
56	US23/Piketon	148
25	Jackson/US35	173
31	Zaleski	204
16	Ash Cave	220
27	Circleville	247

From Bainbridge we head west on US50 about five miles to Cave Road and the fabulous Seven Caves and Highland Nature Sanctuary. This 2,000-acre tract of land is hard to describe with words—you really have to see it for yourself appreciate its beauty. The caves and waterfalls in the Rocky Fork Gorge are just wonderful. The land has just recently been purchased by a private group to preserve it, and they offer tours during the summer months. Cave Road and this attraction aren't well marked. The road runs south from US50 immediately prior to (east of) the bridge over Rocky Fork Creek. You will see lots of signs in this immediate area for the Paint Creek and Rocky Creek State Parks, but Cave Road is easy to miss, and believe me, you don't want to do that. The road itself south to the complex is delightful—narrow and twisty with the creek and gorge next to the pavement. Be very careful, this road is narrow with tight curves, and there will be other traffic. In addition, this is definitely a small group or individual biker activity. The facility cannot accommodate large groups of cars or motorcycles.

If you wish to camp at the Seven Caves facility, call ahead at 937-365-1935 for reservations. If you feel really adventurous and would like a wilderness hiking permit, call 937-365-1600.

We next head west on US50 to Hillsboro, the county seat of Highland County. Perhaps Hillsboro's claim to fame is that for decades it was the home of a company that made steel alloy bells that were recognized as being among the finest in the world. They rang out on church steeples, farmsteads, and ships the world over. In fact, thousands of ship bells made in Hillsboro were on Allied ships involved

Smith's Tannery and Travellers Rest Inn (opposite page) are located across the street from each other in Greenfield.

in the D-Day invasion. Each July Hillsboro celebrates the Festival of the Bells to honor their history (and as an excuse for a several-day party).

In Hillsboro, you'll need to go south just a couple blocks on US62 to state Route 138 and turn right. You will turn left from US50 in Hillsboro at the main intersection, with the courthouse on one side and the old opera house on the other. Route 138 heads southwest through the rolling lands of Highland County, making for a pleasurable ride. Near the crossroads town of Danville, turn right onto Route 131 and take it westerly to the main intersection at US68, where we'll turn left and go south to state Route 32—the Appalachian Highway.

Though the Appalachian Highway may be a primary route across southern Ohio, it certainly is not your typical urbanized four-lane roadway. It's a very pleasant journey for all of the nearly one hundred and ten miles you'll be riding it through the hilly countryside of this region. The riding gets better the further east you travel as the road wends its way through a country of forested hills, rock outcroppings and river valleys.

About midway across US32, you'll cross the Scioto floodplain and come to US23. Immediately east of 23 and just north of Route 32, about one mile south of Piketon, is a set of Indian Mounds that is worth a look. This group of four

mounds, the highest of which is 25 feet, had originally been part of a much larger earthwork that included a long berm that was a half-mile long. Unfortunately, road construction, gravel extraction, and other modern activities have destroyed all but the group of four mounds. The entire earthwork was perched on a terrace on the eastern bluffs of the Scioto River valley.

Our easterly journey on the Appalachian Highway takes us beyond Jackson and Wellston into the seriously forested hills of Vinton County. Almost exactly four miles beyond the intersection of Routes 32 and 160 east of Wellston we turn left onto County Road 43C/Vales Mill Road, taking it north a mile to the cross-roads of Vales Mills. At this point, the road we want to stay on goes basically straight ahead, although it would seem that the main road curves right at this point. This is the only somewhat tricky point on the route. Don't follow the curve to the right and cross the bridge over the creek—take the left fork instead, which takes you north. We'll follow this delightfully hilly and curving road through the forest and along Union Ridge up to US50. Take 50 left/west the short two-mile ride to Route 278 and turn right for big fun. Once on 278 ride it north to the village of Zaleski, and then through the Zaleski State Forest to Route 328, which is just beyond the park headquarters building north of the village.

We'll continue our northerly journey on Route 328, yet another delightful road filled with everything that any biker could ask for—hills, curves, scenery, light traffic, and grin-producing riding. This entire series of roads north of the Appalachian Highway is just great.

At New Plymouth, Route 328 turns east but we want to turn left onto Route 56. This is another fun stretch of road, and you'll see plenty of other bikers out enjoying the delights of this region. Just west of the intersection with Route 374, you will see the signs for Ash Cave, part of the Hocking Hills State Park system and one of several geologic delights found in this area. It is certainly worth a stop and the short walk to the cave and waterfall. I recommend taking this trip during the spring when the flowering trees and bushes that line the road are in bloom and wild flowers carpet the forest floor. Making this run in late April or May has the added advantage of very light traffic on the roads, and the waterfall at Ash Cave is much more impressive with the higher stream levels found in April or May.

Continue west on 56 and near the village of Laurelville notice the landscape changing around you. Wooded and hilly land gradually becomes more open and productive farmland. Follow Route 56 northwest through the fields and rolling landscape of Pickaway County all the way back to Circleville to complete this circular ride filled with fun motorcycling and interesting things to see.

Highways That Made History

OHIO HAS MANY roads with origins dating back to the very earliest days of exploration and settlement. After having played major roles in the history of Ohio, many of these routes have either evolved into main roads with no obvious connection to their origins, or they have disappeared entirely with the passage of time and development. However, the role they played in the development of Ohio and the nation cannot be overstated. Given its geographic location, Ohio is unique in that four of the original "transcontinental" roads of the early twentieth century went through Ohio (The National Road, The Lincoln Highway, The Dixie Highway, and the Yellowstone Trail). I don't believe any other state can make that claim. The stories behind these roads and the culture they created are as fascinating as the roads themselves.

Almost everyone has heard of Route 66—the famous federal highway that linked Chicago and California. The story of Route 66 has become part of our culture and demonstrates the level of passion Americans have for their vehicles and driving them on great roads. While Ohio's grandfatherly roads may not have been the subject of movies, TV shows, and songs (*get your kicks on Route 66*), these routes actually date back far longer than The Mother Road and lack none of the excitement, romance, and charm of fabled Route 66. The historic roads I've chosen to describe here were selected because planners envisioned them as roads that would knit together a young and unconnected nation, would serve to connect distant points for economic and national sovereignty purposes, and would serve to settle unpopulated portions of the country. These early "transcontinental" roads were a manifestation of a young nation's sense of itself—the ultimate application of Manifest Destiny—it could be said. Historical roads I've selected to include are:

- The Lincoln Highway (two versions)
- The National Road
- The Dixie Highway

There are several other roads that also qualify, however, they are not included because they are no longer easily identifiable, they have essentially been buried in large stretches under the concrete of superhighways, or they have been covered on other tours outlined in the book.

It is very enjoyable to research old roads and explore them on your own. Examples of roads that can still be located and ridden in Ohio include the Scioto Trail, the Yellowstone Trail, the Zane Trace southwest from Zanesville to Maysville, KY, and the Three-C Highway, which connected Cincinnati, Columbus, and Cleveland. Take the time to research old Ohio Department of Transportation maps from their earliest available map in 1912 to the 1930s when, except for expressways, the road system looks much as it does today.

Ohio was one of the first states to number roads in order to make some sense out of the many local trails and gravel roads that crisscrossed the state. Many of these local roads were officially joined together to make long distance, albeit circuitous, highways connecting distant cities in the state. You can spot the main highways on the earliest maps by the low number assigned to them by the state during the period prior to 1927, such as Route 1, the National Highway; Route 2 was the Yellowstone Trail; Route 3 was the Three-C Highway; Route 4 was the Scioto Trail; Route 5 was the Lincoln Highway; and Route 6 was the Dixie Highway. This numbering system was preceded by another short-lived attempt to consolidate and identify individual roads with numbers. In 1920, Ohio used Roman numerals to designate the major roads of the time. The Lincoln Highway was Roman numeral II. Starting in 1927 the federal system of numbering roads was put in place, and many road numbers were changed to reflect this new national system.

A person should explore these roads sooner rather than later because the heavy boot print of urban sprawl has already significantly changed them. By their nature, they were the major roads of their day, and these routes became even more important with the passage of time. This meant that they were some of the first roads to be upgraded or realigned and straightened for efficiency.

It must be kept in mind that almost all historic roads, some of which have transformed into jam-packed six-lane behemoths today, started out as game trails and Indian footpaths through the wilderness. The first European explorers and then American settlers followed these native trails rather than hack new routes through the wilderness. The Indian paths connected distant points and were a well-recognized means of travel long before the first white person set foot in what is now Ohio. Let's give credit where credit is due. Native Americans had the same need to travel long distances that we do—for trade, migration, following food sources, warfare—you name it. We didn't invent these human activities. The native footpaths followed the high ground and thus meandered a lot. If you look at any of the older roads, they also meandered across the countryside following the high ground along ancient pathways.

It wasn't until modern transportation engineers straightened and flattened roads that they became boring straight lines between points A and B. The old roads were wonderful examples of byways in no particular hurry, winding across the countryside as if they knew that it was the journey that mattered, not just the destination. I love unimproved and rural roads because they have soul. They're sexy and natural—with hills and curves and lots of character. Modern improved roads have been neutered and are without character. These plain vanilla highways are wide, flat, and straight, and no fun at all!

Certainly, the number of motorcyclists who can remember an Ohio without expressways is getting very small, but there are still folks alive who can recall when these historic roads were the main routes for travel in all directions. Long before station wagons filled with families plied these pre-expressway roads in the 1940s and 1950s, families in horse-drawn carts or in Model Ts followed the very same routes when Ohio was much younger. Given our typically here-and-now view of the world, this history is often unknown or unappreciated by modern day observers.

I think it is important to remember this history. Besides, these roads actually make for enjoyable riding, especially if you take the time to stop and soak in some of the lore that is as much a part of these roads as are the curves, hills, and small towns you travel through. Making these roads even more enjoyable is the fact that the majority of traffic utilizes nearby parallel expressways, resulting in relatively light traffic on many stretches.

You don't just ride these historic roads—you explore them to discover the forgotten gems of yesteryear hidden amongst the modern trappings of today. It could be an 1830s tavern, an 1860s stagecoach inn, sections of brick pavement from World War I, or gas stations and diners from the 1950s. These artifacts are fascinating to discover and to imagine the world in which they were a routine part.

While these roads may not be your cup of tea for riding repeatedly, it's a worthwhile accomplishment to be able to say you've ridden all of Ohio's own versions of Route 66 from beginning to end. One just has to become readjusted to driving the way our parents or grandparents did—at slower, more relaxed speeds on two-lane roads that went through each small town along the way. These roads were the lifeblood of those towns. In fact, most of the towns along the original territorial roads were founded in the first place to provide basic services, such as food and lodging, to the earliest travelers.

So slow down a bit to explore and enjoy these roads the way they're meant to be. You'll be fascinated and more appreciative of your land after you've ridden and rediscovered Ohio on these historic roads.

The Lincoln Highway

THE LINCOLN HIGHWAY was primarily the brainchild of Carl G. Fisher, owner of a company that manufactured lights for automobiles, and Henry B. Joy, owner of the Packard Automobile Company. Fisher also owned the new Indianapolis Speedway. Fisher came up with the idea of a "coast-to-coast rock highway" in 1912 and soon sold others on the merit of a road connecting the two coasts. It was in December 1912 that Fisher, acting on a letter he received from Joy about coming up with a better name for the highway—one that would capture the imagination and patriotism of the populace—that use of Lincoln's name was decided upon. Joy's father had worked in the Lincoln administration and as a child, Joy heard much praise about President Lincoln around the dinner table. It turns out that a highway connecting Gettysburg and Washington, DC, was to have been named the Lincoln Highway, but that project never got off the ground, so its supporters gladly lent their support and name to Fisher's vision of a coast-to-coast road.[1]

Fisher and Joy were automobile enthusiasts and clearly saw the bright future of the Tin Lizzy. In 1913, Fisher and Joy were joined in this daunting endeavor by several other auto executives as well as owners of companies that produced concrete. A notable holdout was Henry Ford, who disagreed with private and corporate donations being used to build the nation's road system. Ford argued that such an important endeavor should be a public program, financed through taxes and user fees. He correctly predicted that funding it in any other manner was simply ignoring the obvious: that it would result in a road system designed by local officials and the wealthy—both of whom had their own agendas that weren't necessarily best for the nation as a whole.

Like most grand schemers, the early advocates of a coast-to-coast highway did have their own self-interest in mind to some degree. If they could demonstrate the feasibility of connecting America with a road system, it would be a tremendous boon to the early automobile and road-building industries. They were also the voice for a growing number of car owners, however. In the period just prior to World War I, automobiles had become reliable and affordable enough that the very first auto-tourists (autoists) were making their presence felt—all that was missing were the roads. Even early motorcyclists were in on the excitement of cross-country travel, which should surprise absolutely nobody! In 1912, the Federation of American Motor Cyclists was preparing for a cross-country motorcycle relay, hoping to set a record for carrying a message from one coast to another.[2]

You might be wondering why it was that private citizens had to be the driving force behind a national road system. The fact is that in 1913 there was no federal money, involvement, or oversight of highways. Roads were a local affair, with their main purpose being to connect farmers with nearby towns for the movement of produce and to connect towns to one another. Henry Ford's insistence that the government, and thus the people, get involved became reality when it soon

---

[1]*The Lincoln Highway*, Drake Hokanson © 1988, University of Iowa Press.
[2]*Ibid.*

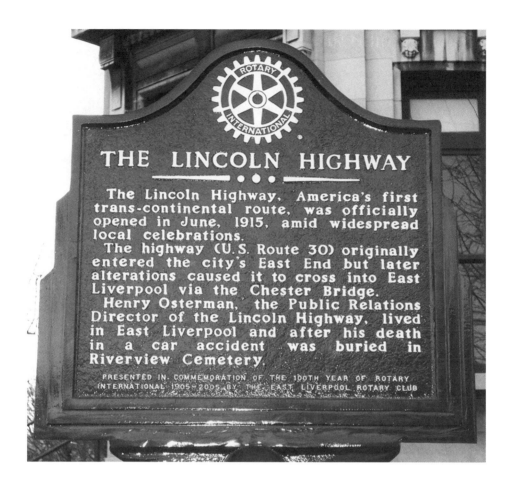

THE LINCOLN HIGHWAY
• ◆ •

The Lincoln Highway, America's first trans-continental route, was officially opened in June, 1915, amid widespread local celebrations.

The highway (U.S. Route 30) originally entered the city's East End but later alterations caused it to cross into East Liverpool via the Chester Bridge.

Henry Osterman, the Public Relations Director of the Lincoln Highway, lived in East Liverpool and after his death in a car accident was buried in Riverview Cemetery.

PRESENTED IN COMMEMORATION OF THE 100TH YEAR OF ROTARY INTERNATIONAL 1905-2005 BY THE EAST LIVERPOOL ROTARY CLUB

became obvious that the road building program was much too large and important to be left to local communities and private donations.

The Lincoln Highway has been appropriately called the "Main Street Across America." That is a very applicable name as it did, in fact, connect towns together across the center portion of the nation. It didn't purposely bypass towns as today's new roads do. The highway stretches about 3,300 miles from Times Square in New York City to Lincoln Park in San Francisco (the actual distance depends on which version of the LH is used).

Fisher and Joy and other highway advocates formed the Lincoln Highway Association and worked with local officials to hook together existing local roads into an identifiable interconnected highway that a driver could follow from one end to the other. This meant that the road had to be well marked along its entire length. This was accomplished with red, white, and blue Lincoln Highway (LH) signs on telephone posts and concrete posts at regular intervals.

This monument in honor of Mr. John Hopley is located just east of Bucyrus. Hopley was a local politician who played a major role in developing the Lincoln Highway, especially in having it routed through Bucyrus.

Association leaders worked closely with local units of government in all states included in the route. This made the job difficult as, of course, every mayor within 50 miles of the proposed route wanted the highway to run through their town and every governor wanted the road to go through their state. The economic benefits of being on the Lincoln Highway were obvious to everyone. This politicization of the process resulted in what seems today to be illogical twists and turns as the developers tried to accommodate local wishes. Though the word "highway" was used in all the speeches, brochures, newspaper articles, and even sermons from pulpits across America, one has to keep in mind that many years would pass before the interconnected but unimproved roads became a highway in any real sense of the word.

Politics and geography resulted in the alignment changing several times over the first 15 years of the highway's life. This makes following the Lincoln Highway today almost impossible to do, because there isn't one highway. Today, when we think of a major highway, I-75 for instance, it doesn't occur to us that stretches of the highway might be rerouted or realigned on a regular basis. Interstate 75 is I-75—its alignment doesn't change without an extreme amount of planning and construction. Such was not the case with the Lincoln Highway.

Between 1913 and 1928, several variations of the highway existed according to maps of that era. There were two primary versions: one that existed prior to

1919 and another with variations that resulted during or after 1919. There were even variations on these two main routes, but the differences were localized and only the most extreme Lincoln Highway purist would be concerned about these minor alternates. I am leaning heavily on Ohio Department of Transportation maps for the period of 1912–1930 and on research done by the Indiana University of Pennsylvania[1] in determining the actual route. It is important to note for riders that there are several versions of this historic road in Ohio, but this book is not the place to try to define the exact routes of all the various Lincoln Highway iterations. To further complicate matters, the Ohio transportation director was given the authority in 1930 to name US30 as the Lincoln Highway—no matter where new construction or bypasses might take US30.

For the purposes of this book, I will describe in as much detail as possible the main pre-1919 route, and the route that is defined as the Historic Byway since there are fairly significant differences in these two routes.

All along this highway, there are fascinating tidbits of Americana. I'll point out some of them, but as you ride the route, be on the lookout for signs of the glory days of the Lincoln Highway (1920s–1960s). They are there in the form of concrete markers, old gas stations, cafes and diners, sections of original brick roadway, and more. Don't be in a hurry—it's a fascinating part of our history that you'll be passing up if you treat this road as simply a means of getting from point A to point B. Enjoy the ride.

Some of the various markers for the Lincoln Highway.

[1] *The Lincoln Highway Resource Guide*, Indiana University of Pennsylvania, Spatial Sciences Research Center and the Geography & Regional Planning Department, August 2002.

The Lincoln Highway Historic Byway

WE BEGIN THE Lincoln Highway trip in downtown East Liverpool at the corner of Fifth and Broadway Streets, where the Highway monuments are placed. This intersection is located about six blocks north of US30 / SR39, which follows the Ohio River shoreline. At the southeast corner are two monuments to the highway—a concrete marker that Boy Scouts and other groups put in place along the road in 1928 and an historical sign giving some detail of the highway. These monuments are located in front of the Ceramics Museum, a popular attraction that memorializes the history of this city.

Follow Fifth Street west to Jefferson—you'll see the white stone building of St. Aloysius Church at that corner—and turn north following the Lincoln Highway signs to SR267. You are on SR39 for a block at the US30 / SR39 interchange and then exit onto 267 northbound. Taking the official Historic Byway route is generally fairly easy because of the signs along the way. Follow SR267 up the long and high hill out of East Liverpool to north of Glenmoor, where you pick up US30 and follow it into Lisbon. The Byway is easy to follow west from this point to Canton. Along the way, there are some things to point out. While on the LH in Lisbon, you will want to at least get a picture of the Steel Trolley Diner on the east side of town and the Crosser Diner a little farther down the road. The Steel Trolley Diner is a 1950s diner and Crosser dates from the 1930s. Both diners have served travelers on the highway for many years. If you're in the mood for coffee or food, you're in luck—either restaurant will take you back to what qualified as "fast food" two generations ago. West of Lisbon the road shows its heritage by meandering across the countryside to Canton. This circuitous route is the result of the original formation of the LH when existing local roads were hooked together. West of Lisbon the road also roughly follows the Sandy & Beaver Canal—a feeder canal that ran east and west connecting locales in western Pennsylvania and eastern Ohio with the main Ohio & Erie Canal that, in turn, connected Lake Erie with the Ohio River. The Sandy & Beaver was a very difficult canal to dig and, amazingly, was in business for less than a decade before being made obsolete by the railroad. Ironically, at the same time one group of immigrants was performing backbreaking work digging the canal, another group

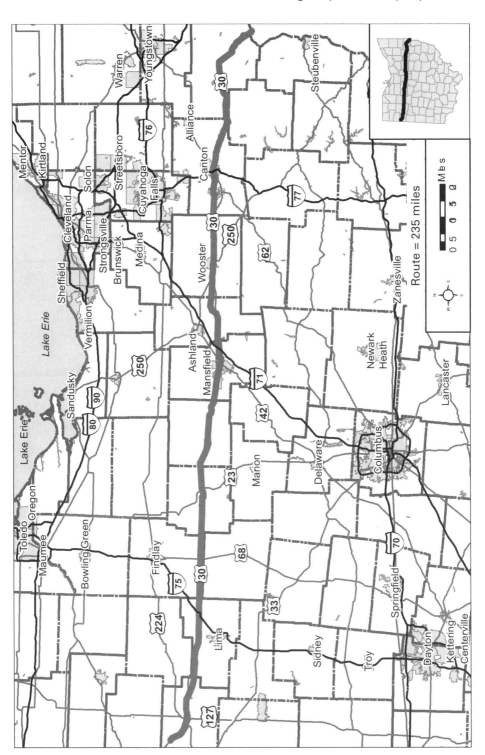

of immigrants was doing equally backbreaking work clearing rights-of-way and laying track for railroads that would negate the work of the canal diggers.

In the small town of Hanoverton, there are two replica markers for the Lincoln Highway. The first is a concrete marker of the same style as those put in place nearly eighty years ago, and the second is a replica of the brick pillars also used to identify the route years ago. You will see several of these brick LH monuments as you progress westward. Just north of the LH on Plymouth Street in Hanoverton, you will find the Spread Eagle Tavern in an 1837 building that has been recently restored.

There are some segments of the old highway in the stretch of the LH between Minerva and Canton that deserve special attention. Just west of Minerva, Historic Byway signs will direct you to a half-mile loop onto Tunnel Hill and Cindell Roads for a short and somewhat rough ride on original roadway. You won't miss a lot if you pass this up. It does give you an idea of the condition of the original road, but it isn't real compatible with all large touring bikes. To me, the best stretch of original road and one you definitely won't want to pass by is Baywood Road just west of the Tunnel Hill loop between Minerva and Robertsville. This wonderful narrow and hilly road, paved with brick, is an absolute delight to the senses as you pass through countryside that travelers of seventy-five years ago would still no doubt recognize. Baywood Road drops you in the village of Robertsville, where you pick up US30 / LH again and continue west. Just west of Robertsville, you'll be directed onto two more short stretches of Cindell Road on the north side of US30. The first is another section of old brick road and the second is asphalt.

Getting through the Canton metropolitan area is actually very easy. Just follow US30 into town and, when you hit SR172, follow it straight west out of town. State Route 172 is called Lincoln Way through the western suburbs. Before you leave Canton, take time to visit a couple of high-priority attractions. They are the Pro Football Hall of Fame and the Canton Classic Car Museum. If you're a football fan, you've no doubt had a visit to the Football Hall of Fame on your long list of things you wanted to do during your lifetime. Well, you will seldom be as close as you are right now. When route 172 intersects with I-77, just get on the 77 and head north a couple of miles. Follow the signs and you will be there in no time. They're open every day except Christmas, and parking is even free. Their phone number is 330-456-8207.

Located downtown at the corner of 6th Street and Market Avenue just south of the Lincoln Highway, the Classic Car Museum is a very convenient stop. They have nearly fifty rare and special interest cars, plus tons of artifacts and cool, car-related gadgets. They're open seven days s week and can be reached by telephone at 330-455-3603.

THE LINCOLN HIGHWAY HISTORIC BYWAY 235 MILES		
Miles	**Destination**	**Total**
0	Pennsylvania State Line	0
14	West Point	14
25	Minerva	39
17	Canton/I-77	56
30	Wooster	86
33	Mansfield	119
25	Bucyrus	144
15	US23/Upper Sandusky	159
39	Beaverdam	198
19	Delphos	217
18	US30 Expressway west of Van Wert	235

As you ride through the Canton area try to imagine what your grandparents saw. The stretch between East Canton and Canton would have been on a dirt lane through pastures and cornfields, not suburbs, and the stretch between Canton and Massillon on the west would likewise have been a narrow road through farms and woods, not endless strip development. What a difference in the span of one long lifetime.

West of Massillon, SR172 will dump you onto US30 for a couple of miles, then you can get on Old 30 to ride through the town of Dalton, where an original roadway monument is preserved. Follow US30 all the way into Wooster where it becomes Liberty Street. Go west on Liberty, which becomes Lincoln Way on the west side. You will be on SR302 for a while, but when 302 turns north, you want to keep going straight west. Outside of Wooster you hit a busy intersection when Lincoln Way crosses US250, but once you get across, you will find smooth sailing on a scenic and fun road all the way to Mansfield. In Ashland County, Lincoln Way becomes County Road 30A—a carryover from when the original Lincoln Highway was labeled as US30 eight decades ago. Now a new and "improved" US30, limited-access highway runs parallel to the old road. You'll enjoy riding this old road as it meanders through scenic countryside westerly through the small towns of Jeromesville, Hayesville, and Mifflin, and through the Charles Mill Lake area. Eventually the LH becomes SR430, taking you into Mansfield.

Located on the east side of town in Lisbon, the Steel Trolley Diner is an authentic 1950s-style eatery.

In Mansfield, there is a section of the LH Byway that I think needs better signage. Follow the Byway straight into town on SR430, which is joined by SR39 and US42 as the road goes west through town as the main east / west street. In downtown Mansfield turn north on Diamond Street / SR13, taking it four blocks north to 4th Street and go west. This street angles in a northwesterly direction on the west side of Mansfield and through the city of Ontario. Signs will direct you to a short loop on Maybee Street, then west again on US30, which we follow to just west of Crestline. West of Crestline you will loop off of 30 onto Leesville Road, past the monument marking the capture location of Colonel Crawford, through the village of Leesville, and then west again where you join up with US30, taking it into Bucyrus.

On the east side of Bucyrus, there are a couple of LH monuments. The first is a 1918 brick pillar along the road at a cemetery, and the next is a large monument to John Hopley, a successful native son who was instrumental in creating the LH through Ohio. The Hopley monument is along the road at the Bucyrus Country Club & Golf Course. Proceed straight west through Bucyrus on Mansfield Street. I suggest parking the bike at the traffic circle in town and walking around a bit to enjoy this small town's ambience. The Crossroads of America mural is unique and needs to be seen up close to fully appreciate it. This huge painting depicts Bucyrus Square as it appeared in 1917.

West of Bucyrus, take Business 30 out to US30, which you cross over and continue west on CR30 through Oceola and into Upper Sandusky. On the east edge of Upper Sandusky, there exists a remnant of the original brick Lincoln Highway that leads down to the old Sandusky River Bridge. An Ohio historical marker and replica LH pillar mark this historic location. Upper Sandusky was a strategically important place in early Ohio history. It was located on the Harrison Trail between Columbus and Fort Stephenson (now Fremont) and was the site of Fort Ferree, built in 1812, one of a series of forts built during the War of 1812 in an attempt to wrest control of the Northwest Territory from the British. There was also a famous spring at the site of Fort Ferree called Indian Spring. Colonel Crawford and his men satisfied their thirst there during those fateful hot summer days of June 1782. The Overland Inn was later built at the spring, and Charles Dickens was once a guest at the Inn.

On the west side of downtown Upper Sandusky, you'll go north four blocks on Warpole Street / SR199 and continue west on CR330 / Business 30. Just west of town you will come to where the new US30 ends and reverts to the old two-lane US30. This stretch of Old 30 will be our companion for many miles as we head west as straight as an arrow through the part of the Ohio mosaic that is well known to many—the flat farmland piece of the picture.

Just kick back and relax as you ride west. There isn't much in the way of special attractions in this stretch—so much so that I found the building in New Stark that is covered with old oil company gas station signs to be worth a stop and a picture. In the twenty-five miles of Historic Byway between Upper Sandusky and State Route 235, there is no modern US30 running parallel to the Lincoln Highway, thus there is a bit more traffic on this stretch than on others. Because of the straight and clear nature of the roadway, I don't view this as a problem since traffic moves well and there is nothing to cause backups or unsafe conditions. West of Upper Sandusky, it's not until you reach Beaverdam that you're shocked back to the twenty-first century. Beaverdam has the misfortune of being at the crossroads of I-75 and US-30, both of which have exits onto the Lincoln Highway. It is also where the Dixie Highway and the Lincoln Highway intersect. The east side of Beaverdam has a large number of facilities servicing interstate truckers, with all the usual fast food restaurants thrown in the mix, all of which creates about a mile of amazing congestion in this wide-open farm country. Beyond Beaverdam, the Byway travels through Cairo and Gomer on its way to the cool canal town of Delphos. In Gomer, note the old gas station at the crossroads and the defunct roadside park just west of the village. These roadside parks were regular features on main roads of pre-expressway America. I recommend taking some time in Delphos to inspect the canal and visit the Canal Museum in town, which is located just south

John Brumback left money to build this beautiful public library for the people of Van Wert.

of where the LH crosses North Main Street. Also, note the beautiful mural on the side of the Delphos Herald building depicting life in Delphos at the heyday of the canal period.

Going west from Delphos to Van Wert there are three attractions of note. The first is a drive-in movie theater! Talk about a feeling of *déjà vu*! A little west of the drive-in, there is a building that I guess to have been a combination service station and restaurant, located in a uniquely shaped metal building built to serve travelers on this highway. A little farther west is a historic marker noting the point where General Wayne's army marched through the wilderness in August 1794 on its way to the pivotal battle at Fallen Timbers. Proceed west on the Byway to Van Wert. While in this pleasant small city, stop to appreciate the magnificent county court-house building. It is one of the most impressive in Ohio, and that's saying some-thing since Ohio has many marvelous courthouses! Just a few blocks west of the courthouse, you will pass by the Brumback Library. Even if you don't go inside, do stop to marvel at this wonderful building, which was built in 1901 thanks to a bequest by Mr. John Brumback who left money for the purpose of constructing a library for the people of Van Wert County. It has to be one of the most impressive small town libraries you will find anywhere. A 1928 concrete LH marker post can be found in Van Wert's Fountain Park.

The official end of this tour is eight miles west of Van Wert at the point where the Lincoln Highway became a victim of the new US30. The old road ends at the new highway (or more correctly, under the new road), and from this point to the Indiana state line you would be riding on a new, limited access highway, not the Lincoln Highway.

You've done it—ridden across Ohio on one of the most famous and celebrated roads in the country. Much of the trip was through the same small towns and through the same town squares in front of the same courthouses and storefronts that travelers saw generations ago. It truly is a wonderful ride through time.

Note: The Ohio chapter of the Lincoln Highway Association is active in preserving the history and physical artifacts of this historic highway. They have placed numerous signs and displays at places such as rest areas and have installed replica marker posts and pillars along the route. They have also developed The Lincoln Highway National Museum and Archives at 102 Old Lincoln Way in Galion, OH. You can call them at 419-462-2212 or find them online at www.lincolnhighwayassoc.org/info/oh/ for more information on this historic road.

The Lincoln Highway Pre-1919 Route

WE BEGIN THIS trip at the same location as the above Historic Byway tour—at the corner of Fifth and Broadway in East Liverpool, in front of the Ceramics Museum, and at the site of two Lincoln Highway markers. Remember, on this earliest version of the LH you will be following roads that are not part of the official Historic Byway, so every now and again you'll have to ignore the Lincoln Highway Byway signs.

Follow the same directions as the previous route to just past Glenmoor where SR267 will make a hard right, becoming Route 7 and crossing US30.

When 267 makes this hard right, you'll want to make a left angled turn onto what becomes County Road 451, which eventually crosses the new and improved US30 and intersects with East Liverpool Road \ old US30 where we turn left. Liverpool Road \ old 30 will itself curve back across US30 and Buckeye Road—which in very short order becomes Roller Coaster Road—and continue straight ahead. This is an original section of the Lincoln Highway that you will want to take. It's more enjoyable than taking US30, which was part of the later alignment. Roller Coaster Road will rejoin US30 and the Historic Byway version just southeast of the city of Lisbon. We will then stay on US30 for some distance through Lisbon and west through many small towns and finally to East Canton.

Just west of East Canton, US30 takes a dip south and SR172 / Tuscarawas Street heads straight west—this is the street you want to stay on. In East Canton watch for one of the 1928 concrete LH pillars.

Stay on SR172 / Tuscarawas, which becomes Lincoln Way in Massillon. Continue on Lincoln Way / 172 past the town of East Greenville where you will join US30 for a short distance, veering off the highway onto Main Street / Lincoln Highway through the city of Dalton. West of Dalton we again occasionally pick up US30 as the LH, and sometimes the original highway will parallel US30 a short distance away. Two 1928 concrete markers have been preserved in Dalton—one is in downtown and the other is just west of town.

Take US30 to the east side of Wooster where you will notice Pittsburgh Street heading off at a northwesterly angle. Pittsburgh Street becomes Liberty Street heading west in town, and Liberty becomes State Route 302, and farther west outside of Wooster it becomes Old Lincoln Road.

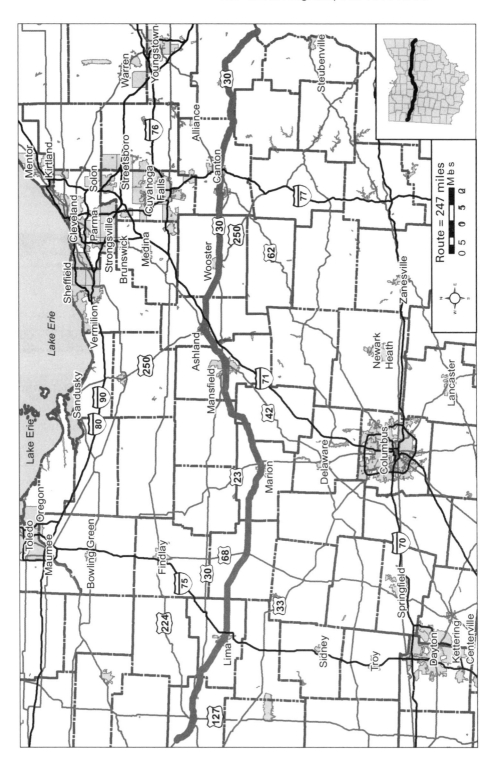

This is the first major divergence of the original alignment from the later version. West of Wooster and just east of Jefferson Old Lincoln Road, US30 and US250 diverge. Signs will say that the Lincoln Highway goes straight ahead on Route 30A, but the old route actually headed northwest, so you'll want to ignore the Byway signs at this point. Take US250 through the towns of New Pittsburgh and Rowsburg and into Ashland. In Ashland, US250 takes a hard right with Claremont Street heading southwest. Take a left onto Claremont which eventually joins with US42. Take this road southwest toward Mansfield. About midway, you will see a bypass for the town of Windsor. The old highway went through the village of Windsor, so you'll want to get off US42 and make a right angle turn onto Township Road 1688—also called Windsor Road—which rejoins US42 west of the small town. Continue on US42 to Mansfield. Just before reaching Mansfield, US42 joins Ohio 39 for a short distance westward. In downtown, US42 makes a ninety-degree turn south and SR39 continues straight ahead—stay on SR39. After a short distance, SR39 turns to the northwest and SR430 (Park Avenue) continues straight ahead—you want to continue straight west on 430. You are essentially just heading straight west through Mansfield—just the names of the roads change.

Continue west on 430 just beyond the town of Ontario to where it joins SR309, which you will take all the way to Marion. In Galion, SR309 jogs south to join Ohio 19, traveling west and then south through town, and then southwest to Marion. Take SR309 through Marion and continue on it as 309 heads to the northwest and then west into Kenton. Remain on SR309, following it through Kenton and continuing all the way to Lima and beyond—on into Delphos.

Looking at a map, it's obvious that the loop described above, which took the LH through the cities of Galion, Marion, Kenton, and Lima, and ultimately to Van Wert, was longer than a straight line from Mansfield to Van Wert. In the early days of the Lincoln Highway, there were decent roads connecting these "major" cities, while roads that connected Mansfield and Van Wert were in poor shape. Henry Joy soon altered the Lincoln Highway, straightening it from Mansfield to Van Wert so as to achieve his goal of a straight-line route whenever possible and also because he felt that the citizens and officials of Marion and Lima, in particular, were not properly supportive of the highway. While the "official" route may have been changed on Mr. Joy's maps, the citizens and local officials along the Marion / Lima route maintained for several years that theirs was the real Lincoln Highway.[1]

On the east side of Delphos, SR309 takes a right turn and heads straight north. Follow this curve and about a half mile later, you'll hit The Lincoln Highway. Turn

[1] *The Lincoln Highway*, Drake Hokanson © 1988, University of Iowa Press.

THE LINCOLN HIGHWAY PRE-1919 ROUTE 247 MILES		
Miles	Destination	Total
0	Pennsylvania State Line	0
14	West Point	14
25	Minerva	39
17	Canton/I-77	56
30	Wooster	86
21	Ashland	107
14	Mansfield	121
37	Marion	158
27	Kenton	185
28	Lima	213
16	Delphos	229
18	US30 Expressway west of Van Wert	247

left on LH and follow it through Delphos and all the way to Van Wert. Mr. Fisher's road is easily followed through Van Wert. About eight miles northwest of Van Wert, it is supplanted by the US30 expressway, which heads into the wilds of Indiana where only the most foolhardy might dare to venture.

The National Road

By THE EARLY 1800s, settlement in Ohio was becoming fairly widespread, especially along the Ohio River, but travel from the east was still difficult. For years, waterways had been the means for traveling to the west but this wasn't always possible, especially in the more southerly routes. Pikes over the Allegheny Mountains of Pennsylvania got travelers from the northeast to Fort Duquesne / Pittsburgh, where they could access the upper Ohio River. However, farther south in the Baltimore and Washington, DC, area, the going was still difficult. The Appalachian Mountains separated the headwaters of the Potomac from the Ohio River, making a water route impractical.

Both Presidents Washington and Jefferson recognized the need for a road connecting these two rivers, not only to aid the movement of settlers and the military into the Northwest Territory but also to counter the effect of the British in the hinterlands west of the mountains. Even after having lost the American War of Independence, Britain was still very active in the newly gained American lands and was fomenting Indian troubles in an effort to block American expansion west of the mountains. In fact, Britain didn't abandon two forts they held in the Michigan Territory until 13 years after the Treaty of Paris awarded the Great Lakes region to the new United States of America in 1783. Washington and Jefferson both understood that to hold these newly won lands they must make it clear that sovereignty was being claimed. What better way to do this, and at the same time encourage settlement, than construction of a road from the capital region to the western wilderness?

Congress passed the National Road Act of 1806, authorizing construction of a road from Cumberland, Maryland, to the Ohio River and appropriated thirty thousand dollars to achieve this goal. It's fascinating to read the degree of specificity that Congress provided for the road's construction. In the legislation providing for the road, they specified how wide it was to be (four rods), what materials were to be used, placement of markers every quarter mile along the road, the construction of roadside ditches, and so on. They even declared that no incline or decline from horizontal could exceed five degrees in grade. Streams were to be crossed by stone

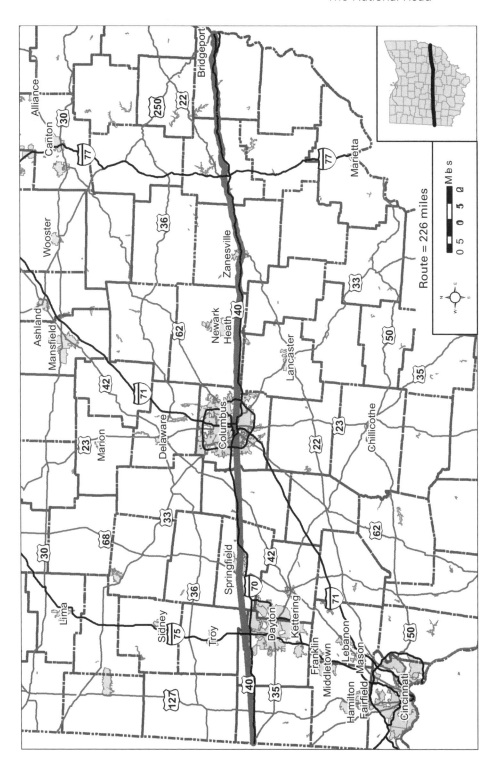

Route = 226 miles

bridges rather than by fording the stream as was the common practice at the time in frontier areas. Work began on the road in 1811 and reached Wheeling in 1818. It was known by several names: the National Road (NR), the Cumberland Road, or the National Pike. It was the first federally sponsored highway and the funds for extending the road across Ohio and Indiana came from sale of public domain lands to speculators and settlers.

By 1838 the National Road extended to Springfield, Ohio, and ultimately to Vandalia, Illinois, in 1841. Originally, the plans called for it to stretch from Baltimore to St. Louis, but the rapid growth of railroads in the mid-1800s made roads such as this less important. Things changed, of course, when the automobile supplanted trains as the transportation of choice for Americans—roads once again reigned supreme.

Even though it never reached the final goal, it did eventually stretch 800 miles in length—a very admirable accomplishment given the time period and conditions encountered by the workers. The original National Road very closely parallels today's Route 40. Driving it is a mobile history lesson. Like most of our historic roads, it isn't the kind of road that motorcyclists would choose for a fun day in the twisties, but it is an enjoyable road in many sections and is certainly one that a person ought to ride slowly and thoughtfully, absorbing the history. It is quite easy to follow and since I-70 parallels it the entire 230 miles across Ohio, traffic is lighter than one might expect. I've found that the only troublesome areas on the road are the outer "sprawl" edges of cities along the highway. It is actually quite interesting riding through the original downtown sections of towns and cities to view the old buildings. The rural portions are enjoyable, as well, with long stretches of minimal development and pleasant scenery.

We begin our ride through history in Bridgeport on the mighty Ohio River. The first stretch is very easy—get on US40 and follow it all the way to Morristown. In this first twenty miles, there are a few attractions. In St. Clairsville, you'll want to visit the Lentz Tavern and Great Western Schoolhouse, which are adjacent buildings. The tavern was built in 1830 and the schoolhouse in 1870. St. Clairsville itself is an old Pike Town built on the original road. Its Main Street has many

Miles	Destination	Total
	THE NATIONAL ROAD **226 MILES**	
0	Bridgeport	0
20	Morristown	20
21	Old Washington	41
20	Norwich	61
13	Zanesville	74
26	Hebron	100
28	Columbus/Scioto River	128
42	Springfield	170
20	Great Miami River	190
36	Indiana State Line	226

historical buildings, and the entire district is listed on the National Register of Historic Places.

Ohio's portion of the National Road actually began life in St. Clairsville. It was there on July 4th, 1825, that a ceremony was held on the grounds of the Belmont County Courthouse marking the beginning of road construction in Ohio.[1] From St. Clairsville the new road followed the existing Zane's Trace to the east and west—straightening, widening, and building bridges as needed. The National Road wasn't going to be just another muddy, narrow, and rough trail through the wilderness. It was designed and built to serve the transportation needs of Ohioans for generations.

Just west of Bridgeport at the town of Blaine, road builders encountered one of the major impediments to the road—notorious Blaine Hill. This steep and high hill required builders to create a series of switchbacks to move travelers out of the river valley and onto the high land to the west. Today, US40 rides over the water and up the hill on a viaduct built in 1933. It's an impressive structure, but the original S-Bridge, which still exists below the viaduct, is every bit as impressive. Built in 1828, it is still in great shape though no longer carrying traffic. At the west end of Blaine, immediately before getting onto the viaduct bridge, turn right

---

[1]*Land of Promise: The Story of the Northwest Territory*, Walter Havighurst © 1946, The Macmillan Company, New York.

Restored bridge and brick pavement at Blaine Hill, located west of Bridgeport. This proved to be a very difficult stretch of road to complete.

onto county road 10 and you'll see the old bridge right ahead of you. It's an enjoyable stop where you can see bridge technology separated by a century of time and light years of technological and societal changes.

Morristown is a bit farther down the road and is also a Pike Town with many old buildings worthy of some of your time. In Morristown, you'll need to follow Main Street through town and then be on US40 again for about three miles west of town. For a short stretch, I-70 is constructed over the NR so you will need to get onto I-70 just west of Morristown and take it a short distance to the next exit (202), where you can exit onto Ohio Route 800. Ride SR800 on its temporary east-west alignment until you come to Township Road 807, which you'll follow through the Village of Hendrysburg.

Just west of Hendrysburg, you'll once again get on SR800 until it turns north, at which point, you should go straight ahead on County Road 40A / Old National Road. Take National Road west to Fairview, where you once again have to get on I-70 until exit 193. When you exit the expressway, go north a very short distance on SR513, quickly turning west onto 690 / Bridgewater Road. Taking this road west, you'll soon see a sign for CR6764 which loops off Bridgewater Road to cross the S-Bridge—a signature bridge style designed for this road—over the Salt Fork River. You'll get back onto CR690 by turning immediately after crossing the bridge and following the road under I-70 and then turning west again on CR670. Following CR670 to County Home Road North will take you back over I-70. A short stretch on Fairground Road will take you back to the National Pike, which goes west into Old Washington. Just east of Old Washington is Peacock Road—a short segment of the original roadway.

Unfortunately, it sounds more complicated than it really is. In this stretch the NR follows I-70 closely and sometimes the Pike switches back and forth on either side of the expressway.

West of Morristown, notice the countryside you're riding through. It didn't always look like this. Decades of strip mining changed this land from one of high, forested hills to the current gently rolling reclaimed landscape of meadows and pastures.

Follow Old National Pike road through the historic town of Old Washington. The style and age of the buildings tell you that this town has been here a long time and has witnessed much history. Some of this history can be further explored if you take Morgan's Way south a couple of blocks to the old cemetery on the hill. You can't miss it. At the top of the hill is a historic marker explaining the events of July 23, 1863, when Confederate forces under General Morgan arrived in town. While Morgan's men were searching the town for supplies, a Union army detachment that had been pursuing them attacked the rebels. Three of the Confederate troops were killed and were buried in the local cemetery. Three small flags of the Confederacy mark the grave stone.

We leave Old Washington on US40 westbound. Through much of the stretch of the Old National Road from Morristown to east of Zanesville, the road is quite nice with decent scenery and riding conditions. You won't mistake it for your favorite motorcycling road, but it certainly gets passing grades.

Take US40 all the way through Cambridge, an attractive old Pike town with many historic old buildings and another S-Bridge from the original road over Wills Creek. West of Cambridge, US22 joins Route 40 and the road changes character, turning into a four-lane highway for a stretch. Take it west through New Concord where you can visit the John and Annie Glenn Historic Site and Exploration Center. The Center is housed in John Glenn's boyhood home, which was moved to this location and made into a museum of twentieth-century American history. It's located at 72 West Main Street in New Concord and is open mid-April through mid-October. Just west of New Concord is the Fox Run S-bridge and a short segment of original road located in a small park on the north side of the road. This bridge and road segment were abandoned in the 1930s when the road was straightened a bit in this stretch. The bridge has been recently restored.

A couple of treats await you near Norwich. A section of the original National Road that was paved with brick loops off of US40 near Norwich, and it is also the home of the National Road and Zane Grey Museum—you won't want to miss either attraction. In Norwich, turn right on Norwich Drive, then left onto Main Street through town. Turn right onto Brick Road and follow it back to US40. The old brick road is very cool. The brick paving is kind of rough, so go slowly and soak in the history. World War I is the main reason that there is brick pavement under your bike's wheels. When America became involved in "the war to end all wars," the state of our nation's roads was little better than during the days of the Wild West. Roads were little more than improved dirt trails, and when the army had to move huge numbers of troops and war materiel across the nation to Atlantic ports, they had serious problems. Paving main roads became a national priority. Several paving methods were tried, including brick. Much of the brick pavement on this and other roads was actually done by convicts conscripted for that purpose. It's quite amazing that this section of road has survived the decades of traffic that it has seen.

The museum is located on US40 / 22 east of the interchange at I-70 (exit 164). Museum hours vary, so call 800-752-2602 for up-to-date scheduling.

Continue west on US40 through Zanesville and over the city's trademark "Y" Bridge, which crosses both the Muskingum and Licking Rivers. This is the fifth

Y-bridge built at this location. The first was built in 1814. Zane's Landing Park is a good place to view the bridge and is adjacent to the bridge on Market Street. Also at the park is the *Lorena* sternwheeler, which offers boat rides on the Muskingum River. Call them at 800-246-6303 if you'd like to do a dinner cruise.

Zanesville is a good place to consider the fact that construction of much of the National Road from Wheeling to Zanesville had its birth several years prior to Congressional action creating the National Road concept. In 1796, Colonel Ebenezer Zane and his brothers carved an improved trail west into the Ohio wilderness beginning at Wheeling, West Virginia. As with most "road" builders, they utilized existing Indian paths to some degree whenever feasible, but theirs was a relatively straight and improved route into the interior of an as yet largely unexplored country. Timing and events were on their side, and their venture could not have happened a few years earlier. It took General Wayne's victory at Fallen Timbers in 1794, Jay's Treaty with the British, and finally the 1795 Treaty of Greenville to pave the way for this road into Indian Country.

It was at the tiny river crossing town of Zanesville that the old Zane's Trace and the new National Road parted company. From Zanesville, Zane's Trace headed southwest through Chillicothe and on to the Ohio River across from Maysville, KY. The National Road proceeded due west through the rapidly developing land of central and western Ohio.

About five miles west of Zanesville, you will find the Smith House and Headley Inn, both of which provided food and lodging for travelers and teamsters on the early National Road. As you progress westward, take three bypasses from US40 through the small towns of Mt. Sterling, Hopewell, and Gratiot to see more of the original road. From Brownsville to Kirkersville, US40 / National Road is a national scenic byway and continues in its pleasant riding condition. Before proceeding west from Brownsville, however, consider a three-mile detour north of town to Flint Ridge State Memorial. Flint Ridge is a fascinating place that contains quarries of very high-grade flint, which was mined for millennia by Native Americans for use as tools and weapons because of its high quality. The museum is closed Mondays and Tuesdays, but the park and walking paths among the quarry pits are always open. If you plan to take the Arrowheads and Superbikes tour, you can leave this activity until that trip.

Immediately west of the village of Brownsville, Eagle Nest Hill Monument marks the highest elevation of the road in Ohio and also commemorates the paving of this stretch of road from 1914 to 1916. Pull over and gaze at the barely discernable carvings on this boulder. Though very difficult to read, the inscription on this large granite boulder states the following:

Old National Road
Built 1825, Rebuilt 1914
Through the efforts of James M. Cox
Governor of Ohio

Also carved in the rock are the outline of a Conestoga wagon and an early car.

West of Brownsville, you will pass through Hebron, a fairly busy area where there is an interchange at Route 79 and I-70 just south of the National Road. Hebron is home to the Buckeye Central Scenic Railroad and the National Road Station. They can be found on US40 just east of Route 79. Go to www.buckeye-centralrailroad.org for more information about rides and special events. This group also has a train operating out of Byesville.

West of Kirkersville, the urban influence of Columbus is felt as you follow the highway west through the capital city. You will be on Main Street until just prior to reaching I-71. At that point, take Champion Street about seven blocks north to Broad Street, where you make a left turn and resume westward travel. The ride through downtown Columbus is quite nice. You will appreciate the historic old buildings that line the road, and it is wide and free flowing through town. As usual, it is the suburban edges where frustration arises due to traffic congestion and stoplights.

The National Road was completed to Columbus in 1833, representing eight years of enormously hard work by thousands of men who, for the most part, were not yet even citizens of this country. Every inch of the road was built by the muscle, sweat, and blood of humans and horses. As we effortlessly motor along on our magnificent horses of steel, this is an important thought to keep in the backs of our minds.

Remain on US40 west of Columbus to Lafayette, where the historic Red Brick Tavern is located at the intersection of US Routes 40 and 42. This magnificent building was built in 1837 to serve the needs of early travelers. It also provided stables for horses and served as one of the stopover points for the early version of the Pony Express that existed in the late 1830s. As a traveler on the National Road, you can also enjoy a meal and respite from the toils of travel in this historic Inn. The name, Red Brick of Yesteryear, is proudly displayed on the building. In the 1800s, taverns and inns were built at intervals designed to accommodate travelers who could cover only a certain number of miles in an average day's travel—usually between ten and twenty miles apart.

West of Lafayette a right turn onto Old US40 will take you through the small town of Summerford. Once past town, a right turn will deposit you back onto US40, which you will continue to follow westward to South Vienna, where a trip

The Red Brick Tavern is located at the intersection of US 40 and 42.

through town on Main Street is recommended. Main Street joins US40 again just west of South Vienna. At the tiny village of Brighton, you'll once again make a slight loop off US40 onto the old road, where you will ride past the Davey Tannery Building, another historic building dating back to 1845. The satellite dish mounted on this building looks out of place, to say the least.

Keep heading west on 40 into Springfield, where a left turn onto Main Street will take you through town. You will know you are close to Springfield when you pass the Melody Drive-In Movie Theater. Right out of the 1960s!

Just past Springfield, Main Street intersects with US40 again, but in town you will parallel US40 a few blocks south. There are two attractions in Springfield that

Look for the Madonna of the Trail monument on the west side of Springfield.

are worthy of some time. The first is the Pennsylvania House Museum, which is a building that stood at the junction of the National Road and the old Dayton-Springfield Pike. The Inn was built in the 1830s and served travelers on these historic roads. The Old Pennsylvania House served primarily the stagecoach traveler of the mid and late 1800s. It originally had stables for horses and a place for freight wagons to be parked. The Museum is located at 1411 West Main Street in Springfield (937-322-7668). As this book is being written, the building is undergoing significant restoration by the DAR, who originally saved the derelict building in the 1930s.

On the west side of Springfield, just west of the entrance to Snyder Park, you will find The Madonna of the Trail, one of twelve similar monuments erected in each of the states through which the road passes. The monument depicts a heroic pioneer mother with her children and symbolizes the important role these women played in settling the American frontier. At ten feet high and weighing five tons, it is an impressive monument!

From Springfield west all the way to the Indiana border, US40 / National Road is an official scenic byway. The final urban area on the NR is through the northern Dayton suburbs. At Vandalia and Englewood, the highway takes a southerly dip as it crosses dams over the Great Miami and Stillwater Rivers. These two loops are very pleasant rides as the land around them is primarily undeveloped parkland. It's a scenic region, not at all what one would expect if they weren't familiar with this area. The historic byway route through these two jogs is well marked, and there is no chance of making a wrong turn.

Once suburban towns such as Englewood and Clayton are left behind, the remaining twenty-five miles on US40 / National Road provides a pleasant ride through western Ohio farmland. Traffic is light and riding conditions are good as the road delivers you to the state line and Richmond, IN.

Well, congratulations. You've completed a 226-mile-long trip in a matter of hours on a road that took many years to build and many difficult days to cross for much of its existence. What I find amazing is that there are so many buildings still standing on this highway that served the needs of pioneers one hundred and fifty or more years ago .

The Dixie Highway

THE DIXIE HIGHWAY (DH) had its beginning at the same time as the Lincoln Highway, and under the same circumstances. Many of the advocates for the highway were even the same, beginning with Mr. Fisher. Carl Fisher was typical of the gutsy people who went from rags to riches chasing the American Dream. A sixth-grade dropout who had to work at age twelve to support a fatherless family, he turned ideas and enthusiasm into reality. His love of wheeled adventure, starting with the bicycle, developed into the Indianapolis 500 Speedway, the Prest-O-Lite Company, the country's first automobile dealership, and of course, the Lincoln and Dixie Highways.

Fisher had a reason beyond pure altruism to push the Dixie Highway. He was the first to see that what is now Miami, FL, could be something other than swampland. After developing Miami as a resort area for cold northerners, he needed a means for people to get there. To accomplish this he built rail lines but also pushed hard for the Dixie Highway, actually a collection of roads and routes that had many legs. From 1914 until 1927 when the federal government took over the interstate road system, the Dixie Highway went from Sault Sainte Marie, MI, to Miami, and another leg from Chicago to Miami. Today, I-75 largely fills the role of moving shivering Midwesterners to the warm, sandy shores of Florida.

While many states that the Dixie traversed actually had two or even three versions of the highway, Ohio's section was pretty straightforward, going from Toledo to Cincinnati. Today, I-75 very closely parallels the Dixie except for the stretch south of Dayton. The close presence of I-75 to the old Dixie is a very good thing because the expressway absorbs the great majority of the traffic, leaving only light traffic on most of the Dixie, especially north of Dayton.

A lot has been written about the importance of the Dixie beyond its value for moving traffic. A hundred years ago, the Deep South and the northern parts of this country were still two very different places socially and economically. This historic road began the process of truly unifying the rural agricultural south with the industrial urban north.

We begin our journey down the Dixie from the north starting on US24 / Detroit Avenue in Toledo. It's easy to pick it up right at the state line if you wish, though the first couple of miles (north of SR51) navigate through an old industrial

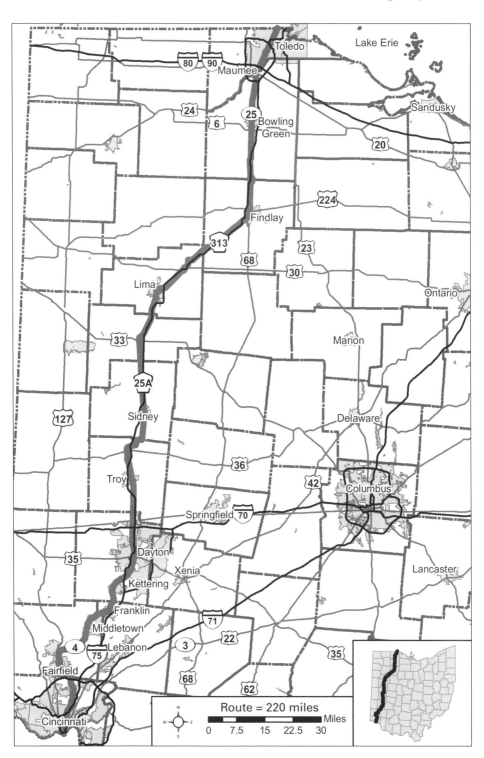

Route = 220 miles

area where the pavement is a bit rough. There are a couple of curves, so watch the signs carefully in this stretch. South of SR51 the road is smoother and easy to follow. In the city of Maumee US24 joins Ohio Route 25, with US24 heading southwest along the historic Maumee River and SR25 going straight south to Bowling Green. We leave US24 at this point and start our southward journey on Route 25, taking it through Bowling Green to the small town of Cygnet. This stretch is a divided four-lane highway with light traffic due to I-75 being right next door, and the sailing is smooth and easy, if not exciting. There is much unseen history on this stretch of road, since long before it was the Dixie Highway or US25, it was the Bullskin Trace, an old Indian trail that extended from the Ohio River to the west end of Lake Erie that was used later as a "road" for settlement and for war.

Between Cygnet and North Baltimore, I-75 covers the original road so you have to get on I-75 at Cygnet and take it south to Exit 167. At that exit, cross over the overpass to the east side and immediately turn onto County Road 220, which runs south on the east side of I-75 and was the original Dixie Highway. Take CR220 south through Van Buren and past Van Buren State Park all the way into Findlay. County Route 220 becomes Main Street in Findlay. Take it to Lima Avenue / CR313 (Dixie Highway) and take this road southwest to Bluffton, OH. Along this stretch, the Norfolk and Western Railroad will be on your right and I-75 on your left. It'll be real hard to get lost!

About two miles southwest of Bluffton, I-75 again buries the DH for a short stretch. Just after passing a golf course southwest of Bluffton and immediately after going under an overpass, you'll notice a short stretch of road going to your right. Take this short road to the stop sign at Hillville Road and turn left. After going west about one and a half miles, you will come to Swaney Road. Turn left on Swaney for a mile to where it drops you back onto the Dixie, which will then take you to the Lincoln Highway at the east edge of the village of Beaverdam. In days of yore, Beaverdam housed a facility that was the relay station for all coast-to-coast telegrams. Today Beaverdam is an old-looking tiny town, but because there is an interchange at I-75 on the east edge of town and several truck stops at the interchange, it can be a busy place if you go east a bit to get gas or food. When you reach Beaverdam,you will stop at the Lincoln Highway. Straight ahead of you will be a monument marking the Lincoln Highway. At this corner, we turn right for a short distance, and in town you'll hit the main intersection of Napoleon Road. Turn south on this road, taking it over the I-75 expressway and under US30. Just beyond the US30 underpass, you will see Dixie Highway heading to your right. In this area, DH parallels I-75 on the east side of the freeway as it angles southwest to Lima.

Just northwest of Lima the Dixie joins with Ohio Route 81, running west into Lima's downtown. Dixie Highway and SR81 share a common roadway through

Miles	Destination	Total
THE DIXIE HIGHWAY 220 MILES		
0	Michigan Border	0
27	Bowling Green	27
24	Findlay	51
24	Beaverdam	75
10	Lima	85
34	Sidney	119
20	Troy	139
19	Dayton	158
25	Middletown	183
37	Ohio River	220

Lima. In the downtown section, you will pass by the magnificent Allen County Courthouse, and seven blocks later, you will see Metcalf Street at a stoplight. Turn left onto Metcalf Street, which continues south of town as the Dixie. The south side of Lima is very interesting with chemical and manufacturing industries, the old Department of Defense Tank Plant, and a very large Marathon oil terminal. Maybe Lima's tough persona explains why it was the birthplace of Phyllis Diller! Lima is also home to some great car and motorcycle events. Throughout the summer a series of cruise-ins are held with prizes for winning cars and motorcycles. In September of each year, the Rebel Run Rod and Custom Nationals are held. This is a major event with some of the best custom cars you're likely to see anywhere. Call the Road Rebels at 419-221-1137 for more information.

The Dixie is very easy to follow south from Lima through Fort Shawnee and Cridersville to Wapakoneta, this stretch being parallel to and west of I-75.

Just northwest of Wapakoneta, the DH and SR67 join forces, heading west into town where they intersect with Business Route 25A (Dixie Highway) heading south. The 25A designation is a carryover from the 1920s when the federal government assumed jurisdiction for interstate highways and assigned them numbers rather than names. The Dixie Highway used to be US25. The Dixie is also called County Road 25A in Auglaize, Shelby, and Miami Counties.

Follow Route 67 as it heads into Wapakoneta, turning right on the main drag—Auglaize Street. Follow Auglaize Street through this very nice downtown,

Two attractions in Cincinnati are the Roebling Suspension Bridge and the Great American Ball Park (opposite page).

past the courthouse, and turn left on Willipie Street, which becomes Route 198 south of town. Route 198 turns into Dixie Highway and CR25A, which heads straight south on the west side of I-75 all the way to Sidney. Along the way, it picks up SR219 as it travels through the villages of Botkins and Anna.

In Sidney, go straight south through town on Ohio Street and exit town on the southeast corner at a pretty amazing railroad bridge over the Miami River that looks more like an ancient Roman aqueduct than a bridge. Five miles south of the river, you'll see Miami-Shelby East Road (at the county line). Take this west and southwest less than two miles to Sidney Road. Turn left onto Sidney Road and continue south to Troy.

Take the Dixie into Troy, go past yet another beautiful Ohio sandstone courthouse, to the roundabout. In the traffic circle, turn right onto Market Street and head south. A half mile south of town, you will encounter a "Y" ahead of you at a stop light. Market Street will make a turn to your right, the Dixie / 25A will go to your left, and straight ahead of you will be a Walgreen's Store. After angling left about one mile, CR25A begins heading straight south again toward Dayton. It crosses I-75 about three miles south of Troy and makes a direct line through the suburban city of Northbridge, over the Great Miami River, and on into the northern suburbs and the city of Dayton.

The Dixie Highway is surprisingly easy to follow through the entire Dayton metropolitan area. You stay on the same pavement even though it occasionally changes names. For much of the stretch, it bears the Dixie name. In Dayton, it will be called Kenowee, which you take into town and turn right onto Monument Street. Head west on Monument past Fifth/Third Field—home of the Dayton Dragons—to St. Clair Street where you turn left / south. St. Clair Street becomes Patterson Street, then Kettering Street, then Dixie Highway again, which then becomes Central, then Main, then the Dayton-Cincinnati Pike, then SR73 / Verity Parkway in Middletown. This entire stretch is very easy to follow and is actually quite a nice ride in much of its length as it parallels the Great Miami River and traverses through open land and parklands.

But hold on just a minute—before leaving Dayton a person just can't be this close to the oldest and largest (and free) aviation museum in the world without paying it a visit. The National Museum of the United States Air Force is an absolute must-see! Its seventeen acres of indoor and outdoor exhibits chronicle every aspect of civilian and military aviation for the last century—literally taking the visitor from Wright Brothers technology to the latest stealth technology. In fact, a B-2 Stealth Bomber is on display. Don't miss the IMAX theatre for an absolutely unreal experience with flight. The museum is on State Route 4 just south of I-70 and just east of I-75 (just northeast of downtown). The Dixie intersects with SR4 in downtown, just after crossing the Mad River. A left turn will get you there. Contact the museum at 937-255-3286 or online at www.wpafb.af.mil/museum. They're open from 9:00 am to 5:00 pm seven days a week.

Through Middletown, you'll once again be paralleling I-75 about a half-mile to the west. Take this to the town of Monroe and Ohio Route 63, where a right turn is needed. Follow SR63 about three miles to the west and turn right on Ohio Route 4, following it south all the way to Carthage, located on the north edge of Cincinnati.

If you aren't intimidated by the challenges of heavy urban traffic, it is possible to wrestle your way through Cincinnati to the Roebling Suspension Bridge, where the Dixie Highway entered Kentucky. Where Ohio Route 4 intersects with I-75 in Carthage, you will notice Vine Street proceeding parallel to I-75 on the south. Take Jefferson Avenue around the home of the University of Cincinnati Bearcats and pick up Vine again, following it to Court Street. A right turn on Court, then a right onto Race, and finally a left on Elm will get you to the Suspension Bridge, as folks in the Queen City refer to it. This last stretch through Cincinnati isn't as difficult to follow as it may seem, but the traffic will test your nerves and clutch. Walking along the river in the downtown district is an enjoyable activity. Cincinnati has long been a great sports city. In 1866, after resolving that little matter of the Civil War, the country's first professional baseball team, the Cincinnati Redlegs, was formed here. Walking along the river, the cityscape is filled with the imposing hulks of Great American Ball Park (home of the Reds) and Paul Brown Stadium (home of the Bengals).

From this vantage point, you can see several riverboat companies on the opposite shore that offer cruises on the Ohio River. Take a quick trip across the Suspension Bridge for a cruise—it would be a great addition to this trip.

And thus ends an exceptional ride down a historic highway. The adventure is made more interesting if you take the time to notice the artifacts left from the glory days of this highway. These small restaurants, gas stations, motels, and other service facilities were the "new thing" back in the days of when this road was young. Many reminders of what our grandparents and great-grandparents saw while traveling this road still remain—we just have to look a little harder for them.

Following the Water

O hio's shape and much of its culture is formed by water. From Lake Erie on the north to the mighty Ohio River on the south and east, as well as the canals that connected cities and villages, Ohio's waters are like arteries in a living body. Ohio's history and its present day economic and recreational opportunities owe much to its water resources. Until the coming of the railroad in the mid-nineteenth century, Ohio's waterways, rivers, and canals were the interstate highway system of the time. After the opening of New York's Erie Canal and several canals in Ohio in the 1820s and 1830s, wheat farmers in western Ohio's prairies were connected with New York City and Europe to the east and New Orleans to the south. As they say, this changed everything.

In this chapter, we will explore this facet of Ohio. I describe a trip entirely around Lake Erie, although a person could just do the Ohio portion, which happens to be the Lake Erie Scenic Byway. Circumnavigating Lake Erie is a wonderful trip, however, so I hope you have the time to do the whole tour. I also plot a ride through the Cuyahoga Valley and along the Ohio & Erie Canal system, as well as along the entire length of the Ohio River, which defines Ohio's southern boundary.

I think you will find the three trips described in this section to be not only very enjoyable from a pure motorcycling perspective but ones which will also heighten your knowledge and appreciation for this state's resources and history as they relate to water.

The Great River Road

THERE'S SOMETHING very special about riding along a river. For one thing, you can almost always be certain that it will be a fun ride, with lots of curves and hills as the road meanders alongside the river through the bluffs and hills created by rivers as they carve deeper into the landscape over time. There is also the enjoyment of playing tag with the river itself, viewing the water and watching the boats—be they canoes, fishing boats, or barges and freighters—that offer the rider something different than the normal daily routine. For me, riding near a river also conjures up images of Huck Finn and Tom Sawyer and of lazy summer days that involved things that you never told your mother. Such images keep me forever young and carefree—even if only in my mind.

When you follow a river, the roads almost always also follow the pathways of history. Early America was explored and settled by means of its waterways. Large or small, rivers were the early highways used by Native Americans, early explorers, and settlers alike. Much drama was played out over the centuries on these very rivers that we are fortunate enough to ride alongside on smooth and winding highways today. This is especially true of the great rivers of America, such as the Hudson, the Missouri, the Ohio, the Mississippi, and other water highways of our nation. The Ohio River, in particular, is truly impressive. It is a muscle-bound, blue-collar working class river making its way through a rugged yet beautiful landscape. In Paris, gentle folk sit on the banks of the Seine and contemplate its splendor while sipping Chardonnay. Along the Ohio River, working men and women toast the river with a Rolling Rock beer and comment to one another about what an amazing badass, hard-working river this is! This is the namesake river for this state—the river that the Iroquois called Ohiiyo—Good River!

This 450-mile ride is a fantastic tour along the mighty Ohio, from the border with Pennsylvania in the northeast to its departure from Ohio as it continues its journey to the Mississippi in the far southwest. Get ready for a very pleasant two-day ride, but honestly, there is so much history along this road and so very much to see and experience all along the route, that it's even better to make it a three- or four-day excursion.

The tour starts at the east end on Ohio State Route 39 at the Pennsylvania border. This border is important because it separates the old from the new in our

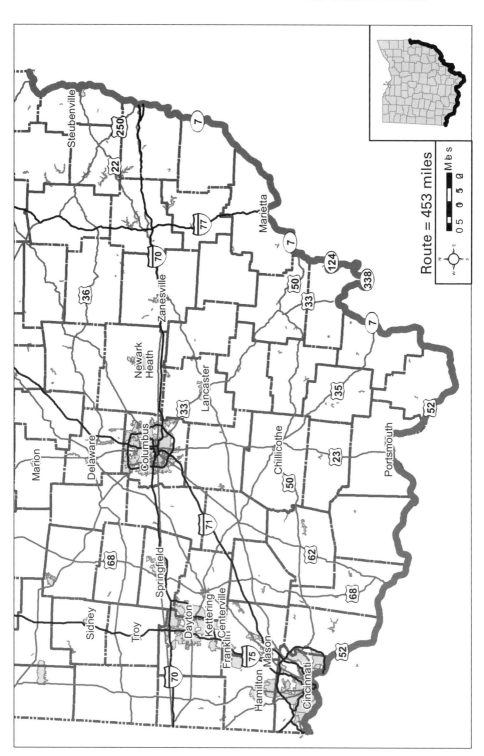

Route = 453 miles

Old Fort Steuben is named after Friedrich Wilhelm von Steuben, a Prussion officer who aided the Americans in the War of Independence.

nation's history and it divides the east from the west—the land that had been a British colony for generations and an upstart region won by wars and the grit of settlers and soldiers. While these lines have been blurred by the passage of time, the historical significance of this border will always be a reality.

State Route 39 will take us into East Liverpool (*aka* America's Crockery City, home of America's ceramics industry from 1840 to 1930), where it is joined by US30. After a short ride through town, we turn west onto Ohio Route 7 and our journey begins in earnest. It doesn't take long for some very interesting scenery to appear. Just south of East Liverpool the road is cut into hills resulting in towering cliffs on the inland side and, of course, the river itself hugging the east side of the road. Once beyond East Liverpool, Route 7 becomes a pleasant roadway as it travels through various small river towns. You get quite a patchwork effect while following the river. One minute you will be surrounded by beauty, with the river on one side and marvelous hills and bedrock cliffs on the other, and then around a curve will be a large power plant or steel mill. The towns along the river all seem congested. I guess when you have only a small amount of flat land between the water and the cliffs you have to squeeze everything into a small space. The first large town encountered is Steubenville—the City of Murals and birthplace of Dino Paul Crocetti—better known to most folks as crooner and comedian Dean Martin. It's certainly worth a ride through downtown to see twenty-five murals

	THE GREAT RIVER ROAD 453 MILES	
Miles	**Destination**	**Total**
0	Pennsylvania Border	0
27	Steubenville	27
22	Martin's Ferry	49
49	Fly/Sisterville Ferry	98
33	Marietta	131
14	Belpre	145
32	Buffington Island	177
35	Middleport	212
64	South Point	276
12	Ironton	288
26	Portsmouth	314
42	Manchester	356
46	Moscow	402
51	Shawnee Lookout Park	453

painted on various buildings. Each mural tells the story of an important event in this historic city. A stop at Old Fort Steuben is also recommended. Construction began on the fort in 1786 when the Continental Congress sent the First American Regiment to the Ohio frontier to guard surveyors as they began mapping the newly won lands west of the river. The Native Americans living and hunting on these lands weren't the least bit happy to see this turn of events, which resulted in settlers beginning to pour across the border, and expressed their displeasure in hostile acts aimed at settlers and surveyors alike. The fort was named in honor of Friedrich Wilhelm von Steuben, a Prussian officer who aided the American cause in the recently ended war of independence.

One of the more amazing sights in Steubenville is to look across the river at the very impressive bare rock cliffs that line the river on the West Virginia side of the river.

Down the road a bit, past Bridgeport and the National Road, is the small town of Bellaire. If you're ready for lunch, a great place to eat would be at the Union Street Station, a depot transformed into a restaurant with a train theme. While in

Bellaire, be certain to admire the fabulous Stone Bridge/B&O railroad viaduct. This amazing piece of work was built between 1867 and 1871 largely by Irish stonemasons, and its forty-three stone arches span one and a half curving miles leading to a bridge across the river!

About ten miles south of Bellaire, Route 7 becomes more scenic and enjoyable as you travel through lightly developed countryside. Less than thirty miles from Bellaire, you will encounter the small town of Hannibal and the Hannibal locks and dam. This is a great place to stop and explore the navigation system on the river by means of a viewing platform and visitor center at the locks. Mighty impressive!

Hannibal's Kiedaish Point Park—an overlook that perches seven hundred feet above the river valley—provides for an absolutely fabulous view of the river and the broad valley it has carved over the millennia.

Upon leaving Hannibal, kick back and relax as you ride along with the river on one side and the Wayne National Forest on the other. At the village of Fly, you may want to stop briefly to consider that the Fly–Sistersville Ferry has been carrying people and freight across the river at that spot since 1817. You will no doubt notice the ferry fighting the mighty Ohio River current as it struggles to reach the opposite shore.

Marietta is next on the menu and a highly recommended stop. Marietta was founded in 1788 and named in honor of Marie Antoinette, then the sitting queen of France. Marietta is filled with history—from the haunting ancient Native American Conus Mound in Mound Cemetery to its historic district, where fifty-three historic sites are to be found on a walking tour. Interestingly, more Revolutionary War officers are buried in Marietta than anywhere else in the country.[1] Marietta is also home to Campus Martius, site of the Northwest Territory Museum, and the nearby Ohio River Museum, where the only surviving steam powered sternwheeler towboat, the *W. P. Snyder*, is located. Campus Martius had its beginnings as a stockade built in 1788 to protect the seat of government of the Northwest Territory as well as to protect settlers who were starting to arrive in the new town. By 1795, it was no longer needed. Call 740-373-3750 for more information and museum hours. These two recommended stops are located off SR7 at the point where the highway bridge crosses the Muskingum River.

Marietta boasts of a footnote in history as being the first city in the Northwest Territory. Well, this is technically true, since it was formed just one year after the Northwest Ordinance of 1787 by which congress created the Northwest Territory. Prior to that, sovereignty of the land upon which the city stands was claimed by

---

[1] *Land of Promise: The Story of the Northwest Territory*, Walter Havighurst © 1946, The Macmillan Company, New York.

France and Great Britain, not forgetting the claim of Native Americans who possessed the land for millennia. Three other cities located in what was to become the Northwest Territory—Detroit, St. Ignace, and Sault Ste. Marie all predate Marietta by a hundred years or more, and Vincennes, Indiana, by over fifty years. Not to diminish Marietta's importance, it did serve as the first capital of the Northwest Territory from which Governor Arthur St. Clair presided over this vast new part of the nation during a period of great danger and upheaval on the frontier.

While driving through Marietta, Route 7 joins company with SR60 for a short time. When heading north through town on 7/60 I recommend a very short side trip to view what is locally called The Castle. This beautiful Victorian-era home is open for tours during the summer months, but it is fun to just ride by and admire the wonderful architecture and style of this stately home. Turn right on Scammel Street and go two blocks to Fourth Street. The Castle is on Fourth Street just north of Scammel.

A more time-consuming attraction in Marietta is the *Valley Gem* sternwheeler riverboat. Take an old-fashioned riverboat trip down the Ohio River to see it up close. Call 740-373-7862 for reservations. They operate Monday through Saturday.

Marietta really is a fabulous place to visit, but sooner or later, we do have to continue with the trip. When you're ready to move on, continue southwest on Ohio Route 7 to the town of Belpre. Just as you enter town, SR7 will make a ninety-degree turn west and US50 will be straight ahead—take US50 south and just before crossing the bridge to West Virginia, you will see SR618 (Washington Boulevard) going west along the shoreline. This is the road you want, not

Treat yourself to a ride on the Valley Gem *steamwheeler in Marietta.*

only because it hugs the shore but because it also takes you past Blennerhassett Island Historic Park—an island in the river that stands in tragic testimony to what lengths some folks will go when tempted by greed, power, and ambition.

Harman Blennerhassett was a wealthy aristocrat who had a mansion built on this wilderness island in 1798. No expense was spared. Try to imagine bringing the finest furniture, oil paintings, carvings, silver doors, French porcelain, and all the supplies and craftsmen necessary to build such a mansion down the Ohio River on flat boats—this in an area where settlers were being massacred and conditions for the vast majority of people bordered on bare survival.

With a beautiful wife and a house filled with servants, most of us would say that Mr. B had it made. A chance meeting with Aaron Burr—who is perhaps most famous for killing Alexander Hamilton in a duel—abruptly changed Blennerhassett's idyllic lifestyle.

Unfortunately, Blennerhassett got caught up in Burr's territorial ambitions and joined him in a scheme to possess an empire of their own comprising what is now Texas and other parts of the southwest. Burr and Blennerhassett conspired to create a country of their own west of the Mississippi, but when President Jefferson caught wind of the conspiracy, he ordered the men arrested for treason. Blennerhassett fled to the very western lands he had hoped to rule some day, but he was captured nonetheless. He served a spell in a Virginia prison and, upon release, his Camelot-like life was ruined. The mansion had flooded while he was gone and then burned to the ground in 1811. It has been beautifully restored based on what could still be found of the foundation and other evidence of its original size and shape.

The park is actually on the West Virginia side of the river but can be viewed from the Ohio shore. It is easily accessible by taking US50 across the river in Belpre.

For railroading buffs, there is a caboose museum in Belpre that might be of interest. It is open by appointment only, so call 740-423-8767 if you're interested. When you've seen all you want to see in Belpre, proceed west on SR618, which joins SR7/US50 just west of the Island. We'll follow 7/50 for just a couple of miles, at which point we leave it again to follow the river as Routes 7 and 50 head inland. Just prior to entering the small town of Little Hocking, SR124 will angle off to the left—that's the road you want. SR124 will follow the river about as closely as you can (without getting water in your gas) through the small towns of Hockingport, Reedsville, and finally the tiny town of Portland. This stretch of 124 is just great. It is often right on the water's edge with high cliffs of rock equally close on the opposite side. There are occasional caution signs in this stretch that warn of rough pavement. They're not referring to the traditional pothole variety of roughness, rather the kind that occurs on many of southern Ohio's roads when the land under the road slips downhill.

The tiny town of Portland is where the Battle of Buffington Island was fought (the battle itself wasn't actually fought on the island, but rather on the Ohio shore of the river). This is the only location of a major Civil War battle on Ohio soil. A four-acre park preserves a small portion of the battlefield, and two monuments honor the event. One of the memorials is in memory of Daniel McCook, a lawyer from Carrollton, Ohio, who died in the battle. The story of "The Fighting McCooks" is an incredible one. In addition to Daniel and his eight sons, Daniel's brother, John, and his five sons all fought for the Union. Three of Daniel McCook's sons were killed. Now there's a family that stood for something! An impressive Conus Indian Mound is also in this park.

Shortly after leaving Portland, SR124 turns inland but SR338 goes straight ahead along the river, so we just keep heading south following the water. After tag teaming the river, SR338 eventually turns back north and meets Route 124 again in the town of Racine. At the south end of a peninsula formed by the curving river, the landscape changes greatly. There is a large, fertile flood plain in this area where specialty crops, such as tomatoes and other vegetables, are grown. It is also an area of large gravel mining operations.

Follow SR124 all the way to the city of Pomeroy, where Ohio Route 7 reappears. State Route 7 actually skirts Pomeroy to the north, so we want the Route 7 Bypass that tightly follows the shoreline through town. Take a few minutes in Pomeroy to see the Meigs County Courthouse. This impressive structure is made even more unique because it is built into the side of a cliff, making all three stories accessible from ground level. Pomeroy is typical of several river towns that

Two of the murals found in Portsmouth.

have struggled economically ever since King Coal was dethroned by mines in West Virginia and Wyoming. Ohio's high-sulfur coal lost favor in the late 1900s due to high pollution emissions when burned. Pomeroy is undergoing revitalization, and like many towns along the river, it is capitalizing on its waterfront location for its resurgence.

The Route 7 Bypass follows the riverfront through Pomeroy and Middleport, joining up with SR7 a couple of miles west of Middleport. We continue to follow Route 7 through Cheshire and Addison, then through the busy US35 intersection and on into Gallipolis—our next stop. The City of the Gauls was settled in 1790 by a large group of French settlers. The late eighteenth century was a period of great unrest and danger in France. The French Revolution was just in its early stages, making it a dangerous place to live, especially for aristocrats and the educated class. This fact, plus highly exaggerated stories and claims by unscrupulous land developers, led a number of French to invest in land on the Ohio River. Upon arrival, the immigrants found the land deeds worthless. Congress eventually helped them acquire land, and the next battle for these urban French was facing the harsh and alien conditions in the wilderness in a place that was named in honor of their home country. Over time, Gallipolis has lost its French flavor. With so many travelers and settlers using the Ohio River as the major highway for that part of the country, it was only natural that a broad mix of people would settle where a town already existed, thus diluting its once unique character. An interesting stop in Gallipolis is the Our House Museum. It was built in 1819 as a tavern and served that purpose for many decades. The three-story brick building is located at First Avenue and State Street in town. A nice park on the river can be found at the south end of town. Gallipolis is a fun place to visit July Fourth when the Gallipolis River Recreation Festival celebrates the holiday with four days of fun and games in the city park. It has been going on for over forty years and always ends with an amazing fireworks show.

Upon leaving Gallipolis, follow SR7 as it winds through a lightly developed area with the river on one side and Wayne National Forest on the other. It makes for very enjoyable motorcycling and sightseeing. Across the river from the large West Virginia city of Huntington, some congestion is encountered again, and at this point we'll pick up US52—our host for the next portion of the trip. Route 52 is a four-lane highway at this point and is easy sailing.

This road will steer us northwest to Ironton, at one time the pig iron capital of the world. Early Welsh immigrants to this area found many minerals that were easily mined, including coal and iron ore. Ironton was a company town formed by the Ohio Iron and Coal Company in 1848. It grew very rapidly, and from 1850 to the 1870s it was the center of the iron mining and steel production region. Many charcoal blast furnaces dotted the countryside, and remnants of many still remain. This region of south central Ohio and northern Kentucky is known as the Hanging Rock Region—named after a high sandstone bluff on the river just west of Ironton—where easily mined iron ore was abundant. Several of the palatial homes built by men who became very rich during the iron and coal heyday still remain in town. A number of large (fourteen by forty feet) murals, painted between 1991 and 2002 on various city buildings, also grace the Ironton cityscape. I recommend getting off the main highway to take Business 52 through Ironton. This is the best way to see the town and the river. Since it also takes you past

Frog Town USA, a favorite biker restaurant and tavern on Business 52 just east of downtown Ironton, you certainly can't pass it up.

Portsmouth, a city of 21,000 people located at the juncture of the Scioto and Ohio Rivers, is the next large town on the route. One of Portsmouth's most notable attractions are the murals depicting two thousand years of history that are painted on two thousand feet of twenty-foot high floodwall. It's an amazing sight! One of the murals includes a very nice motorcycle scene, including an inset painting of the 1913 Portsmouth Motorcycle Club. To get to the murals, follow the signs for south US23. Mural signs will direct you the rest of the way. Upon leaving the west end of the murals, you find the Portsmouth Brewing Company restaurant. It's in an old red brick building and is a very popular brewpub and eatery.

Portsmouth was also the site of a Uranium Enrichment Plant that had both military and civilian uses while it operated from 1952 to 2001—not something every town can claim as part of its pedigree. There are two Hopewell Indian Mounds in Portsmouth. One—the Tremper Mound—is a couple of miles north off of SR104, but the other is just three blocks north of US52, about three quarters of a mile east of US23. Before you reach US23 in Portsmouth, watch for Hutchins Street and take it north off US52 to Mound Park. When you think of Indians, you might also think of Roy Rogers. Portsmouth was hometown to this Western hero, and a museum, open by appointment only, houses memorabilia about this TV and movie star and his famous horse Trigger. Call 740-353-0900 in advance if you're interested in a tour.

The Portsmouth area is fairly congested for a small city, with US52 and US23 intersecting there as well as two busy bridges over the river. However, once past the local congestion, US52 turns into a very nice ride west of the Scioto River where it passes just south of the Shawnee State Forest. In fact, it's a very nice ride all the way from Portsmouth to Cincinnati, with mile after mile of open space, forest-covered hills, and frequent views of the river.

About midway between Portsmouth and Cincinnati, there are three small historic towns. The first is Manchester—the first town incorporated in the Virginia Military District. A little farther west on Route 52 is Aberdeen—the southern terminus of Zane's Trace, the trail built through the Ohio wilderness in the 1790s from Wheeling, West Virginia.

The other historic town is Ripley. Literally the dividing line between slave and free states, the Ohio River witnessed the human struggle for freedom up close and personal. Southern Ohio was the front line for the abolitionists, and Ripley was a well-known point on the Underground Railroad for escaping slaves. Many residents took an active role in making the Underground Railroad work. One man who did more than most was the Reverend John Rankin, whose house

The Rankin House in Ripley was a safe haven for slaves escaping the South.

atop Liberty Hill was a safe haven for many of the two thousand fugitive slaves who escaped through Ripley. The Rankin House, built in 1825 by the Reverend, is today a National Historic Landmark and is open for tours. It is located in the northwest portion of Ripley just off US52. A sign points the way. Rankin House sits on the highest point of land around, and it's a fun ride on a bike up to the house, as if you needed any more reason to go see it. The nearby Signal House, where Reverend Rankin signaled waiting slaves to let them know the way was clear, is now a bed and breakfast.

There are several locations along the Ohio River where Indian Mounds are present, so watch for the signs. One such site is in Stivers Memorial Park in Ripley and another—the Eddington Mound—is near Chilo alongside the highway.

Proceeding west, you will pass the beginning of the Bullskin Trace (roughly, today's SR133). Near Chilo, there are two interesting stops where you can learn a great deal about the river's locks and dam systems. The first is at the Lock 34 Museum and Park, and just down the road are the massive Meldahl locks—they're very impressive structures! A bit farther west, you will cross the Grant Memorial Bridge. Immediately across the bridge, you will see the U.S. Grant birthplace and museum in Point Pleasant.

Continuing on US52 takes you right into downtown Cincinnati where it seamlessly joins up with US50, which is the road you'll take along the river west of Cincinnati. In downtown, US50 turns into a limited access highway for a stretch through the stadium district and leaves the west side of Cincinnati as River Road. It's a nice enough ride along the river between Cincinnati and the state line, quite obviously getting better the farther west you go. (The first couple miles on the west side of Cincinnati are the worst, but they are quickly put behind you.) The road is in good shape west of Cincinnati and makes for a nice ride. All along the

Grant Memorial Bridge near Chilo.

river, you are reminded that the Ohio is a river that earns its way by working hard. It's not a dainty or delicate stream!

Just west of Addyston US50 takes a sharp turn north. Immediately before this turn, you will see a sign for the William Henry Harrison Monument, with Miami Road angling to the right. Take this turn and almost immediately, you will see the large monument for President Harrison. Continue up that road just a short distance to Brower Road, taking it a very short distance to Cliff Road—which is the one you want. Cliff Road very closely follows the river from atop a high, curving bluff, providing magnificent views. Take Cliff Road west to Dugans Gap Road, turning right. Follow Dugans Gap as it winds around and eventually ends at Lawrenceburg Road, where a left turn will take you to Shawnee Lookout County Park. It is in this beautiful, 1,156-acre park on the majestic Ohio River that we will end our trip. Enjoy some time in the park exploring the several historical displays and Indian Mounds in their natural setting. I recommend that you take the walking trail to Miami Fort, located in the far southwest corner of the park at the confluence of the Great Miami and Ohio Rivers. You can't miss it—just keep the five massive power plant stacks in sight as you work your way west. Miami Fort is a fascinating collection of Native American burial mounds, earthworks, habitation sites, and earthen fort. The earthworks encloses twelve acres and is perched high on a bluff overlooking the Ohio River. Once you've seen it, it's easy to understand why the natives chose this location for their amazing structure.

One of the historical buildings located in Shawnee Lookout County Park

Shawnee Lookout Park is a microcosm of the fantastic attractions and history to be found all along this river highway. In fact, the curving and hilly roads in the last few scenic miles of the trip also serve as an example of the great riding to be had all along the mighty Ohio River.

The Lake Erie Circle Tour

BEING SITUATED on Lake Erie is a defining reality for Ohio. The lake contributes immeasurably to the state's culture, history, and economy, and brings the world to Ohio's doorstep. Lake Erie offers endless opportunities for recreation and relaxation along its miles of sandy beaches and maritime vistas. Every Ohioan should celebrate Lake Erie and cherish its many contributions to Ohio's quality of life. I believe that the best way to appreciate the fabulous history and attractions along Lake Erie is to take a trip completely around it. Depending on your itinerary, this tour could easily take three to five days. You could do it in less time, but you would miss out on so much by not stopping at and exploring the many attractions that line the shore.

The Ohio portion of this trip has been designated as the Lake Erie Coastal Ohio Scenic Byway because of the historic and scenic value of the lakeshore route. Many people make the assumption that Ohio's Lake Erie shoreline roads are simply uninteresting and busy highways through large cities, but you should not do the same. The roads that make up this byway are enjoyable motorcycling roads and are lined with many nice attractions.

Let's start the trip in Toledo, located at the mouth of the Maumee River, which just happens to be the largest river draining into Lake Erie. The Maumee River is also steeped in history, and the mouth of the river at present-day Toledo is not only a major Great Lakes (and thus international) port, it also played a major role in the development of Ohio and the Northwest Territory. When in Toledo, take the time to head southwest a few miles along the Maumee River to visit the Fort Meigs site and the Battle of Fallen Timbers Park. These two places had a major impact on the history of the Great Lakes region. Their importance and the brave deeds played out here need to be appreciated and remembered. (Of course, if you take the "On The Trail of Mad Anthony" tour described elsewhere in this book, you'll visit both of these attractions and many more that concern the history and attractions of this corner of the state).

Toledo is a large city of about 325,000 people (over 600,000 in the metropolitan area) and is a major center of trade and manufacturing. The city was first settled in 1817, known then as Port Lawrence, and incorporated in 1833. The Founding Fathers named it after Toledo, Spain—though nobody is quite sure

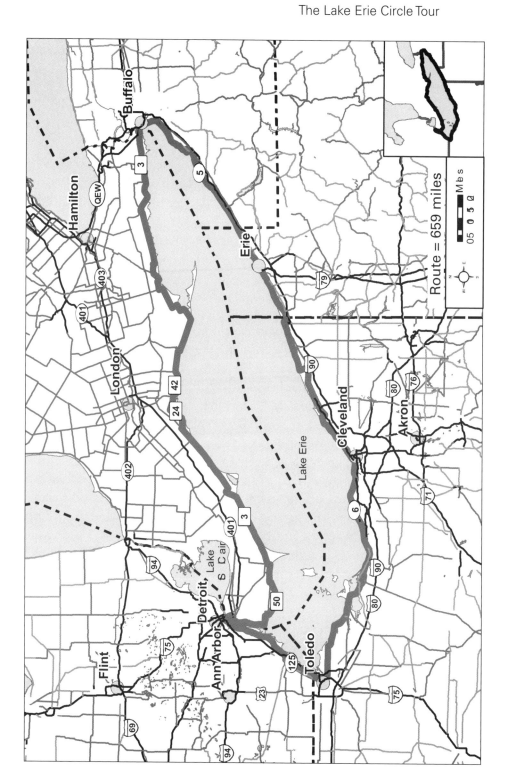

Route = 659 miles

Lake Erie

Lake St. Clair

Buffalo
Hamilton
QEW
3
5
403
401
London
Erie
79
42
24
90
Cleveland
80
76
Akron
402
71
3
401
6
94
Flint
75
Lake St. Clair
Detroit
50
90
Ann Arbor
125
Toledo
80
23
69
94
75

Miles
05 0 50

why. While 1817 may seem a bit late as far as settlement in this region is concerned, there is a reason. The great Black Swamp covered all of northern Ohio from Lake Erie south and southwest. This swamp made travel and exploration so difficult that the area was avoided by settlers, who had plenty of higher and drier land nearby. In fact, in 1803 when Ohio became a state, the area around present-day Toledo was essentially unexplored. Even Native Americans hadn't been real active in this area, and the Northwest Indian Wars and the later War of 1812 were the only significant excursions into the area until settlers finally began arriving around 1820, when the swamp was drained.

Toledo may have a reputation as an industrial city short on attractions and sophistication, but that's just not the case. Take the time to explore this city and you will be pleasantly surprised. There are many attractions, fine restaurants, museums, parks, and things to do in this area.

Toledo is crazy about its minor league baseball team—the Toledo Mud Hens—and their new stadium is a wonderful place to watch a game. Touring the SS *William B. Boyer* museum ship near the river mouth is very interesting, and as long as you're on the water, take a cruise on the *Sandpiper*—a canal boat that will take you on a very enjoyable cruise down the river to the lake. Downtown Toledo has many fine restaurants that make for memorable dining experiences. The Maumee Bay Brewing Company, located in the historic Oliver House building downtown, is such a place. It is a microbrewery in a historic district with a mix of good food and a fun atmosphere.

Unfortunately, heading north between Toledo and Monroe, Michigan leaves a person high and dry as there aren't any good coastal roads that connect the two cities. There are local roads, of course, but no single highway that runs the whole distance on the waterfront. This means that a person must take inland roads, such as I-75 (boring!), or one of the nearby parallel roads. I recommend taking the Dixie Highway, which is Route 125 in Michigan and Detroit Avenue in Toledo. This road has lots of history, and prior to I-75 it was *the* highway that got travelers from cities such as Toledo and Detroit to Florida. It will take you to Monroe and then turn east nearer the water as it proceeds north beyond Monroe. Just after crossing the River Raisin in Monroe, the Dixie makes a one-mile jog to the east along the north shore of the river as State Route 50, and then turns northeast again along the coastline.

The City of Monroe has a long history, having its start in 1780. It also has a strong French flavor, and until 1817, it was called Frenchtown. It may be most famous for being the home of George Custer, renowned General of the Civil War and, of course, remembered mostly for his demise and that of his Seventh Cavalry by the Sioux at the battle of the Little Bighorn. There is a General Custer exhibit

THE LAKE ERIE CIRCLE TOUR 659 MILES		
Miles	**Destination**	**Total**
0	Toledo	0
24	Monroe	24
35	Ambassador Bridge	59
18	Amherstburg	77
35	Leamington	112
5	Point Pelee Provincial Park	117
38	Blenheim	155
36	Wallacetown	191
42	Port Burwell	233
21	Port Rowan	254
23	Port Dover	277
33	Dunnville	310
23	Port Colborne	333
19	Buffalo/Peace Bridge	352
14	Old Lakeshore Road	366
60	Pennsylvania State Line	426
19	Erie	445
44	Ashtabula	489
10	Geneva State Park	499
47	Cleveland	546
40	Vermillion	586
21	Sandusky	607
52	Toledo	659

in the Monroe County Historical Museum that follows the famous General's life from his birth in Ohio through his abbreviated military career. The museum is easily accessible on Dixie Highway / Monroe Street just south of the river. An impressive statue showing the general atop his horse is located on the bank of the River Raisin in town.

A nearly forgotten fact about Monroe and the River Raisin, which runs through town, is that the British and their Canadian allies fought hard after the Revolutionary War to make this river the northern boundary of the new United States. As such, it would have guaranteed control over the upper Great Lakes. The US of A would look very different today had they succeeded. As it was, the British didn't pull out of Detroit and other Michigan Territory forts until thirteen years after they had lost the war. Had we lost the War of 1812, quite possibly everything north of Monroe would now be Canada!

Monroe's long and interesting history is due to its location on the water highway used by the very earliest explorers. Before Frenchtown was established at this site, there were skirmishes involving the French, British, and native tribes for a hundred years. Frenchtown was the site of one of the principal battles in the War of 1812. In what was called the River Raisin Massacre, only thirty-three of nine hundred thirty-four soldiers escaped death or capture in January 1813. This was the largest battle ever fought on Michigan soil. The day after the battle a massacre of wounded and captured soldiers, mostly Kentucky volunteers, took place which enraged the Americans and energized them to fight all the harder. "Remember the River Raisin" became a rallying cry for American soldiers during the remainder of the War. This event actually helped turn the tide of the war, causing the Americans to fight all the harder under the "Remember the River Raisin" mantra, just like "Remember the Alamo" served the same rallying purpose a generation later. A lonely stone obelisk in a vacant lot is all that marks the location today. The River Raisin Battlefield museum can be found at 1403 Elm Street in Monroe.

If you were looking for someplace that offers a good plateful of cooked muskrat (more elegantly known as marsh beef) but didn't want to drive all the way to Louisiana, you've found the place. Eating muskrat has been a tradition for nearly two hundred years in Monroe. Muskrat as cuisine got its start during the War of 1812 when Frenchtown inhabitants were starving. Had it not been for this ubiquitous *Ondatra* providing a source of food, many people would have died of starvation. While it has become difficult to find it in restaurants due to state health regulations, it is still a staple of local barbecues, feasts, and civic celebrations.

Saying *au revoir* to Frenchtown we continue our tour north on the historic Dixie Highway. Because the Dixie is now replaced by I-75, it carries less traffic than it did in the past. Crossing over the Huron River and into Wayne County,

Dixie Highway becomes River Road and then Jefferson Avenue. It follows the Detroit River shoreline very closely all the way to the Ambassador Bridge, where we cross into Canada.

There are a number of small parks along the entire stretch that allow access to the river itself, with its impressive vistas of strong currents, islands, and ocean-going ships heading up and down the waterway. This river now also supports a world-class fishery, thanks to efforts of many in both the public and private sectors who cleaned the river up from its industrial sewer status of fifty years ago to the vibrant and attractive waterway it is today. Only thirty-five years ago, Lake Erie was declared dead. It was little more than a huge cesspool largely unfit for swimming or recreational use. Thanks to a great deal of work, enforcement of environmental laws, and a major financial investment by all involved, the lake is greatly improved. The economic boost that a healthy Detroit River and Lake Erie has brought to northern Ohio and southeast Michigan is immeasurable.

The last few miles of the ride up Jefferson Avenue are an eye-opener. This stretch of road is definitely not the usual byway sought out by motorcyclists, but it isn't very long and it is worth seeing. You will pass by huge industrial complexes in places like Ecorse, River Rouge, and Zug Island that served as the manufacturing backbone of our economy for many decades. Huge factories and steel mills—both active and abandoned—line the road and waterway in this stretch. It's the kind of place not a lot of people see but is critical to our economic well-being. The hard part is ensuring that we have the industrial infrastructure necessary for our modern economy while at the same time making sure that our quality of life and environment aren't harmed. It's a delicate and expensive balancing act to be sure. There are few places where the economic and environmental tug of war has taken place to the degree it has on the lower Detroit River.

Just up the road from Ecorse and River Rouge, you'll see the massive Fort Wayne complex on the east side of the street. Fort Wayne has unfortunately fallen into disrepair, but it has a long and interesting history. The fort was built in 1854 on what is the narrowest stretch of river in that area because of serious border tensions with British Canada. Fort Wayne was to have the latest in artillery to defend shipping lanes and be capable of reaching the opposite shore. The fort was named after General Anthony Wayne.

The fort was fortunately never used in combat, but it did serve as an induction center for every war from the Civil War to Vietnam. Several original buildings at the fort still survive. I still have vivid memories of standing in one long line after another at Fort Wayne on a hot July day in my youth, completing my pre-induction physical.

At this point, just follow the signs to the Ambassador Bridge and head south to Windsor, Ontario. Yes, that's right, south. Detroit is the only border crossing point in the nation where you travel south to get to Canada. The Detroit River turns in an east / west alignment at this point, with Windsor situated on the south shore. The Ambassador Bridge is unique in several ways. First, it is the busiest international crossing point in North America, and second, it is privately owned. One might assume that an international bridge would be a government-owned piece of infrastructure, but that's not the case. The Bridge was built with private funds in 1929 and is jointly operated by The Detroit International Bridge Company and The Canadian Transit Company. Over one-quarter of all Canadian / US trade occurs over the Ambassador Bridge.

Detroit and Windsor share a very close relationship. They are sister cities in many ways, with common links involving families, economics, sports, and recreational activities.

The Windsor area, like Detroit, is also steeped in history. As one might expect, it has a more decidedly British flavor and is graced with beautiful gardens and parks along the riverfront. It has also become famous for its casinos. While in Windsor check out the plaque and small park dedicated to the 1838 Patriot War in which a Michigan militia of Irish descent invaded Ontario, in conjunction with Canadian rebels, in an effort to wrest the southwest peninsula of Ontario from British control. Of course, it was a failed effort but is another interesting chapter in the joint histories of the US and Canada.

Crossing the Bridge will put you on Ontario Route 3, so just stay on it until its junction with Ontario Route 20 / 18, on which you'll start south along the east coast of the Detroit River. Route 20 will initially be Ojibway Parkway and later turn into Front Street for much of its length south to Amherstburg. Going south along the east shore is a bit like downriver Detroit—it is where a good deal of Ontario's chemical industry is located thanks to underground salt deposits.

Fort Malden National Historic Site in Amherstburg is a reconstructed fort, originally built by the British prior to the War of 1812 but abandoned by them in 1813 and occupied by American forces for two years during that war. A restored 1819 brick barracks, earthworks from the 1840s, and various other buildings are preserved at the site. As with other Canadian forts, it tells the other side of the story. This fort, which was built twenty years after the original Fort Amherstburg just south of here at the mouth of the Detroit River, was intended to defend the interests of British North America. The original Fort Amherstburg was a major British base during the War of 1812. It's fascinating to go back two hundred years when the open and welcoming border between our two nations that we all take for granted wasn't the case.

Shortly after passing through Amherstburg, Ontario 20 swings eastward, and shortly after that, you will encounter CR50 heading south to the lake. Take CR50 and follow it along the shoreline all the way to the town of Kingsville, where Ontario 20 rejoins it. Continue east until you reach Leamington and Point Pelee Provincial Park. If you wish, you can spend time in the park and walk to the southernmost point of land on the Canadian mainland. (Fish Point on Pelee Island in Lake Erie is the southernmost point of Canada.) Point Pelee is very renowned for birding during the spring and fall migrations. A few miles west of Leamington, the provincial road makes a ninety-degree turn north, but we'll just stay on County Road 20 straight east to Leamington. When you see the Pelee Island ferry on your right, you'll be at Erie Street—turn north and take this

Port Burwell Lighthouse

into Leamington and Provincial Route 3, once again heading east on 3. Ontario Route 3 will be your host for about eighty miles to the small town of Wallacetown. In between Leamington and Wallacetown, there are many attractions. You may be surprised at how lightly the north shore of Lake Erie is developed in this region— it certainly makes for very pleasant and enjoyable riding with light traffic and good roads. This is a region of agricultural specialty crops, and fields of tomatoes and other vegetables are common. This is also Canada's tobacco-growing region. Many fine vineyards have also developed in this southwest peninsula. Canada has many wonderful people, places, and attractions but is lacking in sunny southern resorts. This is Canada's south coast!

In Wallacetown you will turn south on County Road 8 to Route 16, which will take you to Route 20, a one-mile jog south on CR22 just northeast of Port Stanley, and then continue east on CR24. The route numbers change occasionally, but if you just stay on the road that follows the coastline the most closely, you'll be all right. Route 24 will take you along the coast to Route 42. This stretch of road from

Wallacetown east to Port Rowan takes you past four Ontario Provincial Parks that are located on the lakeshore. Other attractions include the Port Burwell light-house and many small parks located in the villages that are located on the shore. You will find yourself on OR73 for a few miles near the Port Bruce Provincial Park but don't pay it any mind—you want to continue east on CR42 when Ontario 73 turns north.

In Port Rowan, CR42 turns north two miles and then turns east again. After three miles turn left on CR16 for two and a half miles and turn right on provincial Route 24. Take Route 24 eleven miles and after it turns northward, Ontario Route 6 will turn east taking you to Port Dover.

Follow Route 6 east out of Port Dover to Rural Route 3 (Dover–Dunville Road) and follow this road all the way through the town of Dunville. Please note that in Dunville, RR3 joins provincial Route 3 for a mile or so. Provincial 3 veers northeast on the east side of Dunville. You want to stay on RR3, which is Taylor Side Road, and then Main Road on the east side of Dunville. Rural Route 3 heads southeast where OR3 turns northeast. We want RR3, which will continue along the shoreline (known as Lakeshore Road in the stretch east of Dunville) and, after twenty-two miles, will deliver you back to Ontario Route 3 in Port Colborne (where the Welland Canal enters Lake Erie after bisecting the Niagara Peninsula from Lake Ontario). Once back on Provincial Route 3 follow it to Fort Erie, where you will cross the Niagara River to Buffalo, NY.

Fort Erie, Ontario, is a nice place to take a break and discover a little about Ontario history and learn more about our own history at the same time. The Old Fort Erie—another major War of 1812 site—is an interesting place to visit, especially for Americans. It provides a glimpse into the Canadian and British side of that war. Two American warships were captured at Fort Erie (the *Ohio* and *Somers*). Lake Erie, of course, played a very significant part in the war with Commodore Oliver Perry's crucial victory against the British in a fierce naval battle on the lake in an attempt to free Detroit and Lake Erie from British control.

The nearby Ridgeway Battlefield Museum also describes a fascinating period of history from the Canadian perspective, which most Americans probably aren't aware of. In 1866, a group of Irish-American Civil War veterans (the Fenian Brotherhood) invaded British North America (now Canada) in an attempt to obtain freedom for Ireland. Obviously, it was a doomed attempt, but it is an example of the continuing animosity between the British and Americans during that time period, and of course, it shows that the British/Irish issue has been stewing for a very long time. There were several other excursions into what was to become Canada during that period, all of which had the effect of speeding up the process of confederating Canada as a nation to preserve its territorial integrity.

After crossing over the Peace Bridge into Buffalo, follow I-190 / Route 5 south out of town. Of course, if you wish, this is the time to take I-190 north to Niagara Falls for a hectic but always impressive trip to this mighty cataract on the Niagara River connecting Lakes Erie and Ontario.

Continuing south on the tour, after just two miles, I-190 will head east and Route 5 turns southwest along the shoreline taking you all the way to Ohio. Take Route 5 for twelve miles to the Wanaka Country Club, where you'll see Old Lakeshore Road quartering off to your right front. This road hugs the shoreline for fifteen miles while Route 5 goes inland in this stretch. Just after riding through Evangola State Park, you'll see Lotus Point Road—turn left and take it the short distance back to Route 5 and head west / right again.

Very shortly after getting back on Route 5, it will join company with US20 for a short distance, then 20 parts company temporarily. Stay on Route 5 and follow it through Erie, where the road takes a one-half mile jog to the south and then continues west.

Erie is an interesting city with a number of museums, lighthouses, parks, and monuments—including the Commodore Perry monument—that are of interest. It's a good place to do a little wandering on the shoreline.

Continue west on Route 5 until just before the Ohio border where Route 5 joins US20. Stay on 20 for just a few miles until Conneaut, Ohio, where you'll get on Route 7 (Mill Street) going north to Ohio State Route 531. The stretch of coastline between Conneaut and Ashtabula is the least developed shoreline on all of Lake Erie in Ohio. The road follows a high bluff overlooking the lake and traverses through

Fairport Harbor Lighthouse

an area where there is still a lot of wooded land. The lake is almost always visible. State Route 531 will take you to Ashtabula with its bustling harbor and the Great Lakes Marine and US Coast Guard Museum. It is located at 1071 Walnut Drive in Ashtabula. Continue on to Geneva State Park where Route 531 meets State Route 534 and turns south to US20 at the town of Geneva (birthplace of Ransom E. Olds—inventor of the venerable Oldsmobile with its Rocket V8). Stay westbound on US20 roughly 14 miles and just east of Painesville where Ohio Route 2 angles off to the right.

If you have an interest in marine artifacts and would like to climb a historic lighthouse to get a fantastic view of Lake Erie and the mouth of the Grand River, take the Painesville exit off US2. Head north on Richmond Street, which then becomes High Street and finally Water Street in Fairport as you follow the river out to the Fairport Harbor Marine Museum and Lighthouse. It's a fun and interesting stop and climbing old lighthouses is always a treat.

Take SR2 west about eight miles and near Mentor you will notice SR615 (Center Street) heading north toward the Lake. Take 615 a short distance and it'll deliver you to Route 283 (known locally as Lakeshore Boulevard,) which will be your riding host for many miles. Mentor has one of the nicer local parks on the lake. On the east side of Cleveland, in Gordon City Park at the intersection

Cleveland is home to the Rock and Roll Hall of Fame and Museum—a must-see for any Baby Boomer.

of Martin Luther King Drive, Lakeshore Boulevard joins I-90 for a short distance through downtown. This immediate area has several fine attractions, including lakeshore parks, the 1819 Dunham Tavern Museum, the *USS Cod* Submarine (which sank over a dozen enemy ships in WWII), the steamship *William G. Mather*, the Rock & Roll Museum, and more. You're also just a short ride from several worthwhile attractions in the north of Cleveland, including the Auto-Aviation Museum, Jacobs Field, and more. To visit these downtown and lakeshore attractions, get off at the 9th Street exit. Most of these sites are between the highway and the lakeshore and are really easy to reach. By the way, did you know that the character Superman was created in Cleveland in 1933? Impress your friends with that little piece of trivia! Cleveland really does rock!

Interstate 90 will leave and head south, but you will want to stay on what is now Ohio Route 2/US6/US20 heading west along the shoreline. This stretch of road is called the Cleveland Memorial Shoreway, then Clifton Boulevard. and then Lake Road after crossing the Rocky River. Shortly after crossing the Rocky River just west of Lakewood, Routes 2 and 20 part company and our ride continues west along the shoreline on US6 all the way to Sandusky. Notice the Charles Berry Memorial Bridge when crossing the Black River in Lorain. It's the largest bascule,

Tony Packo's Cafe, made famous by Corporal Klinger, is located in the heart of Toledo—check out the sausage sandwich and chili specialties.

or lift, bridge in the United States. Built in the late 1930s and opened for traffic in 1940, it was later renamed to honor Mr. Berry, a Lorain resident and Medal of Honor recipient killed at Iwo Jima. Be on guard when crossing the bridge as all four lanes consist of metal grid. Just make sure you have got a good grip on the bars. In my mind, Lorain is one of the nicer towns along the shore west of Cleveland. For one thing, it has a very nice public park on the lake (Lakeview Park) in an area where public lake access is unforgivably scarce.

A destination I recommend for anyone with an interest in the history of the Great Lakes is the Inland Seas Maritime Museum, located a few blocks north of US6 in Vermillion at the corner of Huron and Main Streets. Turn north at the corner of US6 and SR60 / Main Street in town. An unusual obelisk monument with a clock in it at this corner makes it easy to find.

In Huron, we once again pick up Route 2 to cross Sandusky Bay to Marblehead Peninsula and the many attractions to be found there. (If you want to explore historic Sandusky, fighting a lot of urban traffic, you can take US6 right through Sandusky and meet up with Route 2 west of town.) The Lake Erie Islands and the Marblehead Peninsula are unique in Ohio and wonderful places to explore. Getting out to Marblehead Lighthouse (the oldest light on the lakes) will require heading east from SR2 on Bay Shore Road. Ferries out to the islands are available at three places on the peninsula between Marblehead and Port Clinton. These side trips are highly recommended (especially to Kelley's Island, the largest freshwater island in America) to view the fascinating glacial grooves carved into the island's limestone 30,000 years ago during the last Ice Age and Indian pictographs on Inscription Rock. A ferry trip to South Bass Island, where attractions include the spectacular Perry Victory and International Peace Monument, Crystal Cave, Perry's Cave, state parks, and much more, should also be high on your to-do list.

When you've done and seen all that you can fit into your schedule, take 163 back to Route 2 west of Port Clinton. Route 2 will take you all the way to the east side of Toledo and Woodville Road / SR51 / SR65, which we'll use to cross the Maumee River. This route takes us across the Anthony Wayne Suspension Bridge—a very impressive structure. It's much more interesting crossing the river on this bridge than taking the expressway. While still on the east side of the river, you might want to head to the internationally famous Tony Packo's Café for their sausage sandwich and chili specialties—highly recommended by no less than Corporal Klinger himself! This iconic restaurant is located just off I-280 at exit 9, then right / east on Front Street. It's less than two miles north of the SR2 / I-280 interchange.

Thus, we complete this very interesting and scenic tour around a great lake. I hope you enjoyed it. One lake down, four more to go?

The Cuyahoga Valley Canal Tour

THIS GREAT RIDe follows the waterways that helped form Ohio during the last two centuries. Two of the state's great rivers—the Cuyahoga and Tuscarawas—are almost always right by your side on this tour, but there's more. We'll follow the Ohio & Erie Canal, from near Cleveland almost all the way to Coshocton, and visit port towns where the Pennsylvania & Ohio Canal and the Sandy & Beaver Canal met the O&E. However, it isn't just water in its liquid form we'll follow. Steam played a major role in the movement of people and goods in the 19th century, so we will explore a fabulous railroad museum and yard in Dennison where steam reigned supreme for decades. And let's not forget the charming town of Canal Fulton, named in honor of the inventor of the steamboat.

Although this route, at two hundred and twelve miles, could feasibly be done in one day, it really would be a shame to try to squeeze it into just a day trip. It should be at least two days, since there is so much to see, so many fascinating places to stop for exploration, and so much history to discover. The icing on the cake is that the majority of roads are just great!

We begin our passage of discovery at the northeast corner of the Cuyahoga National Park, near the city of Garfield Heights, where Rockside Road meets the Ohio & Erie Canal and the Cuyahoga Scenic Railroad. There is a station for the railroad located at this juncture. The train running through the park has been immensely popular and is a wonderful way to see the valley from Cleveland south to Canton. Train operators offer a wide variety of special events, such as a murder mystery train, a wine-tasting trip, and of course, fall color runs. They also offer educational rides that focus on local history events, such as the Underground Railroad and canal history.

Cuyahoga National Park is a recent addition to our nation's park system, and it came along just in time. Dedicated in 1974, authorization of the park was a battle against time and urban sprawl. The Cuyahoga Valley was being rapidly developed in the 1960s, and this irreplaceable piece of landscape and history was about to become just another urbanized area of look-alike houses and malls. Thanks to the efforts of concerned local citizens, Congress responded and created the Cuyahoga Valley National Recreation Area within the national parks system. As a result, the canal, towpath, twenty-two miles of the river, and

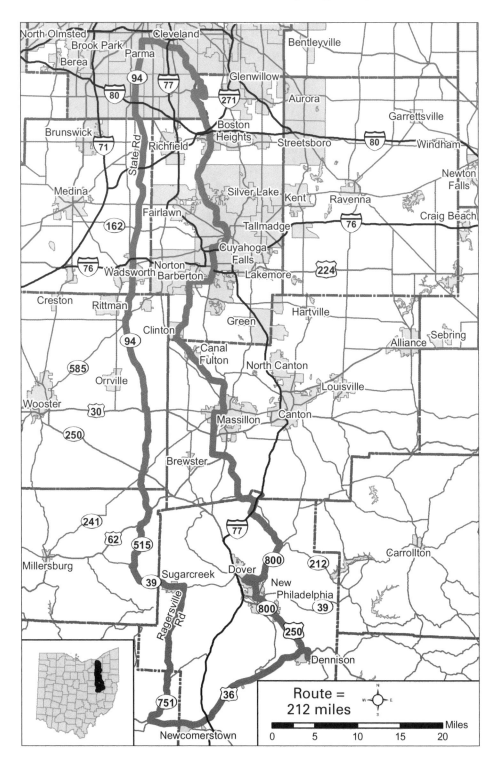

Route = 212 miles

Miles
0   5   10   15   20

OHIO
HISTORICAL
MARKER

CANAL TUNNELS

Southeast of this point are the Big and Little
Tunnels. They were links in the 73-mile Sandy
and Beaver Canal which connected the Ohio
River with the Ohio and Erie Canal. Shifts of
Irish laborers worked day and night with hand
drills and blasting powder to cut the 1060-yard
Big Tunnel which opened for commercial use
in 1850 and was abandoned 2 years later, a
victim of the railroad.

THE OHIO HISTORICAL SOCIETY
WITH
THE COLUMBIANA COUNTY HISTORICAL ASSOCIATION
AND
THE CANAL SOCIETY OF OHIO
1964   3-15

thirty-three thousand acres of the beautiful Cuyahoga Valley are there for all of us to enjoy.

Begin the trip by going south on Canal Road, part of the very picturesque Canalway Scenic Byway. There are byway signs all along this portion of the trip between here and Dover to help guide you. Canal Road throughout the length of the park is an enjoyable ride, although not one where speed is an option. During the warm months this park sees heavy use, and there are many vehicles—two- and four-wheeled, powered and unpowered—plus a number of places where the canal tow path trail crosses the road. Enjoy the scenery, the river, the canal, the occasional sightings of the valley train, and take in all that this gem of a park has to offer, but save the road racing for another day.

As you might guess, there are many attractions and places to stop in the park. It's fun just riding through without stopping, but the occasional stop to learn about the canal and the river valley's long history make the trip even more intriguing. A visitor's center is located just a couple miles south of the start point, and this is a good place to pick up brochures and view various displays and maps. The staff is very knowledgeable and can enhance your experience, not only in the park but also by providing useful information about the entire length of the canal byway.

We leave the park just north of Akron but the canal byway is easy to follow right into downtown. Follow the signs, but if you want to trace it out on a map: exit the national park on Riverview Road, which turns into Merriman Road south of the park, from Merriman turn left onto Memorial in Akron, then right on Cuyahoga, followed by another right on Howard Street. Howard becomes Main Street downtown—follow it right through town to Thornton Street, where you turn right/west.

Remember, there are signs all along the route, and even though it sounds complicated, it really isn't. The streets are well marked and some of the turns are obvious because of T intersections.

Follow Thornton west across the canal and the Innerbelt Expressway to Manchester Road (also SR93) and follow it south four miles to Robinson Road. Go right on Robinson Road 2.4 miles through Barberton to Van Buren Road and

THE CUYAHOGA VALLEY CANAL TOUR 212 MILES		
Miles	Destination	Total
0	Cuyahoga National Park/North Boundary	0
20	Cuyahoga National Park/South Boundary	20
17	Barberton/Van Buren Avenue	37
26	Navarre	63
21	Dover	84
14	Dennison/Depot	98
23	State Route 751	121
18	Sugar Creek	139
19	Mt. Eaton	158
23	Wadsworth	181
31	Rockslide & Canal Roads	212

turn left. This road gets you out of the urban area and offers a pleasant riding road along the canal that takes you through the canal town of Clinton and into Canal Fulton.

Canal Fulton is one of those must-stop towns. It's a place where you'll want to walk to appreciate its brick streets and many historic buildings. At Community Park, you can ride on the *St. Helena III*, a replica canal boat, and at the Old Canal Days Museum you can learn about the history of the town and Ohio's canal system. The museum is at 116 South Canal Street. Calling 330-854-3808 will get you information on the museum and about a ride on the canal boat. Just south of town on Erie Avenue, Lock 4 Park is a recommended stop to view functioning locks and a canal keeper's cabin. Continue south on Erie Avenue toward Massillon to continue the trip. The canal and Tuscarawas River will be at your side the entire way.

Erie Avenue will deposit you on First Street in Football Town (*aka* Massillon). Where First Street meets Lincoln Way, there is a wonderful mural about Massillon's place in the game of football. (Another really neat mural is one block west and one block south of this corner—it's on the back side of a building and not readily visible but definitely worth going over to see.) The Ohio Military History Museum is on Lincoln Way just east of First Street and features military artifacts and displays that highlight the military role of Ohio's citizens throughout its history. On a lighter note, Massillon hosts a series of Saturday night cruise-ins that include all variety of classic cars and motorcycles during the summer.

Going through Massillon on the canalway is easy: just follow First Street to Tremont Street where you turn right, taking Tremont over the river and maybe a total of two miles to 17th Street / Carmont Road, where you make a left turn. While following Carmont south through the countryside, you'll see a sign point east to "Old Canal Trail"—this isn't us, so don't take it. Just continue straight south to the T at Elton Road. Go left on Elton Road into Navarre. In Navarre, Elton Road becomes Wooster Street. Take this to Route 62, which you take south three blocks to Canal Street. A left on Canal will continue the tour. Canal turns into Hudson Street, which you take less than a mile and a half to Riverland Road, where you turn right. Riverland is a fun road that closely follows the meanderings of the Tuscarawas River. It traverses a heavily wooded countryside and is right next to the canal for much of the way. One note of caution—there is a rough railroad crossing on this stretch that is marked only by the old X railroad warning sign. Slow down when you see it ahead.

When Riverland Road forms a T at Route 212, turn left and take it into Bolivar. At the south end of Bolivar, Route 212 parts company and heads east. At this point we just continue straight south on County Road 102, past Fort Laurens (which I talk about in another ride) to Towpath Road / CR111. Very shortly after turning, you'll go over the expressway. County Road 111 becomes a joy to ride east all the way, where it dead ends at Dover–Zoar Road. You have to make a couple of clearly marked (and obvious, once you see them) jogs here, and the road will ultimately make a T at Route 800. Turn right on 800, taking it south along the Tuscarawas River to Dover.

Upon leaving Massillon, pretty much this entire part of the tour is on roads that are an enjoyable ride. The river is never far away and the roads follow the canal closely. Because the roads are often in the river valley, there are many trees to add to the scenic delight, and the roads curve a lot to keep up with the river.

At Dover, we leave the official canal byway. It ends in Dover anyway without any fanfare, so we go east at Dover rather than follow the byway signs into town. Stay on Route 800 as it turns east through New Philadelphia. East of New Philadelphia, you will think you've lost track of Route 800 as there aren't any road signs for it until you get way out to the east. At the Ohio Highway Patrol post by US250, you will finally see a sign confirming that you're on the right road.

I find the area by Uhrichsville to be one of the more unpleasant of the whole trip. It has got a congested strip where several major roads converge (800, 36, and 250). Just make your way through the brief stretch of ugliness and go east on US250 toward Dennison. Follow the brown tourist signs to the Dennison Depot

The Dennison Depot and Museum is one of the best railroading museums in Ohio and has specially scheduled train rides.

and you'll arrive there with no problems. This museum and depot is just great. It has to be one of the best railroading museums in Ohio, with rolling stock and other displays to make a railroading buff out of even the most uninterested person. There are specially scheduled train rides available from the depot and a gift shop that caters to railroading devotees. There is also an adjacent 1940s restaurant should you decide you need a cup of Joe and a snack to tide you over till your next meal. Go to www.dennisondepot.org for more information.

Leave Dennison the same way you came into town, but when you hit the highway, go west on US36 where it splits off of US250 at Urichsville. After a couple of miles of four-lane divided Highway 36 becomes a very nice two-lane road. Since it is built in a broad valley, there are tree-covered hills on both sides all along its length that make for a scenic ride.

Along the way is the historic village of Gnadenhutten (which you've already read about in the Colonel Crawford tour). The monument and museum are located just south of Route 36 and are easy to get to. It makes for an interesting and educational stop. Going into the village, the first thing you see is a large factory—not exactly evocative of a missionary village in the eighteenth-century wilderness. The village itself is more historic and looks older. The memorial is at the south end of town, actually located within a cemetery. It's not a big or bustling place, rather a somber reminder of a shameful day in our history.

West of Gnadenhutten the road gets seriously nice. As you ride on a roadway carved through the hills, you will see signs stating "Land Slides" and "Rock Slides," which will remind you that you're not in Ohio anymore, Toto. But wait, we *are* in Ohio. It's just another part of the state that most people don't see because they're spending too much time driving like maniacs on the expressways!

Take Route 36 past Newcomerstown to State Route 751. Route 751 is just great! It'll remind you of Route 555 in southeast Ohio, albeit a somewhat less hyperactive version of 555. It's a curving and undulating blacktop through a beautiful rolling countryside that'll have you grinning ear to ear in no time. Be aware, however, because there are several tight curves that can catch you off guard, and there's the occasional curve unexpectedly awaiting you at the crown of a hill. It's a relatively short stretch of road but a really nice one. When you arrive at the village of Bakersville, turn left at the large farm implement dealer and then make another right onto CR97 just a quarter mile later. Go past the white church on CR97 and continue north into the open countryside. You will cross the county line into Tuscarawas County just north of Bakersville, and this county road becomes much better with newer blacktop as well as being wider and smoother. This leg of the trip is a series of county roads with very light traffic that will continue the fun you were having on 751 (though a bit more sedate). A few miles north of Bakersville, you'll come to a fork in the road at the site of a large red barn—you want the left fork (CR44) which will take you to its end at Ragersville Road. Turn right on Ragersville and it will delight you all the way north to the village of the same name. Slow down in Ragersville—in fact I recommend you stop to take a good look and maybe even a walk through the local general store and gas station that'll have you believing you've been time-warped back to the 1950s. Very cool.

Beyond Ragersville you make a right jog then continue north again up to Route 39, where a left turn takes you into the Swiss village of Sugar Creek. For a Swiss village Sugar Creek strikes me as a bit untidy, but maybe the whole thing about Swiss tidiness is overblown. In reality, Sugar Creek is a somewhat sprawling small town that belies its country town / Swiss village facade. Sugar Creek is the center of Ohio's Swiss cheese industry and hosts an annual Swiss cheese festival. Sugar Creek's residents certainly don't have feet of clay. No, they use that clay for better purposes. The town is home to two very large brick factories—Belden and Finzer.

The red clay brick should enjoy official status in Ohio. All across the state there are beautiful buildings of brick. The official old-fashioned farm home in Ohio should be the stately red brick, two-story house that is ubiquitous across the countryside and small towns alike. Whereas other states' schoolhouses are white and wood-framed across their rural landscapes, Ohio's are built of red brick. Take a look around on your travels and marvel at the wonders that this simple fired clay block has made possible. And now you know where many of those bricks were made.

Continue west on Route 39 to Walnut Creek and SR515. West of Sugar Creek you'll note that this is the heart of Ohio's Amish Country. Amish craft shops are everywhere, and horse and buggy combos are frequent travelers on all local roads. Route 515 north of 39 is certainly no exception. Follow 515 north through the rolling Ohio countryside to US62, turning right to the village of Winesburg. From the main intersection in Winesburg continue east on US62 just about exactly one mile to County Road 186 / Winesburg Road and turn left. You will shortly pass the Logenberger Mennonite Church and continue straight north to Mt. Eaton. This stretch of road is through the heart of Amish farmlands and you will need to be watchful for buggies and bicyclists on the road.

Winesburg Road ends at Route 241 which we take right into the village of Mt. Eaton. At the stoplight where 241 hits Route 250 in Mt. Eaton, we continue right straight across on what is now SR94. Route 94 will be our riding partner for many miles—in fact, all the way north to the sprawling town of Wadsworth, once a country town but now part of the western suburbs of Akron. The countryside between Mt. Eaton and Wadsworth is a nice ride—not spectacular but certainly passable. The only real congestion you'll encounter between Mt. Eaton and Wadsworth is at US30 at Dalton. That changes at the north side of Wadsworth and the interchange with I-76 / US224. Just continue straight north on SR94 and one-half mile north of I-76 you will see Reimer Road going right. Turn onto Reimer and then immediately make a left turn onto State Road. Stay on State Road as it works its way north. This is still a real nice stretch of road, although I suspect its days as a good biking road are getting numbered given the amount of development (mostly in the form of half-million dollar homes) taking place along it. Be that as it may, it's still a good road that you'll enjoy. It certainly beats parallel major routes. Beware of the junction with SR18, which is a busy four-lane highway where State Road crosses it. Be patient as traffic on 18 can keep you waiting a couple of minutes.

North of I-80, without as much as a blink of the eye, State Road becomes Route 94 once again. Beware of speed traps in this section as the speed limit suddenly drops from fifty-five to thirty-five, with a favorite spot for concealed patrol cars being just north of the turnpike. As you continue north on 94 into Parma the landscape becomes urban, and when you approach the road where we turn right (Snow Road), you will see a beautiful Ukrainian Orthodox Church (St. Vladimir's) with its trademark domed spires. Snow Road is just a couple of blocks beyond the church, and a right turn is needed when you get there. As you travel east, Snow Road turns into Rockside Road. (At the corner of Rockside and Brecksville Road take a gander at the McDonalds at the southeast corner of the intersection—I'll wager it's the fanciest McDonalds you've ever seen!)

Continuing east on Rockside delivers us back to Canal Road and signals the end of this fabulous trip along Ohio's historic waterways.

Some Fun Local Rides

THERE ARE, of course, many hundreds of miles of enjoyable roads in Ohio that are great for a quick ride when the chance arises. They are located across the state. I've listed these not because they're the best of what's available but because they are among the best and are, for the most part, not included in the long tours laid out in the book. If you're in the area these roads make for a fun afternoon ride.

1. If you're in Vinton County and want an amazingly fun ride, take Route 278 from beginning to end. It really is a great biking road through a wonderfully scenic landscape. This continuously curving road takes you over hills and through valleys in a forested landscape pretty enough to have come right out of a Courier and Ives painting of rural America.

2. Ohio Route 775 from Proctorville on the Ohio River north to Ohio Route 141. This is a fantastic ride through the Wayne National Forest and the hills and valleys of Lawrence and southern Gallia Counties.

3. In southwestern Ohio, Route 247 between Hillsboro and the Ohio River is great fun. Midway be sure to take a two-mile detour east on Grace Run Road, located a couple miles south of Ohio 32, to see the Harshaville Covered Bridge. This historic bridge was built in 1855 and was used by General Morgan and his Raiders when the confederates moved through this area during the Civil War.

4. Route 151 from Station 15 near Dennison southeasterly to its juncture with Route 7 just south of Steubenville.

5. Another great road in east-central Ohio is State Route 164 from Lisbon southwest to Leesville. It is twisty and great fun through nice countryside.

6. US24 from Waterville near Toledo and southwest along the Maumee River to the Indiana State Line. Not a really technical road but, in most stretches, is very pleasant, scenic and fun.

7. Route 73 between Hillsboro and Portsmouth winds through very pretty countryside ,with enough hills and river valleys to make for a really interesting and enjoyable ride. Again, not really technical but definitely a delight.

8. Straight south of Zanesville, Ohio Route 78 runs between the small towns of Murray City on the west and Bristol on the east end—a scenic and fun road.

9. The Windsor–Mechansville Road in western Ashtabula County runs parallel to and between State Routes 45 and 534. Beginning at the village of Mechanicsville and the covered bridge of the same name, it runs generally straight south through a nice landscape. It's an enjoyable road, even if not really exciting, for its entire 15-mile length.

10. The Defiance Trail is one that might be best for adventure bikers. It can be done on a typical street bike, but there are stretches where a rider may wonder what they're doing on a road such as this.

    This stretch of historic road follows the west side of the Auglaize River and is one of the oldest roads in this part of the state. Its origins are as a military road hacked out of the wilderness. Today, it can be followed quite easily from the Spencerville/Fort Amanda area all the way north to Defiance. Along the way, you'll see historical sites ranging from the locations of Fort Brown and Fort Jennings, built during the War of 1812, to a Johnny Appleseed nursery location.

    The name of this road changes often as it twists and turns south from Defiance. The best bet is to get a county map book and trace out the road before you ride it. It begins at Defiance as State Route 111, going southwest along the river. After several miles, Route 111 heads straight west and the fun begins as you follow CR171 paralleling the river. About eight miles south of the point where you leave Route 111, you'll come to the Fort Brown memorial. Southeast of here the road becomes Township Road 207 and then TR123, becoming a narrow and fairly rough township road—great fun on a KLR or Ulysses. Between Cloverdale and just east of Delphos, you'll ride on state routes for short stretches, and northeast of Delphos you'll find Fort Jennings. Between Fort Jennings and Route 309, you'll be on TR23. South of Route 309, the road is well marked as the Defiance Trail and is suitable for any bike. There is nothing really spectacular about this stretch of road—but riding it from Fort Amanda (another 1812 fort) to Defiance is a fun exercise in retracing military history. As you ride along, imagine the tired, hungry, and no doubt scared soldiers who hacked this trail out of the swamps and forests two hundred years ago as they made their way north to do battle.

11. I normally try to avoid federal roads because they are usually busier, wider, flatter, and straighter than their state or county counterparts. In other words, they're not nearly as much fun. Between Zanesville and the Cincinnati area,

US22 is a pretty nice road, and if you have to make this trip, it's infinitely better than the I-70 / I-71 alternative. Further east, the stretch between Cadiz and Cambridge is also nice.

12. Any or all of Route 800 between Dennison and the Ohio River. It winds through and over hills, river valleys, forest, and farmlands, and in general, is challenging in some parts and just plain fun in the rest. Route 800 is like SR555, SR26, and a few others in that it's a destination ride—folks come a long way to ride these roads.

13. State Routes 325 and 233 between Rio Grande and Oak Hill in Gallia and Jackson Counties.

14. The approximately twenty-mile length of SR12 from Benton Ridge (just southwest of Findlay) southwest to Vaughnsville. Jog south on SR115 a half mile, then continue southwest on Old Route 12 a few more miles to the Lincoln Highway.

15. Nine miles north of where US35 and SR104 intersect just north of Chillicothe, you will see Williamsport–Chillicothe Road heading west. Take this road as it follows Deer Creek all the way to the small town of Williamsport. Continue straight north out of Williamsport on Chillicothe Road, jogging west a block or two on Yankeetown Road, then continuing north on Darbyville–Williamsport Road to the crossroads village of Pherson at Route 56. Continue straight across 56 and head northeast a short distance, then left on CR3 into Darbyville. Jog left a block in Darbyville, then north on London Road/CR3 along Darby Creek all the way past I-71. Eventually, the road curves westward as CR4, and if you have time, take it all the way to London. For most of the trip the road curves along Deer and Darby Creeks, through pretty countryside.

16. A roughly twenty-two-mile triangular ride to the south of Loudonville is very nice. Just southwest of Loudonville off of SR3, take the Wally Road Scenic Byway as it twists through pretty countryside along the Mohican River down to SR514. Between parks and campgrounds, the road alternates with the river on one side and hills or cliffs on the other. To complete the triangle, go east on 514 to the tiny town of Nashville and then back northwest on 39/60 to Loudonville. This is heavy-duty resort country ,so try to time your rides on other than peak weekend periods.

17. Holmes County has many fine riding roads through its bucolic countryside. Several its roads are already included in long tours described in the book. A very nice ride begins on SR39 heading east out of Millersburg and turning south on

SR557 a few miles east of town and riding it southeast to SR643. Leave 643 at New Bedford and go north through the tiny burg on CR600, which shortly becomes CR59 and then CR58 as the roadway meanders northwest back to US62 just south of Millersburg. This is a ride that's great early in the morning or in the evening (actually, it's a great ride any time of day, but rides through this kind of countryside are especially nice early or late in the day).

18. South of Steubenville, take SR150 west from Route 7 to US250 and jog north a couple of miles, then proceed west again on SR519. Take 519 to US22 and head west a couple of miles again to County Road 33, taking this north to CR20, which in turn heads west and becomes SR799 near Clendening Reservoir.

19. From Jackson, take SR776 southwest to SR335. From this point go west on county roads to Wakefield, near US23. When you hit 335, continue straight west on Dewey Road, then a bit north on Germany Road, and west again on Owl Creek Road. Owl Creek turns into Salt Creek Road and goes to Wakefield and US23. A fun ride filled with curves and very light traffic.

20. This can be an hour ride or an all-day ride, depending on how much time you have. From Coshocton take SR83 south, which goes almost to Marietta so it can also be a great longer ride—even an overnight trip. Virtually the entire stretch is fabulous riding, with hills, curves, great scenery and plenty of nearby attractions if only you can force yourself to park the bike and spend some time exploring!

Resources for the Ohio Motorcyclist

HAVING SPENT beaucoup years wandering North America on two wheels, I long ago learned that there were some basic items I needed to carry with me on trips—be it an hour ride in familiar countryside or a ten-day excursion across the country. These items included many that most motorcyclists carry in their tank bag or saddlebags: miscellaneous objects ranging from aspirin to tire patches. I always tried to have one additional article with me—that is, a list of emergency phone numbers, including police, wrecker services and motorcycle dealers. Thankfully I didn't need these numbers very often, but when I did, they were invaluable.

It is my intent that this book be of a size that every motorcyclist riding in Ohio can carry it with him or her, and thus I want it to contain all those pieces of information that I wished I had available on a trip. Therefore, in the following pages you will find emergency phone numbers for Sheriff Departments and Highway Patrol posts across the state, major hotel and motel reservation numbers, lost credit card reporting phone numbers, and motorcycle dealer information for as many brands of bikes as I can locate. I hope you never need the emergency numbers, but hopefully it'll provide peace of mind on your motorcycling adventures knowing you have them just in case. Sheriff Department numbers are especially valuable should you need help on a rural road.

In this new age of computer resources I have also provided a lengthy list of web sites of interest to motorcyclists.

Handy Web Sites

MOTORCYCLE CLUBS

11th Cavalry Motorcycle Club of America: 11thcavalrymc.com/
ABATE of Ohio: www.abate.com
Airheads Beemer Club: airheads.org/
All American Indian Motorcycle Club: allamericanindianmotorcycleclub.com
American Biker Association: americanbikerassociation.com/
American Firefighters Motorcycle Association: aff-mc.com/
American Gold Wing Association: agwa.com/
American Historic Racing Motorcycle Association: ahrma.org/
American Motorcycle Network: americanmotor.com/
American Steel Motorcycle Club: americansteelmc.com/
American Veterans MC: aaa-ammo.com/avmc-1.htm
Antique Motorcycle Club of America: antiquemotorcycle.org/TheClub/theclub.html

Aprilia USA Owner's Club: aprilia-usa.com/
Bald Guys Motorcycle Club: baldguysmc.com/
Bent Wheels Competition Club: bentwheels.com/1/bw/index.asp
Bikers Against Child Abuse: bacausa.com/
Bikers For Kids: bikers4kids.org/
Blood Brothers MC: bloodbrothersmc.org/
Blue Knights International: blueknights.org/
BMW Motorcycle Owners of America: BMWMOA.org
BMW Oilheads Club: oilheadsclub.org/
BMW Riders Association: bmwra.org/
Bonneville Owners Club: autos.groups.yahoo.com/group/
    bonnevilleownersclub/
Brothers of the Third Wheel: btw-trikers.org/uploads/home.php
BSA Owners' Club: bsaoc.demon.co.uk/
Buckeye Beemers Club: www.buckeyebeemers.org
Buell Riding Club (BRAG): buell.com/en_us/brag/bragmain.asp
CB 750 Preservation Society: cb750.org/
Chillicothe Enduro Riders Association: ceraenduro.com
Christian Motorcyclists Association: cmausa.org/
Christian Motorcyclists Association of Ohio: cmaohio.20m.com
Christian Riders Ministry: christianriders.org/
Christian Sportbike Association: christiansportbike.com/
Cincinnati Cavaliers MC: cincinnaticavaliers.motorcyclecity.net
Columbus Biker: columbusbiker.com
Combat Veterans Motorcycle Association: combatvet.org/
Concerned Motorcycle Riders of Ohio: /www.abatecmro.org/
Concours Owners Group: concours.org/
Dayton Motorcycle Club: daytonmc.com
Ducati Enthusiasts Sport Motorcyclists of Ohio: desmohio.com
Ducati Women: ducatiwomen.com/home.html
Ducatis Unlimited Connection: duc.org/
Excelsior—Henderson Riders Club: ehridersclub.com/
Fellowship Riders: fellowshipriders.org/
FJR Owners Club: fjrowners.ws/fjro4/usa.html
Gold Wing Road Riders Association: gwrra.org/
Harley Owners Group: harley-davidson.com/ex/hog/template.
    asp?fnc=hog&bmLocale=en_US
Herd of Turtles Motorcycle Club: pjgillam.tripod.com/herd_of_turtles.htm
Hocking Valley MC: hockingvalleymc.org

Hogs In Ministry: h-i-m.org
Honda CB1100R Owners Group: eskimo.com/~carcosa/1100R.html
Honda Rider's Club of America: hondamotorcycle.com/hrca
Honda Sport Touring Association: ridehsta.com/
Honda VTX Owners Association: vtxoa.com/
Husqvarna Motorcycle Club: huskyclub.com/
In Country Vets Motorcycle Club: icvmc.com/
Indian Motorcycle Club of America: indian-motorcycles.com/
International Brotherhood of Motorcycle Campers: ibmc.org/
International CBX Owners Association: cbxclub.com/
International Norton Owners Association: inoanorton.com/welcome.htm
International Order of Old Bastards MC: home.inreach.com/ioob/index.htm
Internet BMW Riders: ibmwr.org/
Iron Butt Association: ironbutt.com/about/default.cfm
Iron Butt Goldwingers Association: ironbuttgoldwingers.com/
Iron Indian Riders: ironindian.com/
Iron Pigs MC—Black Swamp: ironpigsmcblackswamp.com
Jus Brothers Motorcycle Club: jusbrothersmc.com/
Kawasaki Good Times Owners Club: kawasaki.com/gtoc/main.html
Latin American Motorcycle Association / Women's Section: latinbikers.com/
    Damas/Damas.htm
Latin American Motorcycle Association: latinbikers.com/
Leathernecks Motorcycle Club: leathernecksmc.org/
Long Riders Association: longridersmc.org/
Long Riders MC Magazine: longridersmagazine.com/index_lr_online.htm
Magna Riders Association: magnariders.com/
Marines Motorcycle Club: marinesmc.com/
Maumee Valley Iron Indian Riders: ironindian.com
Military Veterans Motorcycle Club: militaryveteransmc.com/
Moto Guzzi National Owners Club: mgnoc.com/
Motor Maids, Inc.: motormaids.org/
Motocross site for girls: www.MXgirls.com/
Motorcycle Beginners: motorcyclebeginners.com/
Motorcycle Touring Association: mtariders.com/
Norton Owners Club: nortonownersclub.org/
Ohio Bikers: www.ohiobikers.com/
Ohio Motorcycle Clubs List: ohiobikers.com/clubs
Pioneer Motorcycle Club, Inc.: pioneermc.homestead.com
POW_MIA Riders MC: powmiariders.com/

Pride Motorcycle Club (Corrections Personnel): pridemc.org
Proud Veterans Motorcycle Club: kevinandteri.com:8080/pvmc/html/
Red Knights Motorcycle Club: redknightsmc.org/
Ride Motorcycle Club: ridemotorcycle.com/
Ride To Work Association: ridetowork.org/home.php
Riders Association of Triumph: triumphrat.net
Rolling Thunder, Ohio: rollingthunderohio.com
Shadow Club USA: shadowclubusa.com/
Sister Cycle: sistercycle.com/
Southern Cruisers Riding Club: www.southerncruiser.net/chapters.htm
Sportsbike Web Site: sportbikes.ws/index.php
Star Touring & Riding Association: startouring.org/
Suzuki Owners Club: soc-usa.org/
Trike Riders International: trikes.org
Triumph International Owners Club: members.aol.com/JohnTIOC/tioc.htm
Triumph Online Motorcycle Club: autos.groups.yahoo.com/group/triumphmo-
    torcycleclub2/
Triumph Owners Motorcycle Club: tomcc.org/index.html
United Sidecar Association: sidecar.com/
United States Patriots M/C: uspatriotsmc.com/
USA Highway Riders M/C: usahighwayriders.com/
Valkyrie Owners Association International: valkyrie-owners.com/
Valkyrie Riders Cruiser Club: valkyrieriders.com/
Venture Motorcycle Club: venturers.org/
Veterans of Vietnam MC / National Chapter: www.vovma.org/VOVMA.html
Victory Motorcycle Club: thevmc.com/start.html
Victory Riders Association: victory-usa.com/product/vic/vra
Viet Nam Vets MC / Ohio: www.vnvmcoh.org/
Vincents Owners Club: voc.uk.com/sections/index.html
Vintage BMW Motorcycle Owners Club: vintagebmw.org/current/
Vintage Japanese Motorcycle Club: vjmc.org/
Virago Owners Club: viragoownersclub.org/
V-Max Owners Association: v-max.com/
V-Twin Sports Riders: geocities.com/flootiebuell/
Warrior Brotherhood Veterans MC: warriorbrotherhood.com/
Wide Open Sport Bikes.Com: wideopensportbikes.com/WOShomepage.htm
Wolverines Motorcycle Club: wolverinesmc.com/
Women In The Wind, Inc.: womeninthewind.org/
Women on Wheels: womenonwheels.org/

Women's International Motorcycle Association: wimausa.org/
Women's Motocross Association: www.womensmotocrossassociation.com/
Yamaha Owners Club: autos.groups.yahoo.com/group/yamahaownersclub/
Zen Riders: zenriders.com/main.htm
Zen Riders—Ohio: zenriders.com/ohio/

MAGAZINES AND JOURNALS

American Iron Magazine: americanironmagazine.com/
American Motorcycle Network: americanmotor.com
Beginner Bikers Magazine: beginnerbikes.com/
Bike Week Report: bikeweekreport.com/
Biker Threads Magazine: bikerthreadsmagazine.com/
Cycle News Magazine: cyclenews.com/
Cycle World Magazine: cycleworld.com/
Easy Riders Magazine: easyriders.com/
Hot Bike Harley-Davidson Magazine: hotbikeweb.com/
Metric Bikes Magazine: metricbikes.com/index.htm
Midwest Motorcyclist: midwestmotorcyclist.com/
Motorcycle Consumer News: mcnews.com/mcn/
Motorcycle Cruiser Magazine: motorcyclecruiser.com/
Motorcycle Daily Magazine: motorcycledaily.com/
Motorcycle Explorer Internet Magazine: motorcycleexplorer.com/
Motorcycle USA: motorcycle-usa.com
Motorcyclist Magazine: motorcyclistonline.com/
Rider Magazine: riderreport.com
Road Racing World Magazine: venus.13x.com/roadracingworld/
RoadRUNNER Cruising & Touring Magazine: rrmotorcycling.com/
Superbike Magazine: superbike.co.uk/
Twistgrip Magazine: www.twistgrip.com/

MANUFACTURER

American Ironhorse Motorcycle Company: americanironhorse.com
Aprilia Motorcycle Company: aprilia.com/portale/eng/company02.phtml
Benelli: www.benelli.com/page.do
Big Dog: bigdogmotorcycles.com
BMW Motorcycle Company: bmwmotorcycles.com/home
Boss Hoss Motorcycle Company: bosshoss.com
Britten Motorcycle Company: britten.co.nz/
Buell Motorcycle Company: buell.com/selector.asp

Cagiva MotorcycleCompany: cagivausa.com/

Ducati Motorcycle Company: ducati.com/

Harley-Davidson Motorcycle Company / US: harley-davidson.com/en/homef. asp?bmLocale=en_US

Honda Motorcycle Company: powersports.honda.com/motorcycles/

Husqvarna Motorcycle Company: husqvarnausa.com/

Kawasaki Motorcycle Company: kawasaki.com/

KTM Motorcycle Company: ktmusa.com/frameset.asp

Kymco Motorcycle Company USA: kymco-usa.com

MV Agusta USA: mvagustausa.com/web-mvagusta/news_columbus04.html

Norton Motorcycle Company: nortonmotorcycles.com/

Royal Enfield Motorcycle Company: enfieldmotorcycles.com/

Suzuki Motorcycle Company: suzukicycles.com/Products/Motorcycles/Default. aspx

Titan Motorcycle Company: www.titanmotorcycles.com/

Triumph Motorcycle Company: triumph.co.uk/

Ural Motorcycles: ural.com/

Vento: www.vento.com/

Victory Motorcycle Company: victorymotorcycles.com/victory/default.aspx

Yamaha Motorcycle Company: yamaha-motor.com/products/categories/2/mcy/ yamaha_motorcycles.aspx

MISCELLANEOUS

Ed Youngblood's MotoHistory: www.motohistory.net

Enforcers Motorcycle Links: enforcersmc.com/links.htm

Fasttrack Riders: fastrackriders.com/

FIM (English Version): fim.ch/en/default.asp?

International GPS Waypoint Registry: waypoint.org/default.html

Motorcycle Events: gmasw.com/bikelist.htm

Motorcycle Resources and Reviews: powersportsnetwork.com/ ?d=d&menucat=Enthusiasts

Motorcycle Hall of Fame Museum: amadirectlink.com/museum/index.asp

National Motorcycle Museum: nationalmcmuseum.org/default.asp

Ohio Bed & Breakfast Association: ohiobba.com

Ride To Work: ridetowork.org/home.php

Sturgis Motorcycle Museum & Hall of Fame: sturgismotorcyclemuseum.org/

WERA Racing: wera.com/

Woman Biker.Com: womanbiker.com/home.php3

MOTORCYCLE INSURANCE

Motorcycle Insurance—Allstate: auto-insurance.allstate.com/motorcycle

Motorcycle Insurance—Auto-Owners: auto-owners.com/our_prods/car_products/rv.htm

Motorcycle Insurance—Foremost: foremost.com

Motorcycle Insurance—Geico: geico.com

Motorcycle Insurance—GMAC: gmacinsurance.com

Motorcycle Insurance—Markel / BikeLine: protectmybike.com/

Motorcycle Insurance—Progressive: motorcycle.progressive.com/motorcycle_homePolicyAccess.asp

Motorcycle Insurance—Sentry: sentry.com/consumer_auto_specialty_insurance.htm

Motorcycle Racing Insurance—Armor: amadirectlink.com/ATVA/ARMOR.htm

MOTORCYCLE RENTAL

Motorcycle Rental—Cruise America: cruiseamerica.com/motorcycle_rentals/default.asp

Motorcycle Rental—Eagle Rider: eaglerider.com/

MOTORCYCLE SHIPPING

Motorcycle Shipping—1AA Motorcycle Transport: 1aamotorcycles.com/

Motorcycle Shipping - American Auto Transporters: shipcar.com/motorcycle-shipping.html

Motorcycle Shipping—Auto Car Transport: auto-car-transport.com/

Motorcycle Shipping—Dependable Auto Shippers: dasautoshippers.com/dasnew/web_order/lp/movecars.asp

Motorcycle Shipping—Discount / American Baggage: discount-shipping.net/vehicles/motorcycles.cfm

Motorcycle Shipping—Federal: funtransport.com

Motorcycle Shipping—JC Motors Transport: motorcycleshippers.com

Motorcycle Shipping—Moving.com: moving.com/guide/moving/motorcycle.asp

Motorcycle Shipping—The Auto Mover: theautomover.com/motorcycle.htm

ORGANIZATIONS

American Motorcyclist Association: ama-cycle.org/

Canadian Motorcycle Association: canmocycle.ca/

Motorcycle Riders Foundation: mrf.org/

Motorcycle Safety Foundation: msf-usa.org/
National Coalition of Motorcyclists: aimncom.com/

TRAINING AND SCHOOLS

CLASS Motorcycle Schools: classrides.com/
Keith Code Motorcycle School: superbikeschool.com/
Motorcycle Ohio: www.motorcycle.ohio.gov/
Motorcycle Racing School—Ed Bargy: edbargyracingschool.com/
Motorcycle Racing School—Kevin Schwantz: schwantzschool.com/
Motorcycle Racing School—Penguin Roadracing School: penguinracing.com/
Motorcycle Rides in America Track Days & Schools: motorcycleridesinamerica.
    com/schedules.htm
Northeast Sportbike Association: nesba.com/

Emergency Phone Numbers

Ohio Highway Patrol
Motorist Help: 1-877-7PATROL
CB Call Letters (Channel 9): KNN-3083

Ashland 419-289-0911	Lisbon 330-424-7783
Ashtabula 440-969-1155	Mansfield. 419-756-2222
Athens 740-593-6611	Marietta. 740-374-6616
Batavia. 513-732-1510	Marion. 740-383-2181
Bucyrus 419-562-8040	Marysville 937-644-8811
Cambridge 740-439-0187	Massillon 330-833-1055
Canfield. 330-533-6866	Medina 330-725-4921
Canton. 330-433-6200	Milan 419-499-4808
Chardon 440-286-6612	Mt. Gilead 419-768-3955
Chillicothe. 740-775-7770	New Philadelphia 330-339-1103
Cincinnati 513-777-5547	Norwalk. 419-668-3711
Circleville 740-983-2538	Piqua 937-773-1131
Cleveland. 216-587-4305	Portsmouth 740-354-2888
Columbus 614-466-2660	Ravenna. 330-297-1441
Dayton. 937-832-4794	St. Clairsville 740-695-0915
Defiance. 419-784-1025	Sandusky 419-625-6565
Delaware 740-548-6011	Springfield. 937-323-9781
Elyria 440-365-5045	Steubenville. 740-264-1641
Findlay. 419-423-1414	Swanton. 419-826-1729
Fremont. 419-332-8246	Toledo 419-865-5544
Gallipolis. 740-446-9498	Van Wert 419-238-3055
Georgetown. 937-378-6191	Walbridge 419-666-1323
Granville 740-927-0065	Wapakoneta 419-738-8010
Hamilton 513-863-4606	Warren. 330-898-2311
Hiram 330-527-2168	W. Jefferson 614-879-7626
Ironton 740-377-4311	Wilmington. 937-382-2551
Jackson 740-286-4141	Wooster 330-264-0575
Lancaster 740-654-1523	Xenia 937-372-7671
Lebanon. 513-932-4444	Zanesville 740-453-0541
Lima. 419-228-2421	

Ohio Sheriff Departments

Adams County	937-544-2314	Huron County	419-668-6912
Allen County	419-227-3535	Jackson County	740-286-6464
Ashland County	419-289-3911	Jefferson County	740-283-8600
Ashtabula County	440-576-0055	Knox County	740-397-3333
Athens County	740-593-6633	Lake County	440-350-5517
Auglaize County	419-738-2147	Lawrence County	740-532-3525
Belmont County	740-695-7933	Licking County	740-349-6400
Brown County	937-378-4435	Logan County	937-592-5731
Butler County	513-785-1000	Lorain County	440-329-3701
Carroll County	330-627-2141	Lucas County	419-213-4784
Champaign County	937-652-1311	Madison County	740-852-1332
Clark County	937-328-2523	Mahoning County	330-480-5020
Clermont County	513-732-7500	Marion County	740-382-8244
Clinton County	937-382-1611	Medina County	330-725-0028
Coshocton County	740-622-2411	Meigs County	740-992-3371
Columbiana County	330-424-1104	Mercer County	419-586-7724
Crawford County	419-562-7906	Miami County	937-440-6085
Cuyahoga County	216-443-6066	Monroe County	740-472-1612
Darke County	937-548-3399	Montgomery County	937-225-4192
Defiance County	419-784-1155	Morgan County	740-962-4044
Delaware County	740-833-2860	Morrow County	419-946-4444
Erie County	419-625-7951	Muskingum County	740-452-3637
Fairfield County	740-653-5223	Noble County	740-732-4158
Fayette County	740-335-6170	Ottawa County	419-734-4404
Franklin County	614-462-3360	Paulding County	419-399-3791
Fulton County	419-335-4010	Perry County	740-342-4123
Gallia County	740-446-1242	Pickaway County	740-477-6000
Geauga County	440-286-4031	Pike County	740-947-2111
Greene County	937-562-4801	Portage County	330-678-7012
Guernsey County	740-439-4455	Preble County	937-456-6262
Hamilton County	513-946-6400	Putnam County	419-523-3208
Hancock County	419-424-7097	Richland County	419-774-5678
Hardin County	419-673-1268	Ross County	740-773-1186
Harrison County	740-942-2197	Sandusky County	419-332-2613
Henry County	419-592-8010	Scioto County	740-354-7566
Highland County	937-393-2212	Seneca County	419-447-3456
Hocking County	740-385-2131	Shelby County	937-498-1111
Holmes County	330-674-1936	Stark County	330-430-3801

Summit County 330-643-2111
Trumbull County 330-675-2508
Tuscarawas County ... 330-339-2000
Union County........ 937-645-4100
Van Wert County 419-238-3866
Vinton County 740-596-5242

Warren County....... 513-695-1280
Washington County... 740-373-2833
Wayne County 330-287-5750
Williams County...... 419-636-3151
Wood County........ 419-354-9137
Wyandot County 419-294-2362

Major Hotel & Motel Toll-Free Numbers

Adam's Mark Hotels.. 800-444-ADAM
Americinn............ 800.634.3444
AmeriHost Inn 800.434.5800
Baymont Inn.......... 866.999.1111
Best Inns and Suites ... 800.BESTINN
Best Western 800.780.7234
Clarion Hotels......... 877.424.6423
Comfort Inns 800.4CHOICE
Courtyard by
    Marriott 800.321.2211
Days Inn 800.329.7466
Doubletree Hotels 800.222TREE
EconoLodge 800.55ECONO
Embassy Suites 800.EMBASSY
Fairfield Inn 800.228.2800
Four Seasons
    Hotels 800.819.5053
Hampton Inns 800.HAMPTON
Hawthorn Suites....... 800.527.1133
Hilton Hotels 800.HILTONS
Holiday Inns 800.HOLIDAY
Howard Johnson....... 800.446.4656
Hyatt Hotels 888.591.1234
Knights Inn........... 800.843.5644

La Quinta Inns 866.725.1661
Marriott.............. 888.236.2427
Microtel Inns 888.771.7171
Motel 6 .... 800.4MOTEL6
Omni Hotels.......... 888.444.6664
Quality Inns 877.424.6423
Radisson Hotels 888.201.1718
Ramada Inn.......... 800.2RAMADA
Red Roof Inns....... 800.THEROOF
Red Carpet Inn 800.251.1962
Regent International ... 800.545.4000
Renaissance Hotels.... 800.HOTELS1
Residence Inn 800.331.3131
Rodeway Inns 877.424.6423
Sheraton Hotels 800.598.1753
Shoney's Inn 800.552.4667
Signature Inn 800.822.5252
Super 8 Motels 800.800.8000
Suisse Chalet......... 800.5CHALET
Travelodge............ 800.578.7878
Westin Hotels
    & Resorts 888.625.5144
Wyndham Hotels/
    Resorts 800.822.4200

Lost or Stolen Credit Card Phone Numbers

American Express: 1-800-668-2639
Diner's Club: 1-800-2DINERS
Discover: 1-800-DISCOVER
Mastercard: 1-800-MASTERCARD
Visa: 1-800-847-2911

Ohio Motorcycling Regulations

(Check with your local police department, Ohio Department
of Motor Vehicles, or the Motorcycle Ohio Program / Department
of Public Safety for the latest legal requirements)

On-Road

License Endorsement: Required

Safety Helmet: Required by law for novice riders and under age 18.

Rider Education: Required under age 18. Available for all eligible persons.

Eye Protection: Required unless motorcycle equipped with windshield.

Headlight: Required on road. Modulating headlight permitted. Daytime use
legal.

Passenger seat: Required if carrying a passenger.

Passenger age restriction: None

Passenger footrest: Required if carrying a passenger.

Mirrors (L & R): Required by state law.

Helmet speakers: No restrictions.

Radar detector: No restrictions.

Periodic safety inspections: Random—required by law.

Turn Signals: Required if manufactured in or after 1968.

Muffler: Required.

Maximum Sound Level: Local units of government may establish regulations
concerning noise levels. (Title 45, 4513.221) 82dBA at 35 mph or less; or
86dBA at more than 35 mph.

Insurance Requirements: Compulsory Liability with minimum limits.
(12.5/25/7.5k)

Handlebar height: Maximum of 15" above seat.

Waiver for Rider Education: Yes—skills test.

Motorcycle endorsement from other states accepted: Yes

Number of Motorcycles per lane of travel: Two abreast maximum.

Lane splitting: Not addressed in Code or Statutes.

Off-Road

Safety Helmet: Not required

Eye Protection: Not required

Minimum Operator Age: Ages 12—16: Direct supervision of a licensed adult
over age of 18 required.

Rider Education Certification: Not required.

Operator License: Required.
Headlight: Required if operated after sunset.
Taillight: Required if operated after sunset.
Muffler: Required.
Spark Arrestor: Not required.
Maximum sound level: No limit.
Registration: Required.
Vehicle title: Not required.

Motorcycle Dealers & Repair Facilities

AMERICAN IRONHORSE

North Coast Motorcycle
9750 Clark Drive
Rossford, OH
877-NORTHCOAST

APRILIA

Cycle Specialties, Inc.
6175 Harrison Avenue
Cincinnati, OH
513-574-7878

Hinds Performance Motorsports
5838 Columbus Pike Road
Lewis Center, OH
614-545-2213

Honda East
1230 Conant Street
Maumee, OH
419-891-1230

State 8 Motorcycles
100 Cuyahoga Falls Ind. Pkwy
Peninsula, OH
330-929-8123

South Avenue Cycle
7661 South Avenue
Youngstown, OH
330-965-2453

BIG DOG

Performance Cycles
24202 Aurora Road
Bedford Heights, OH
440-439-2577

Easyriders of Cincinnati
7220 Dixie Highway
Fairfield, OH
513-860-3279

Big Dog Motorcycles of Columbus
611 East Broad Street
Columbus, OH
614-224-9400

North Coast Motorcycle
9750 Clark Drive
Rossford, OH
877-NORTHCOAST

BMW

Holt BMW
9000 Cycle Lane
Athens, OH
740-593-6690

Roman Cycle Shop, Inc.
4994 Mahoning Avenue
Austintown, OH
330-270-2697

BMW Motorcycles of Columbus
3810 East Main Street
Columbus, OH
614-239-1269

Mathias BMW Cycle
851 Commercial Avenue SW
New Philadelphia, OH
330-343-6411

Roman Cycle Shop
4494 Mahoning Avenue
Salem, OH
330-270-2697

Competition Accessories
345 West Leffel Lane
Springfield, OH
800-543-3535

BMW Tri-State Motorcycles
4810 Peter Place
West Chester, OH
513-860-1114

All Seasons Sports Center
2700 Akron Road
Wooster, OH
330-264-7735

BOSS HOSS
Lima Auto Mall
2100 North Cable Road
Lima, OH
800-541-5015

DUCATI
Crooked River MCs
1915 Brittain Road
Akron, OH
330-630-9430

JD Performance
5784 Filview Circle
Cincinnati, OH
513-574-1470

Domiracer Distributors
5218 Wooster Road
Cincinnati, OH
513-871-1678

Ducati Columbus
3810 East Main Street
Columbus, OH
614-239-1269

Cycle Search International
4142 Anson Drive
Hilliard, OH
614-527-4650

Hinds Power & Motorsports
5838 Columbus Pike Road
Lewis Center, OH
614-545-2213

Cleveland-Akron European
  Connection
7300 Fair Oaks Road
Oakwood Village, OH
440-735-2000

Competition Accessories
345 West Leffel Lane
Springfield, OH
800-543-8190

EXCELSIOR-HENDERSON

Beechmont Motorsports
Excelsior-Henderson
646 Mt. Moriah
Cincinatti, OH
513-752-0088

Cleveland Motorcycle Co.
Excelsior-Henderson
7429 Tyler Blvd.
Mentor, OH
440-974-6900

Toledo Excelsior-Henderson
4942 West Alexis
Sylvania, OH
419-882-0005

Penton Excelsior-Henderson
1423 Footer Park Rd.
Amherst, OH
440-282-5108

HARLEY-DAVIDSON / BUELL

Liberty Harley-Davidson
32 East Cuyahoga Falls Avenue
Akron, OH
330-535-9900

Athens Harley-Davidson
165 Columbus Road
Athens, OH
740-592-1692
800-592-4464

Lake Erie Harley-Davidson/Buell
38401 Chester Road
Avon, OH
440-934-5000

Southeast Harley-Davidson/Buell
23105 Aurora Road
Bedford Heights, OH
440-439-5300
877-766-SEHD

High Point Harley-Davidson
288 Stockyard Road
Bellefontaine, OH
937-599-4550

Valley Harley-Davidson
41255 Reco Road
Belmont, OH
740-695-9591

Baxter Harley-Davidson
1900 Jackson Pike
Bidwell, OH
740-446-6336

Liberty Harley-Davidson
334 East Hines Hill Road
Boston Heights, OH
330-650-2799

Harley-Davidson of Youngstown
4478 Boardman-Canfield Road
Canfield, OH
330-702-1010
888-686-1010

Joe Carson Harley-Davidson
2930 Helena Drive
Carroll, OH
740-756-1900

Harley-Davidson/Buell of Chillicothe
818 Eastern Avenue
Chillicothe, OH
740-773-8826
800-306-HOGS

Eastgate Harley-Davidson/Buell
699 Old State Route 74
Cincinnati, OH
513-528-1400

Harley-Davidson of Cincinnati
4601 Eastgate Boulevard
Cincinnati, OH
513-752-7890

Cincinnati Harley-Davidson
1799 Tennessee Avenue
Cincinnati, OH
513-641-1188

Harley-Davidson Sales
14550 Lorain Avenue
Cleveland, OH
216-252-3111

A. D. Farrow Harley-Davidson/Buell
491 West Broad Street
Columbus, OH
614-228-6353

Warren Harley-Davidson
2102 Elm Road
Cortland, OH
330-395-4700

F & S Harley-Davidson/Buell
7220 North Dixie Highway
Dayton, OH
937-898-8084
800-783-2222

Adventure Harley-Davidson
1465 Route 39 NW
Dover, OH
330-364-6519

Elyria Harley-Davidson/Buell
561 Cleveland Street
Elyria, OH
440-365-7354

Tri-County Harley-Davidson
5960 Dixie Highway
Fairfield, OH
513-874-4343

Lima Harley-Davidson/Buell
3255 Fort Shawnee Indiana Drive
Lima, OH
419-331-3027

Hale's Harley-Davidson/Buell
1400 Harrington Memorial Road
Mansfield, OH
419-522-8602

Carlton Harley-Davidson
11771 State Route 44
Mantua, OH
330-274-3141

Marietta Cycle Center/Buell
1100 Pike Street
Marietta, OH
740-374-7070

Aces & Eights Harley-Davidson
2383 Kings Center Court
Mason, OH
513-459-1777

Century Harley-Davidson
3053 Eastpointe Circle
Medina, OH
330-721-1702

Jim's Harley-Davidson Sales
7172 Route 707
Mendon, OH
419-795-4185

Western Reserve H-D/Buell
8567 Tyler Boulevard
Mentor, OH
440-974-6900

Roeder Harley-Davidson
3684 US Route 20 West
Monroeville, OH
419-465-2546

Harley-Davidson Sales & Service
862 American Road
Napoleon, OH
419-592-7123

Freedom Harley-Davidson/Buell
7233 Sunset Strip Avenue NW
North Canton, OH
330-494-2453

Ben Breece Harley-Davidson
242 West 4th Street
Ottawa, OH
419-523-4274

Centennial Park Harley-Davidson
12477 Broad Street SW
Pataskala, OH
740-964-2205
800-798-3544

Tim Sherman's Signature H-D
1176 Professional Drive
Perrysburg, OH
419-873-2453
888-444-2753

Grover Harley-Davidson/Buell
1501 East Ash Street
Piqua, OH
937-773-8733

C & A Harley-Davidson
7610 Commerce Place
Plain City, OH
614-873-4604

Roeder Harley-Davidson
3976 Harbor Light Landing Drive
Port Clinton, OH
419-732-6282

Roeder Harley-Davidson
5316 Milan Road
Sandusky, OH
419-621-1046

Mid-Ohio Harley-Davidson
2100 Quality Lane
Springfield, OH
937-322-3590
800-527-4972

Toledo Harley-Davidson/Buell
7960 West Central Avenue
Toledo, OH
419-843-7892
888-743-3373

Thiel's Wheels Harley-Davidson
350 Tarhe Trail
Upper Sandusky, OH
419-294-4951
800-292-4951

Neidengard's Harley-Davidson
284 Canton Road (SR 43)
Wintersville, OH
740-266-6188

Buckminn's Harley-Davidson
1213 Cincinnati Avenue
Xenia, OH
937-376-3344
866-218-1452

Fink's Harley-Davidson
2650 Maysville Pike
Zanesville, OH
740-454-0010

HONDA

Harding's Park Cycle
4330 Kirby Avenue NE
Canton, OH
330-454-6171

Joe Carson Honda
2930 Helena Drive
Carroll, OH
740-756-1900

Honda of Chillicothe
818 Eastern Avenue
Chillicothe, OH
740-773-8826

Beechmont Motorsports
646 Mt. Moriah Drive
Cincinnati, OH
513-752-0088

Harley Davidson/Honda Sales
14550 Lorain Avenue
Cleveland, OH
216-252-3111

ASK Powersports
2450 Park Crescent Drive
Columbus, OH
614-759-9300

Classic Cycles
2657 Morse Road
Columbus, OH
800-244-9368

McCarthy's Honda
8373 North Route 66
Defiance, OH
419-782-4883

Honda of Fairfield
5467 Dixie Highway
Fairfield, OH
513-858-1000

Honda of Middletown
3711 Commerce Drive
Franklin, OH
866-671-7044

Shiets Motors
1557 Oak Harbor Road
Fremont, OH
419-332-9902

ASK Powersports
4075 Hoover Road
Grove City, OH
614-871-3711

Huron Outdoor Shop
1803 Sawmill Parkway
Huron, OH
419-433-6979

Honda Suzuki of Jackson
2223 Clary Road
Jackson, OH
740-286-4956

ASK Powersports
2535 Columbus Road
Lancaster, OH
740-654-3456

Haas Honda
826 Pike Street
Marietta, OH
740-374-4044

Honda East
1230 Conant Street
Maumee, OH
419-891-1230

Just For Fun Honda
15255 Kinsman Road
Middlefield, OH
866-346-3281

Paradox Motorsports
66665 Morristown Road
Morristown, OH
800-814-9132

Mid-Ohio Honda
494 Harcourt Road
Mt. Vernon, OH
877-640-6446

Boulevard Cycle
938 Cookson Avenue SE
New Philadelphia, OH
330-308-8900

Andrews Cycles
13134 State Route 62
Salem, OH
888-554-4371
330-332-8534

Competition Accessories
345 West Leffel Lane
Springfield, OH
800-543-3535

Ray Gollan's Honda
1300 Youngstown Road
Warren, OH
866-369-3700

All Seasons Sport Center
2700 Akron Road
Wooster, OH
330-264-7735

Ray Gollan's Honda
519 Market Street
Youngstown, OH
330-744-1325

HUSQVARNA
Dover Race Ready Cycles
2174 State Route 516 NW
Dover, OH
330-602-9219

Beaver Creek Cycle
13172 State Route 7
Lisbon, OH
330-386-7353

INDIAN
Performance Cycles
24202 Aurora Road
Bedford Heights, OH
440-439-2577

Indian Motorcycle
155 West Kemper Road
Cincinnati, OH
513-587-1635

North Coast Motorcycle
9750 Clark Drive
Rossford, OH
877-NORTHCOAST

Indian & Titan Motorcycles
20660 Route 6
Weston, OH
419-669-4709

South Avenue Cycle
7661 South Avenue
Youngstown, OH
330-965-2453

KAWASAKI
Action Sport Cycles Inc
11333 North Union NE
Alliance, OH
330-821-8777

Athen's Sport Cycles, Inc.
165 Columbus Road
Athens, OH
740-592-1692

A & B Xtreme Kawasaki
5310 Guernsey Street
Bellaire, OH
740-676-2900

Rileys Suzuki & Kawasaki
40309 National Road
Belmont, OH
740-782-1015

Harding's Park Cycle
4330 Kirby Avenue NE
Canton, OH
330-454-6171

Cycle Specialties Inc.
6175 Harrison Avenue
Cincinnati, OH
513-574-7878

ASK Powersports
2450 Park Crescent Drive
Columbus, OH
614-759-9300

Classic Cycles
2657 Morse Road
Columbus, OH
614-471-3511

Kawasaki Motorcycle & ATV
2450 Park Crescent Drive East
Columbus, OH
614-759-9300

ASK Powersports
4075 Hoover Road
Grove City, OH
614-871-3711

J & J Sales and Service
1001 Sprowl Road
Huron, OH
419-433-2523

John's Kawasaki
State Route 93
Jackson, OH
740-286-4907

ASK Powersports
2535 Columbus Road
Lancaster, OH
740-654-3456

Hinds Performance Motorsports
5838 Columbus Pike Road
Lewis Center, OH
614-545-2213

McCune Cycle World
327 Ashland Road
Mansfield, OH
419-524-2222

J & J Motors
11893 Lincoln Way West
Massillon, OH
330-837-3595

Honda East
1230 Conant Street
Maumee, OH
419-891-1230

Mid-Ohio Kawasaki
494 Harcourt Road
Mt. Vernon, OH
877-640-6446

Boulevard Cycle
938 Cookson Avenue SE
New Philadelphia, OH
330-308-8900

McCarthys Cycle
8373 State Route 66
North Defiance, OH
419-782-4883

Norwalk Motorsports
226 Milan Avenue
Norwalk, OH
419-668-1688

J & J Sales and Service
475 Southeast Catawba
Port Clinton, OH
419-734-2754

Andrews Cycles
13134 State Route 62
Salem, OH
330-332-8534

Competition Accessories
345 West Leffel Lane
Springfield, OH
800-543-3535

All Seasons Sport Center
2700 Akron Road
Wooster, OH
330-264-7735

Doug Kane Motorsports
303 West Monroe Street
Zanesville, OH
614-452-5438

KTM

Athens Sport Cycle
165 Columbus Road
Athens, OH
800-592-4464

Mathias Cycle Sales
3787 State Route 800 NE
Dover, OH
330-343-6411

Honda Suzuki of Jackson
2223 Clary Road
Jackson, OH
740-286-4956

Black's Motorsports
708 Division Street
Parkersburg, WV
304-428-0606

KYMCO

AC Motors
6845 Whipple Avenue NW
North Canton, OH
330-492-5200

Beechmont Motorsports
646 Mt. Moriah
Cincinnati, OH
513-752-0088

Dick's Suzuki
11400 US62 South
Leesburgh, OH
937-780-7165

Fischer Cycle Sales
2907 North Bend Road
Ashtabula , OH
440-997-4166

McCarthy Yamaha, Inc.
8373 SR66 North
Defiance , OH
419-782-4883

Outdoor Adventures, Ltd.
657 East Canal Street
Nelsonville, OH
740-342-7600

Pride of Cleveland
2078 West 25th Street
Cleveland, OH
216-737-0700

Terry Walker Cycle Sales
639 West Main
McArthur, OH
740-596-9696

Trails End Sports
161 North Broadway
New Philadelphia , OH
330-364-4933

Zoot Scoots
1057 West 5th Avenue
Columbus, OH
614-298-9668

MOTO-GUZZI

Mid-Ohio Motorcycles
494 Harcourt Road
Mt. Vernon, OH
877-640-6446

Eish Enterprises
11041 Opal Road NE
Salineville, OH
330-738-3944

Speaker Cycles
1255 State Route 213
Steubenville, OH
740-282-5399

MV AGUSTA

Classic Cycles
30478 Groesbeck Highway
Roseville, MI 48066
586-447-1340

Fast By Ferracci
1901 Davisville Road
Willow Grove, PA 19090
215-657-1276

North American Warhorse
1000 Dunham Drive
Dunsmore, PA
866-222-2453

RED HORSE

Canton Custom Cycle
2909 Cleveland Avenue NW
Canton, OH
330-493-5444

Turismo Cycles of Ohio
555 West High Avenue, #168
New Philadelphia, OH
866-318-0336

SUZUKI

Action Sport Cycles
11333 Union Avenue NE
Alliance, OH
330-821-8777

On the Edge Suzuki
300 Rice Industrial Parkway
Amherst, OH
440-985-3343

Athens Sport Cycles, Inc.
165 Columbus Road
Athens, OH
740-592-1692

Jeff Wyler Cycle World
4383 Glen Willow Lake Lane
Batavia, OH
513-752-3447

RideXtreme Suzuki
5310 Guernsey Street
Bellaire, OH
740-676-2900

Rileys Suzuki & Kawasaki
40309 National Road
Belmont, OH
740-782-1015

Harding's Park Cycle
4330 Kirby Avenue NE
Canton, OH
888-454-6171

Suzuki of Chillicothe
818 Eastern Avenue
Chillicothe, OH
740-773-8826

Cycle City
10801 Montgomery Road
Cincinnati, OH
513-489-3463

Cycle Specialties, Inc.
6175 Harrison Avenue
Cincinnati, OH
513-574-7878

Shipps Yamaha Suzuki
11530 Springfield Pike
Cincinnati, OH
513-772-2803

ASK Powersports
2450 Park Crescent Drive East
Columbus, OH
614-759-9300

Columbus Suzuki
3065 Morse Road
Columbus, OH
614-471-3511

Cycle Sport Center
16943 National Road
Cridersville, OH
419-645-4726

F & S Suzuki
7200 North Dixie
Dayton, OH
937-898-7703

Southside Suzuki
4790 South Dixie Drive
Dayton, OH
937-294-1577

Shipps Suzuki
7220 Dixie Highway
Fairfield, OH
513-860-3232

American Powersports
1311 Trenton Avenue
Findlay, OH
419-422-9253

Shiets Motors
1557 Oak Harbor Road
Fremont, OH
419-332-9902

North Ridge Cycles
5929 North Ridge Road
Geneva, OH
440-466-2712

ASK Powersports
4075 Hoover Road
Grove City, OH
614-871-3711

Jones Power Sports
2020 South Eire Highway
Hamilton, OH
513-894-0081

Maximum Street Performance
1697 Hebron Road
Heath, OH
740-788-9212

Suzuki Northwest
3747 Park Mill Run Drive
Hilliard, OH
614-771-0771

J & J Sales and Service
1001 Sprowl Road
Huron, OH
419-433-2523

Honda Suzuki of Jackson
2223 Clary Road
Jackson, OH
740-286-4956

ASK Powersports
2535 Columbus–Lancaster Road
Lancaster, OH
740-654-3456

Dick's Suzuki
11400 US Route 62 South
Leesburg, OH
937-780-7165

Hinds Performance Motorsports
5838 Columbus Pike Road
Lewis Center, OH
740-548-5448

Metro Motorsports
11558 State Route 44
Manatua, OH
330-274-0100

McCune Cycle World
327 Ashland Road
Mansfield, OH
419-524-2222

J & J Motors
11893 Lincoln Way West
Massillon, OH
330-837-3595

Honda East Suzuki
1230 Conant Street
Maumee, OH
419-891-1230

Mentor Suzuki
Mentor, OH
440-602-2222

Mid-Ohio Suzuki
494 Harcourt Road
Mt. Vernon, OH
740-397-5272

State 8 Motorcycles
100 Cuyahoga Falls Indiana Parkway
Peninsula, OH
330-929-8123

Andrews Cycles
13134 State Route 62
Salem, OH
888-554-4371

Adrenaline Motorsports
1101 North Vandermark Road
Sidney, OH
937-497-1103

Competition Accessories
345 West Leffel Lane
Springfield, OH
937-323-0513

Blackhawk Powersports
8396 Fort Laurens Road
Strasburg, OH
330-878-7060

Midwest Powersports
3747 Massilon Road
Uniontown, OH
330-896-9007

Tegtmeyer's Suzuki
Wilmington, OH
937-486-2405

All-Seasons Sports Center
2700 Akron Road
Wooster, OH
330-264-7735

Ray Gollan's Suzuki
1306 Youngstown Road
Youngstown, OH
330-369-3700

TITAN

Easyriders of Cincinnati
7220 Dixie Highway
Fairfield, OH
513-860-3279

Indian & Titan Motorcycles
20660 Route 6
Weston, OH
419-669-4709

TRIKES

Honda Suzuki of Jackson
2223 Clary Road
Jackson, OH
740-286-4956

Mid-Ohio Motorcycles
494 Harcourt Road
Mt. Vernon, OH
740-397-5272

Indian & Titan Motorcycles
20660 Route 6
Weston, OH
419-669-4709

Cumberland Bikes & Trikes
3484 Old Wheeling Road
Zanesville, OH
740-450-3970

TRIUMPH
Harding's Park Cycle
4330 Kirby Avenue NE
Canton, OH
330-454-6171

North Coast Motorcycle
9750 Clark Drive
Rossford, OH
877-NORTHCOAST

Hinds Performance Motorsports
5838 Columbus Pike Road
Lewis Center, OH
614-545-2213

URAL
No dealers found in Ohio

Crawford Sales Company
10138 Colonial Industrial Drive
South Lyon, MI 48178
248-437-8107

Lear Unlimited
2204 North Wolfe Street
Muncie, IN 47303
765-282-6273

Lewis Cycle
122 West Jefferson Street
Tipton, IN 46072
765-675-9090

Etowah Motor Company
5930 MacCorkle Avenue SW
St. Albans, WV 25177
304-201-2065

VENGENCE
North Coast Motorcycle
9750 Clark Drive
Rossford, OH
877-NORTHCOAST

South Avenue Cycle
7661 South Avenue
Youngstown, OH
330-965-2453

VENTO
Creager Cycle Center
580 Broadway Avenue
Bedford, OH
440-439-6666

Atkins Powersports
21172 Power Road
Defiance, OH
419-782-7973

Cycle Search International
5750 East State Route 37
Delaware, OH
740-369-3232

Ed Heston Auto Repair
227 Cedar Hill Road
Lancaster, OH
740-654-2025

Exotic Sports Products
10593 Main Street
Middletown, OH
330-542-9930

A C Motors
6845 Whipple Avenue NW
North Canton, OH
330-492-5200

Andrew's Cycles
13134 State Route 62 West
Salem, OH
330-332-8534

VICTORY
South East Polaris
23361 Aurora Road
Cleveland, OH
440-786-2230

ASK Powersports
2450 Park Crescent
Columbus, OH
614-759-9300

ASK Powersports
4075 Hoover Road
Grove City, OH
614-871-3711

J & J Sales and Service
1001 Sprowl Road
Huron, OH
419-433-2523

ASK Powersports
2535 Columbus Road
Lancaster, OH
740-654-3456

Hinds Motorsports
5838 Columbus Pike
Lewis Center, OH
614-545-2213

Honda East
1230 Conant Street
Maumee, OH
419-891-1230

Century Motorsports
1609 Medina Road
Medina, OH
330-239-1950

McCune Cycle World
327 Ashland Road
Mansfield, OH
419-524-2222

J & J Sales and Service
475 South East Catawba
Port Clinton, OH
419-734-2754

Andrews Cycles
13134 State Route 62
Salem, OH
888-554-4371

South Avenue Cycle
7661 South Avenue
Youngstown, OH
330-965-2453

YAMAHA

Midway Yamaha
3254 Manchester Road
Akron, OH
330-644-2185

Action Sport Cycle
11333 Union Avenue
Alliance, OH
330-821-8777

Athens Sport Cycle
165 Columbus Road
Athens, OH
800-592-4464

Harding's Park Cycle
4330 Kirby Avenue NE
Canton, OH
330-454-6171

Lancaster Sport Cycles
4646 Old Columbus Road NW
Carroll, OH
740-756-9650

Shipps Yamaha Suzuki
11530 Springfield Pike
Cincinnati, OH
513-772-2803

ASK Powersports
2450 Park Crescent
Columbus, OH
614-759-9300

Schiets Motors
1557 Oak Harbor Road
Fremont, OH
419-332-9902

North Ridge Cycles
5929 North Ridge Road
Geneva, OH
440-466-2712

ASK Powersports
4075 Hoover Road
Grove City, OH
614-871-3711

Huron Outdoor Shop
1803 Sawmill Parkway
Huron, OH
419-433-6979

J & J Sales and Service
1001 Sprowl Road
Huron, OH
419-433-2523

John's Yamaha
State Route 93
Jackson, OH
740-286-4907

ASK Powersports
2535 Columbus Road
Lancaster, OH
740-654-3456

Hinds Motorsports
5838 Columbus Pike
Lewis Center, OH
614-545-2213

Yamaha of Columbus
12555 Worthington Road
New Albany, OH
740-927-9944

Hinds Performance Motorsports
5838 Columbus Pike Road
Lewis Center, OH
740-548-5448

Hale's Sport Center
1400 Airport Road
Mansfield, OH
419-522-8602

J & J Motors
11893 Lincoln Way West
Massillon, OH
330-837-3595

Honda East
1230 Conant St.
Maumee, OH
419-891-1230

Paradox Motorsports
66665 Morristown Road
Morristown, OH
800-814-9132

Mid-Ohio
494 Harcourt Road
Mt. Vernon, OH
877-640-6446

Boulevard Cycle
938 Cookson Avenue SE
New Philadelphia, OH
330-308-8900

McCarthy's Cycle
8373 State Rte. 66
North Defiance, OH
419-782-4883

Norwalk Motorsports
226 Milan Avenue
Norwalk, OH
419-668-1688

State 8 Motorcycles
100 Cuyahoga Fall Ind. Parkway
Peninsula, OH
330-929-8123

S & S Sales and Service
475 SE Catawba Road
Port Clinton, OH
419-734-2754

Competition Accessories
  MC Superstore
345 West Leffel Lane
Springfield, OH
800-543-3535

Yamaha of Warren
4867 Mahoning Avenue
Warren, OH
330-847-7644

Clinton County Yamaha
6002 North US68
Wilmington, OH
937-283-2220

All Seasons Sports Center
2700 Akron Road
Wooster, OH
330-264-7735

Doug Kane Motorsports
303 West Monroe Street
Zanesville, OH
800-224-7890